The Bulgarian Communist Party from Blagoev to Zhivkov

D0732635

Histories of Ruling Communist Parties
Richard F. Staar, editor

The Bulgarian Communist Party from Blagoev to Zhivkov

JOHN D. BELL

Hoover Institution Press
Stanford University
Stanford, California

Hoover Press Publication 320

Copyright 1986 by the Board of Trustees of the
  Leland Stanford Junior University

First printing, 1986

Manufactured in the United States of America

90 89 88 87 86   9 8 7 6 5 4 3 2 1

Library of Congress Cataloging in Publication Data
Bell, John D., 1942–
   The Bulgarian Communist Party from
Blagoev to Zhivkov.
   (Histories of ruling Communist parties)
   Bibliography: p.
   Includes index.
   1. Bŭlgarska kommunisticheska partiĩa—History.
   2. Bulgaria—Politics and government—1944–
   I. Title. II. Series.
JN9609.A8K61482 1985   324.2497′7075   85-17744
ISBN 0-8179-8202-7

Design by Lorena Laforest Bass

Contents

Tables

Editor's Foreword

John D. Bell's study of the history of the Bulgarian Communist Party is the tenth volume in our series on the histories of ruling communist parties throughout the world. It represents the first comprehensive survey published outside Bulgaria on this most important subject.

Dr. Bell has utilized not only primary sources in the Bulgarian language but also literature by Bulgarian émigrés and defectors. His is a most thoroughly documented study that brings the record down to the most recent events of the Zhivkov era.

That period is drawing to a close, since in 1984 Zhivkov celebrated his seventy-third birthday and three decades as leader of the Bulgarian Communist Party (BCP). His thirty-year rule has included the destalinization process, an ineffective plot that involved ten persons who may have desired a more nationalist regime, and the current situation, in which the politburo is divided between older and younger generations.

The younger generation includes many more members possessing higher levels of education and expertise in administration and economic affairs. Actuarial tables indicate that this group may succeed the current Bulgarian leadership. If the Communist Party of the Soviet Union is the model, the successor to Zhivkov will come from the next generation of emerging leaders. In any event, the BCP's desire for continuity and unity seems to be influencing developments in Bulgaria. A younger man, Alexander Lilov (age 50), was suddenly removed in September 1983 from both the politburo and secretariat. He may have been perceived as a threat to the leader. At 32, Zhivkov's son Vladimir appears too young to succeed his father.

Of all the East European ruling parties, the BCP has demonstrated the most consistent loyalty to the Soviet Union, which has rewarded Bulgaria with extensive infusions of economic assistance over the years. If any independence movement exists within the BCP, it has not been heard from since the six years before Stalin's death, when almost one-fourth of all party members were purged.

Speaking at the celebration of the fortieth anniversary of the seizure of power that occurred on 9 September 1944, Zhivkov boasted that Bulgaria is one of the countries that has most successfully demonstrated the viability and attractiveness of the socialist system. Although few outsiders would agree that the BCP has overcome every difficulty, and though conflicts now hidden may surface in the post-Zhivkov era, it would nevertheless appear that the ruling communist movement in Bulgaria may avoid the problems that led to the disintegration of fraternal parties in Hungary (1956), Czechoslovakia (1968), and Poland (1981). This volume explains why.

Richard F. Staar

Hoover Institution
Stanford University

Preface

Three excellent monographs are available to the English-speaking reader interested in the history of Bulgarian communism. In 1959 Joseph Roth-schild published *The Communist Party of Bulgaria: Origins and Development, 1883–1936*, which explored the conditions that gave rise to a socialist movement in Bulgaria, the Narrow Socialist tradition, and the career of the Bulgarian Communist Party (BCP) through the middle of the 1930s. Nissan Oren's *Bulgarian Communism: The Road to Power 1934–1944*, published in 1971, carried the story to 9 September 1944. And James F. Brown's *Bulgaria Under Communist Rule*, published in 1970, dealt with the impact of destalinization through the decade of the 1960s.

This volume, which aims at surveying a longer period of time, must necessarily sacrifice much of the detail that informs the arguments and interpretations of these works. Nevertheless, the passage of time has brought the present author several advantages. Inside Bulgaria the 1970s saw the publication of the three long volumes of Tsola Dragoicheva's memoirs, which provided a rare glimpse into the higher councils of the party during the late 1930s and the period of the Second World War. Moreover, Bulgaria's cultural policies in the 1970s were reflected in markedly improved historical scholarship. Although certain themes and the study of the recent past remained off limits to serious investigation, Bulgarian scholars have added a great deal to our knowledge of BCP history, particularly with regard to the period of the Second World War and the "revolutionary process" of 1944–1948. In addition to their published works, many Bulgarian scholars have shared their knowledge and ideas with me in formal symposia and informal conversations in both my country and theirs. Although I often disagreed with their conclusions or analytical framework, I came to respect their desire for honesty. I hope they will see the same desire in this work.

In 1973 Nissan Oren lamented the silence of Bulgaria's political emigration, which had as yet contributed little to the West's knowledge of Bulgaria's recent history. Since that time, the situation has changed significantly as individual Bulgarians and emigré groups have responded to his challenge. The historian Petŭr Semerjeev in Israel has produced valuable studies of Georgi Dimitrov and the trial of Traicho Kostov. Atanas Slavov in the United States has given an insider's view of Bulgarian intellectual life through the 1960s. And in England, before his murder in 1978, Georgi Markov contributed remarkable essays on Bulgarian society, politics, and the creative intelligentsia.

Bulgaria, along with Albania, is the East European country that has been least known to the West, a fact that has had no small impact on that nation's fate. In recent years Bulgarians both inside and outside the country have told us much about themselves. It is a major purpose of this book to present some of this information to the English-speaking audience.

Note on Alphabets, Dates, and Place Names

In transliterating the Bulgarian and Russian alphabets in the text, I have generally employed the Library of Congress system without any diacritical marks except for the Bulgarian ŭ. The second i, however, is omitted in final -ii constructions, and proper names that begin with Io-, Ia-, or Iu- are presented here as Yo-, Ya-, or Yu- (Yordanov, Yankov, or Yugov). Names of scholars who have published in English are used in accordance with their chosen spelling.

The Julian calendar was in use in Bulgaria through 31 March 1916. In the nineteenth century it was twelve days behind the Gregorian calendar; in the twentieth century, thirteen days.

In cases where localities have undergone changes of name, the modern name, in parentheses, follows the original; for example, Gorna Dzhumaia (Blagoevgrad). The Bulgarian administrative regions *okrŭg* and *okoliia* are rendered here as "province" and "district," respectively.

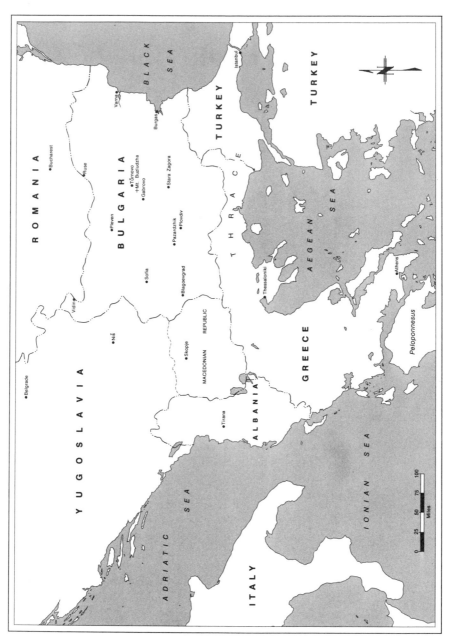

Prepared by Victoria Taylor, UMBC Cartographic Services.

1

Origins
to 1917

Bulgaria, a nation composed primarily of peasant smallholders in the last two decades of the nineteenth century, would seem an unlikely setting for the emergence of a socialist movement. But if the classic prerequisites—industry and a self-conscious proletariat—were lacking, the substitutes frequently encountered in the underdeveloped world were not. Bulgarian Marxism was born in the ranks of the country's young intelligentsia, and it was nurtured there until forces from outside the society brought it to power.

BACKGROUND

In the decades before the liberation of 1878, a quickening of economic life in the Bulgarian lands, the spread of literacy and education, and the creation of a press and ultimately an independence movement saw Bulgarians break out of the shell of isolation that had marked five centuries of Ottoman and Phanariot domination. Bulgarian communities in Constantinople, Romania, and Russia fostered and supported this national revival. Many who participated in it, especially those young Bulgarians who studied in Russian schools or universities, encountered socialist or *narodnik* (populist) ideas. Several of Bulgaria's future statesmen, including some of its most conservative leaders, passed through a stage of infatuation with some form of socialism, most often of a vague or utopian variety. For example, the poet-martyr Khristo Botev, claimed today as a precursor of Bulgarian Marxism, wrote moving indictments of social injustice, but his work was in the age-old tradition of those who side with the weak against the strong; Botev's poetry was not the product of a "scientific" analysis of society. In any case, by the 1870s most educated Bulgarians focused on the achievement of national independence as a solution to all problems.[1]

And the liberation did bring fundamental political, social, and economic changes. National liberation was achieved. The Tŭrnovo Constitution promised Western-style government, with civil rights, limited monarchy, and a National Assembly elected on the basis of universal male suffrage. Turkish landlords fled or were driven from the country, and their estates were broken up for distribution to the peasantry.[2] It seemed that the dreams of the national awakening were being realized, and that Bulgaria would find its place in the mainstream of European civilization. But Bulgaria was not to become the "Belgium of the Balkans." In the following years neither its economy nor its democracy flourished.

Bulgarian Marxist historians have officially designated the years from 1878 to 1900 as the "era of the development of capitalism." They point to the abolition of feudal relations in the countryside; the decline of handicraft production; and the creation of a state apparatus, banking system, and other institutional forms characteristic of a capitalist society.[3] These changes were *structural*, however, and were not matched by actual *development*. As Alexander Gerschenkron concluded from his study of the Bulgarian economy before World War I: "All causes [for industrialization] were present, but the effects failed to materialize."[4] His view is supported in both the 1895 report of the Bulgarian Economic Society, which complained of declining argriculture and stagnant industry, and the recent (1982) authoritative study of Balkan economic history by John R. Lampe and Marvin Jackson.[5] Bulgaria remained a country composed overwhelmingly of peasant smallholders, with fewer than 6,000 factory workers according to the statistics of 1894. Between 1880 and 1910 the proportion of the population in towns of over 2,000 inhabitants actually declined slightly.[6]

Nor was the picture brighter in political life. The Bulgarian historian Ilcho Dimitrov has argued forcefully that Bulgaria never became a genuine "bourgeois democracy." On the contrary, the effort to transplant Western political forms to countries such as Bulgaria, which lacked Western traditions or a comparable economic and social base, produced only stillbirths or deformities.[7] The reign of Prince Alexander Battenberg (1879–86) was marked by a struggle between Liberals and Conservatives over the limits of royal authority, the suspension and restoration of the constitution, union with Eastern Rumelia, and the victorious war against Serbia. It concluded with the kidnapping and abdication of the prince himself. Beneath the turbulent surface of Bulgarian political life a tide was running whose effect was to undermine the country's fragile, paper democracy.

From the beginning, authority was actually in the hands of a politically active elite composed of the country's few large landowners, merchants, lawyers, clergymen, officers, teachers, and those educated in Bulgarian communities abroad. After the liberation, these men took the reins of government, staffing the civil service and officer corps of the new state.[8] By the mid-1880s their number had expanded beyond the country's capacity to find useful work for them, and each year the educational system produced a new crop of intellectuals and lawyers seeking careers in the civil or military bureaucracies. This overproduction turned politics into a struggle for patronage and caused a proliferation of political parties. The Liberal Party suffered its first schism in 1884, when its conservative wing, under Dragan Tsankov, broke away to form the Progressive Liberal Party. Two years later the party split again, this time between the followers of Petko Karavelov and Stefan Stambolov. Repeated fission eventually produced, besides the Progressive Liberals, the Democrats under Karavelov, the National Liberals under Stambolov, the Young Liberals under Dimitŭr Tonchev, the Liberals under Vasil Radoslavov, and the Radical Democrats under Naicho Tsanov. The remnants of the Conservative Party regrouped as the National Party, led by Konstantin Stoilov. There were few or no differences in principle among these parties, as their shifting blocs and alliances came to attest. The goal of each was to secure the power of patronage and access to the state treasury for the party "chief" and his supporters. They became "corporations for the exploitation of power."[9] The broad population lacked the education, organization, and experience to act as a brake on political degeneration. Its role in government was reduced to paying taxes and casting ballots in what were more and more frequently rigged or meaningless elections.

After the abdication of Prince Alexander, actual power passed to Stefan Stambolov. As president of the National Assembly, regent after Alexander's abdication, and prime minister, he secured the unification of the country, found an occupant for Bulgaria's vacant throne, fought off Russia's heavy-handed attempts to dominate the government, and acquired in the process an international reputation as one of Europe's "strong men." Under his rule political life lost its comic-opera features and acquired a more sinister complexion. Establishing a virtual dictatorship, Stambolov executed, imprisoned, or exiled his political enemies and suspended freedom of the press. Although many of the repressive features of his regime ended after he was deposed in 1894, subsequent political standards did not rise even to the level that preceded Stambolov.

The beneficiary of Stambolov's legacy was Prince Ferdinand I of Saxe-

Coburg-Gotha (1886–1918), whose character and policies shaped Bulgarian and Balkan politics to the end of the First World War.[10] Possessed of a high order of political cunning, Ferdinand remained in the background during the first eight years of his reign. In 1894 he suddenly dismissed Stambolov and had him murdered the following year. By encouraging the fragmentation of the political parties and cultivating the good will of the military, Ferdinand extended his personal authority over the government, especially in the field of diplomacy, where he was obsessed with the dream of making Bulgaria the dominant power in the Balkans. Through "his skill in calculating the psychological moment for driving each batch of swine from the trough of power," he made the political parties the pillars of his regime.[11] During Ferdinand's reign, vast public corruption was added to the evils of Bulgarian political life. Nearly every minister who served under him was later charged with filling his pockets at public expense. According to the report of the Russian ambassador in 1915, "the corruptness of the men in power here, and in general of the leading figures in politics and society, is so great and so instilled in their flesh and blood that I am able to confirm that it is difficult to achieve anything here without bribery."[12]

The economic stagnation and political degeneration that characterized this era inspired the popular saying "*Ot tursko—po losho*" (worse than the Turkish times). Among those members of the intelligentsia who were outside of the political establishment—the country's schoolteachers were the core of this group—the conditions inspired an inclination toward more radical programs and ideologies.

Dimitŭr Blagoev and the Founding of Bulgarian Social Democracy

Dimitŭr Blagoev was born on 14 June 1856 in Zagorichane, a large Bulgarian village in the Kastoria region of southern Macedonia, which now belongs to Greece.[13] His father was a poor peasant, who soon migrated to Constantinople to supplement the family income with work as a dairyman. Although far from the centers of the Bulgarian national awakening, Zagorichane was not untouched by it. In 1868 Georgi "Dinka" Konstantinov, an ardent Bulgarian patriot who had absorbed revolutionary ideas in Russia, settled in the village as a teacher, "planting the first seed of human consciousness in many young hearts" [as Blagoev wrote later] before he was expelled from the village in 1870. In that year Blagoev, too, left Zagorichane to join his father in Constantinople. For two years he worked as an apprentice cobbler and then entered the Bulgarian school run by Petko R. Slaveikov, one of the great figures of the Bulgarian national revival.

Slaveikov was on the lookout for able young Bulgarians, particularly ones from Macedonia, who could be trained to promote the national cause. He found in Blagoev an apt pupil. In 1875 Slaveikov arranged for Blagoev to enter the high school in Gabrovo, but his studies were interrupted by the April 1876 uprising in which Blagoev took part. When the Turks crushed the rebellion, Blagoev escaped to Stara Zagora, but with the outbreak of the Russo-Turkish war he was uprooted again. He fled to Tŭrnovo, where he found Slaveikov, who arranged for him to finish his studies in Russia. When Blagoev arrived penniless in Odessa at the end of 1878, the Bulgarian community there helped him to enter the local seminary, where he met Yanko Sakŭzov, son of a Shumen merchant and later his principal rival for the leadership of Bulgarian socialism. Neither man found the seminary appealing. Both soon left—Sakŭzov for Western Europe, Blagoev for an Odessa high school and then, in 1880, for St. Petersburg.

As a student first in the faculty of physical science and mathematics and then of law, Blagoev was quickly drawn to radical student circles and narodnik ideology. When the assassination of Alexander II in 1881 failed to transform Russia, Blagoev, like many other narodniki, including Georgi Plekhanov, became skeptical of prevailing revolutionary assumptions and began to seek new answers. During the winter and spring of 1882–83, after reading works by Lasalle and the first volume of Marx's *Capital*, Blagoev became a socialist. During the following winter, he won over a group of about ten persons who worked to agitate for Marxism among the students and to make contact with workers. This was the first organized Marxist group to be formed on Russian soil.

Calling itself the Party of Russian Social Democrats, Blagoev's group debated adoption of a program and a further course of action. The nature of this program was influenced by Plekhanov's *Socialism and the Political Struggle* and the program of Plekhanov's own Liberation of Labor group, both of which Blagoev discovered during 1884. When adopted in January 1885, the program of Blagoev's circle reflected Plekhanov's outlook on the inevitability of capitalist development in Russia, and the program was in fact sent to the Liberation of Labor for comment.[14] Blagoev's group also began to issue a newspaper, *Rabochi* (Worker), the second and last issue of which included articles sent by Axel'rod and Plekhanov. This attempt to establish a Social Democratic press in Russia won the later acknowledgment of Lenin and the immediate attention of the tsarist police.[15] Blagoev was arrested in February and promptly deported.

Arriving in Sofia in the spring, Blagoev found a minor government post and married Viktoriia (Vela) Zhivkova, a student whom he had first met in St. Petersburg. He formed a small circle of radical friends and in the summer began to publish anonymously *Sŭvremeni pokazatel* (Contemporary Index), an eclectic collection of articles on social science that included translations of Marx and the Russian progressive thinkers. This work was interrupted by the events connected with the unification of northern and southern Bulgaria and the war against Serbia. Unlike most Bulgarians, Blagoev did not hail the union of the two Bulgarias, for he thought it of benefit to the prince rather than the people. His lack of patriotic ardor alienated him from his circle of friends, one of whom exposed him as the publisher of *Sŭvremeni pokazatel*, thus causing Blagoev's discharge from his government post.

In the fall of 1886 Blagoev moved to Shumen, where he taught elementary school and was for a time reunited with Yanko Sakŭzov. Sakŭzov's road from the Odessa seminary had taken him to Germany, Paris, and London, where he had been strongly influenced by the practices of the Western Social Democratic parties. The two men were separated the next year, when Blagoev moved to another position in Viden. He remained there until 1890, trying to win converts to Marxism among the teachers and other members of the local intelligentsia.

By this time Blagoev was no longer alone. Besides Sakŭzov, in Gabrovo was the teacher Evtim Dabev, who had begun to publish *Rositsa*, a weekly paper with a Marxist slant. In Tŭrnovo the lawyer Nikola Gabrovski formed an evening school for workers where socialist ideas were discussed. Also in Tŭrnovo, the teacher Spiro Gulabchev formed *Siromakhomilstvo* (Pauperophilia), a secret society modeled on the Russian populist group, the People's Will. Although it was more narodnik than Marxist, it included several young men who soon turned to Marxism. A circle of Bulgarian students that formed in Geneva maintained close contacts with Plekhanov. In 1889, members of a second Bulgarian student circle in Brussels participated in the founding congress of the Second International in Paris, which was also attended by Gabrovski.

In 1890 Blagoev was fired and nearly jailed after making public remarks against the prince. He moved to Tŭrnovo, his wife's home town, where he formed a close relationship with Gabrovski. The two men were convinced that the time had come to found a party, but the repressive atmosphere of the Stambolov regime led others to fear the consequences of coming into the open. In May 1891 the question was discussed by eight representatives from various socialist circles who gathered at Gabrovski's home under the cover of Easter celebrations. No agreement was reached except to meet again in the summer. In the meantime, Blagoev and Gabrovski prepared a charter modeled on those of the Belgian and French parties.

Since political assemblies were then under ban, Blagoev and his colleagues decided to hold their meeting to coincide with the August 2 commemoration of the death of revolutionary hero Khadzhi Dimitŭr, who had perished on the slopes of Mount Buzludzha, south of Tŭrnovo. Gathered

on the mountainside the evening before, Blagoev and a few friends thought
of themselves as direct descendants of Khadzhi Dimitŭr's band. When the
meeting was held the next day, it was attended by about twenty people,
including Blagoev, Gabrovski, Dabev, and delegates from several socialist
circles, as well as a few local "workers, artisans, teachers, and youths." [16]
Some still argued that the formation of an open party would only bring
police repression, but the fifteen delegates who had the right to cast ballots
voted 12 to 3 to proceed. Blagoev and Gabrovski's charter was adopted,
Yanko Sakŭzov's newspaper *Den* (Day) was chosen as the party paper, and
it was also decided to undertake the publication of a "Bulgarian Social
Democratic Library" to make basic ideological works available to the Bulgarian public. The meeting also elected a general council to be head-
quartered in Tŭrnovo. The exact composition of the council is not known,
although it certainly included Blagoev and Gabrovski.

Toward Schism

In September 1891 the Bulgarian Social Democratic Library issued as
its first publication a brochure prepared by Blagoev (but published under
the name D. Bratanov), *What Is Socialism and Is There a Basis for It Here?*, the
first public statement of a socialist program by a Bulgarian author. Initially
inspired by Zakhari Stoianov's newspaper articles stating that the natural
riches and egalitarian structure of the countryside rendered European socialism superfluous in Bulgaria, it argued the same case that Plekhanov had
made for Russia in *Our Differences*, namely, that the traditional peasant-arti-
san economy was disintegrating as the country entered the stage of capitalist development. Intensified exploitation would lead to socialism, defined as
a planned economy with social ownership of the means of production. In a
section that he later recanted, Blagoev argued that there was no basis in
Bulgaria for socialist extremism, that is, for those who saw revolution as
"bombs and dynamite." Rather, the task for socialists was to concentrate on
organization and agitation among the intelligentsia and among workers,
poor artisans, and tradesmen, who were "tomorrow's proletarians."

Open activity of any kind on the part of the young party was not easy.
An attempt on the life of Stambolov in March 1891 was followed by an
intensified crackdown on the political opposition that included an effort to
stamp out socialism. Stiff censorship, surveillance, and jailhouse brutality
led some of Blagoev's colleagues to reconsider their decision to form a
party. Sakŭzov and Dabev began to argue that this step had been premature, and that overt political activity should be abandoned in favor of a
campaign for improved wages and working conditions for the proletariat.

Slavi Balabanov and Krŭstiu (Christian) Rakovski from the Bulgarian colony in Geneva concurred and proposed a Russian model in which questions of politics and ideology would be left to the Bulgarian socialists in Switzerland. Blagoev, demonstrating the stubborn rigidity that was to be both a strength and a weakness for Bulgarian socialism, was unalterably opposed to any change of course.

The issue came to a head in August 1892 at a party congress in Plovdiv. When they were unable to sway Blagoev, Sakŭzov and his allies seceded from the party to form the Social Democratic Union, dedicated to a nonpolitical, educational-economic approach. The majority of socialist circles affiliated with the Social Democratic Union, which also took with it the socialist press. Blagoev and Gabrovski were obliged to begin a new paper, *Rabotnik* (Worker), and to struggle to rebuild a network of party cells. A year later the third congress of the Bulgarian Social Democratic Party, meeting in Tŭrnovo, revised the party program and accepted the Erfurt Program of German Social Democracy, with its minimum and maximum positions and avoidance of revolutionary phraseology. The Tŭrnovo congress also decided that the time had come to enter politics, and "class candidates," forbidden to enter into any kind of deal with another party, ran in districts where the socialists had a local organization. They garnered a total of 571 votes.[17]

It soon became apparent to both sides that the split in the tiny socialist movement was of benefit to no one. The election campaign had seen the Stambolovist boot come down indiscriminately on members of both the Social Democratic Party and the Social Democratic Union. Blagoev himself was arrested in November 1893 on trumped-up charges of plotting against the life of Prince Ferdinand. After his release he held a series of talks with Sakŭzov, which resulted in an agreement to reunite, although the convening of a unification congress was delayed until July by Sakŭzov's arrest. When the delegates finally assembled in Sofia, they faced a political situation transformed by the dismissal of Stambolov in May, the relaxation of his repressive measures, and the prospect of new, relatively honest elections. As Sakŭzov and Blagoev had previously agreed, the Social Democratic Party and the Social Democratic Union merged to form the Bulgarian Social Democratic Workers' Party, retaining Blagoev's adaptation of the Erfurt Program as its charter. A five-member central committee was elected that included Blagoev and Sakŭzov.[18] Gabrovski's *Rabotnik* was made the official party organ, Sakuzov's *Den* became its monthly journal, and Dabev's *Drugar* (Comrade) became the party's working-class publication.

Despite their renewed collaboration, Blagoev and Sakŭzov continued to hold fundamentally different views on the issues of collaboration with other parties, the place of nonproletarians in the party, and the party's relationship to the trade-union movement. This eventually led to the second, decisive split in 1903.

In 1894, however, Sakŭzov succeeded in overcoming Blagoev's objections and persuaded the congress to adopt a policy of endorsing "honest and progressive" candidates in electoral districts where the Social Democrats had no chance of winning. Later on, Sakŭzov and his supporters carried this policy further by cooperating with opposition deputies in the National Assembly, even adding their signatures to protests addressed to the prince. To Blagoev, who never distinguished among bourgeois parties or individuals, this implied recognition of the legitimacy of Ferdinand's authority.

Of deeper significance than Sakŭzov's willingness to play the parliamentary game was his determination to extend the appeal of socialism beyond the ranks of the proletariat and intelligentsia. The party's relationship to "other small-scale producers," that is, the peasantry and artisan classes, was the subject of sharp debate at the unity congress. Unable to reach agreement, the delegates postponed a decision and allowed Social Democratic candidates and agitators to take any position so long as it did not contradict the basic party program. Sakŭzov and Nikola Gabrovski were elected in rural districts after waging campaigns "whose socialist character was absolutely invisible."[19] This success, which was repeated in national elections two years later, inspired thoughts of uniting socialism with the aspirations of "the entire exploited people," in Gabrovski's words. In the party press and in local meetings, Sakŭzov and Gabrovski introduced the peasant question and called for the development of at least a minimal program supporting measures that could attract peasant voters, such as the expansion of cheap credit in the countryside, state subsidies for the mechanization of farms, the elimination of certain taxes, and so on. Blagoev fought fiercely against this idea:

> It may well be that a special "peasant program" will win the laboring peasant masses to our side [he wrote in 1895], but for us, I believe, it is vital to consider the means used to win them over. With such a program we would be attracting the peasant not to our ideas but only to the program itself, most of whose points will of necessity bit by bit be enacted by the bourgeois parties. For us, what is important is that the laboring rural population sympathizes with our ideas, understands our aspirations and how it can benefit from them. Consequently, in my opinion, our propaganda among the peasants must be purely socialist, and outside the general program of the party there is no need for any other special programs.[20]

Looking for support outside the working class would turn the party into "a conglomerate, a congeries of the most varied elements, intelligentsia and petit bourgeois, without any kind of discipline or unity."[21]

Despite Blagoev's arguments, in the early years Sakŭzov's supporters were in the majority. As conditions in the countryside worsened in the long rural depression of 1895–1899, and as the indifference of the government headed by Dimitŭr Grekov began to radicalize the village, they saw an opportunity to expand the Social Democratic constituency. Six Social Democratic deputies were returned from rural districts in the 1899 elections, and at the end of the year Sakŭzov, Gabrovski, and a delegation of about 150 Social Democrats attended the founding congress of the Agrarian Union, where they angled for a peasant alliance.[22] Although the Agrarian congress was cool to socialism, Social Democrats continued to find the village their main source of electoral support. In 1900 Sakŭzov founded the journal *Obshto delo* (Common Cause) to argue the case for a union of "all productive strata" behind a general reform program. When, in 1902, Prime Minister Danev accused the Social Democrats of advocating the abolition of private property, *Obshto delo* hastened to assure the peasant that the party would socialize only large capitalist enterprises and had no designs on the peasant's land, home, or livestock. Blagoev, however, agreed with Danev and wrote that the party would fight to abolish private property "from the biggest machine to the tailor's needle, from the large tracts of land to the last inch of land."[23]

With regard to the relation between the party and the country's fledgling trade unions, Sakŭzov believed that the unions should be politically independent and open to all workers. Self-interest and growing class consciousness would in the long run impel both unions and their members to join the Social Democratic camp. Blagoev did not recognize the independence of the workers' political and economic struggles, and he advocated that the unions be strictly subordinate to party control and open only to party members.[24]

Bulgarian Marxist historians view the conflict between the Blagoev and Sakŭzov wings of the party in terms of the Bolshevik-Menshevik split in Russian Social Democracy, an interpretation that is given superficial plausibility by the coincidence that the Bulgarian party formally divided in 1903, the same year that Russian socialism split. In fact, the Bulgarians were unfamiliar with the conflicts in the Russian socialist movement, and Lenin had little influence among them until 1917. Although in 1902 Blagoev cited passages from *What Is to Be Done?* in an attack on opportunism, he believed that "Lenin" was another of Plekhanov's pseudonyms.[25] Bulgarian socialism borrowed its conflicts as well as its program from German experience. Sakŭzov's ideas approximated the outlook of Eduard Bernstein, and it was not accidental that Bernstein's chief Bulgarian disciple, Dimitŭr Dimitrov, became a collaborator on *Obshto delo*. For his part, Blagoev borrowed many of his arguments from the attacks on Bernsteinism that appeared in the German socialist press.

In 1897, after Sakŭzov gave up publishing *Den* to devote more time to the National Assembly, Blagoev seized the opportunity to introduce a new monthly journal, *Novo vreme* (New Era), the title taken from Karl Kautsky's *Neue Zeit*. Blagoev used the journal as a forum to attack the "broad," social-collaborationist policy of Sakŭzov and his allies. They in turn accused Blagoev of interpreting socialism narrowly, a charge that he fully admitted. The exchange gave rise to the use of the terms "Broad" and "Narrow" to characterize the two factions and later the separate parties.[26]

Because the Bulgarian party drew its active support primarily from the intelligentsia, Blagoev's emphasis on doctrinal purity carried weight, particularly after Bernstein was condemned as a heretic in the German socialist movement. Blagoev was also able to gain support from a number of able younger party members such as Georgi Bakalov, Georgi Kirkov, Khristo Kabakchiev, Vasil Kolarov, and Georgi Dimitrov. The last two, who were to inherit the leadership of the party, were of very different backgrounds. Kolarov was born into an artisan family in Shumen in 1877. (Shumen was renamed Kolarovgrad after Kolarov's death in 1950; its original name was restored in 1964.) A brilliant student, Kolarov first became a schoolteacher and then studied law in Switzerland. Upon returning to Bulgaria in 1900, he was already a rigid opponent of "opportunism." Dimitrov, born in 1882, was raised in a large, though not wealthy, family of Bulgarian Protestants. Forced to leave school because of poor health, he eventually became a printer, thus entering the profession that spearheaded trade-union organization in the country. Although his Protestant connections led him to become for a while the director of the press of the American College in Samokov, he broke with evangelical Protestantism in favor of socialism and became Blagoev's primary deputy in the trade-union movement.[27]

By 1901 Blagoev had a majority of the party's central committee on his side. At the eighth and ninth party congresses in 1901 and 1902 his supporters introduced resolutions condemning Sakŭzov and his doctrines, but on both occasions the blow was deflected by a coalition of Sakŭzov's allies and a middle group that sought to avoid an open split. In March 1903, without waiting for another congress, 53 of Blagoev's followers defected from the Sofia party organization, accused its leadership of paying insufficient attention to the party's proletarian base, and appealed for official recognition. After a "stormy discussion,"three of the five members of the central committee voted to extend recognition to the defectors and to disband the old organization, on the grounds that its members "have become unworthy of the name of socialists." [28]

The fissure opened in Sofia quickly widened into a complete break. When Sakŭzov and Dabev, the minority members of the central committee, circulated a secret appeal to the local organizations, the majority demanded that those organizations pledge their allegiance to Blagoev's faction. On 6–12 July 1903 Blagoev convened a congress of his followers in Ruse and formally expelled Sakŭzov and his allies. They in turn held their own congress. Henceforth, there were two Bulgarian socialist parties, the Narrow Socialists and the Broad Socialists.

The majority of the local party organizations sided with the Narrow Socialists, although the larger ones, with a majority of the preschism membership, went with the Broad Socialists. Four of the seven Social Democratic deputies in the National Assembly also declared for the Broad Socialists. During the summer of 1904 both parties formed trade-union organizations, the Narrow Socialists creating the General Federation of Trade Unions (GFTU) with approximately 1,500 members, and the Broad Socialists founding the Free Trade Union Federation with about 1,200 members.[29]

Growth and Development to the Balkan Wars

Attempts to reunite the two factions of Bulgarian socialism in succeeding years foundered on the intransigence of Blagoev and his followers. The Broad Socialist Party continued to advocate compromise—Sakŭzov even published a small paper called *Edinstvo* (Unity) to press this cause—and in 1910 appealed to the Socialist International for mediation. The International assigned this task to Rakovski and Leon Trotsky. Trotsky attended the 1910 congress of the Narrow Socialist Party and concluded that the split in Bulgarian Social Democracy was due to the primitive social conditions of Bulgaria, particularly the lack of a strong proletarian base for socialist activity. He did not endorse the Broad Socialists or the Narrow Socialists, whom he referred to as "seminarians" for their doctrinal rigidity, but Trotsky deplored the split for its effect on the nascent trade-union movement.[30]

On his arrival the following year, Rakovski at first inclined toward the Broad Socialists and criticized the Narrow Socialists for "orientalism, hairsplitting, and factional egotism." During the summer he began publishing his own paper, *Napred* (Forward), to propagandize for reconciliation. The Narrow Socialists ignored Rakovski, and he also became disillusioned with the Broad Socialists, eventually concluding that their policy of socialist collaboration led to mongrelization and a loss of socialist "honesty and dignity." Rakovski left the country early in 1912.[31]

Both the Narrow and the Broad Socialist parties grew slowly during these years. Membership statistics presented at annual Narrow Socialist Party congresses are provided in Table 1.

The Narrow-affiliated GFTU also grew. Its membership exceeded

TABLE 1   MEMBERSHIP IN NARROW SOCIALIST PARTY,
          1903–1912

Year	Membership	Proletarian Members
1903	1,174	480
1904	1,195	613
1905	1,475	774
1906	1,234	748
1907	1,795	1,189
1908	1,661	1,103
1909	1,870	1,230
1910	2,126	1,230
1911	2,510	—
1912	2,923	—

SOURCE: Joseph Rothschild, *The Communist Party of Bulgaria: Origins and Development, 1883–1936* (New York, 1959), p. 41; and *Istoriia na Bŭlgarskata komunisticheska partiia* (Sofia, 1981), pp. 660–64.

2,000 in 1908 and 5,000 in 1912, but it had only limited success in organizing strikes. Nor was the picture brighter in the political arena. Owing to a change in the electoral law that substituted single-member constituencies for proportional representation, not a single Social Democrat was returned in the thirteenth National Assembly elections in 1903. Only 8,101 votes, less than 1 percent of the total, were cast for Social Democrats in the fourteenth National Assembly elections five years later.[32]

Nor was the Broad Socialist Party any more successful, in spite of Sakŭzov's goal of creating a genuinely popular movement. Between 1904 and 1911 party membership grew from 1,210 to just over 3,000.[33] The primary obstacle to the growth of Broad Socialism lay in the rise of the Bulgarian Agrarian National Union (BANU) as the party of the peasantry. During the first years of the new century, the Agrarians found in Alexander Stamboliski a remarkable theorist, organizer, and spokesman—a man capable of building a powerful mass movement. Stamboliski developed an orginal analysis of Bulgarian society, one far more realistic and sophisticated than the sterile formulas borrowed by Bulgaria's Marxists. Stamboliski's ideas provided the foundation for the Agrarian Union's program and organizational tactics. By 1908 the BANU had already become the largest opposition party, polling over 100,000 votes.[34] The Broad Socialists, although wishing for peasant support, had always viewed the peasants as auxiliaries to the workers' movement. Consequently, they were unable to compete with the Agrarians for village votes. It was to be the chronic problem of the Broad Socialist Party that it could never stake out substantial terrain between the Narrow Socialists and the Agrarians, a fact that all too often led its members into compromise with royalist and conservative forces.

Although there is a tendency to exaggerate the parallels between Bolshevism and Narrow Socialism, there is one that is entirely justified: in the years before the First World War, internal factionalism, heresies, and witch hunts absorbed a large share of the time and attention of the party leaders. Just as Lenin waged war on conciliators, liquidationists, god-builders, and others, so Blagoev had to deal with various dissenting movements among the Bulgarian party intelligentsia. And, in both cases, the personality of the party leader and his desire for complete authority became issues of debate.

The first conflict within Narrow Socialism arose in 1905 and concerned control over the party press. At this time the party was publishing *Rabotnicheski vestnik* (Workers' Newspaper) as its official newspaper and *Novo vreme* as its theoretical journal. Another journal, *Rabotnichesko delo* (Workers' Cause), published by central committee member Georgi Bakalov, was directed at trade-union members and had semiofficial status. There were other publications edited by party members on their own initiative. Because Bakalov's position on the Broad Socialists was softer than Blagoev's, and because Bakalov also favored looser ties between the party and the trade unions, Blagoev's supporters in the party leadership called for a reform of the party press. They proposed that Bakalov's paper be suspended and that all party publications be subject to central committee approval. Bakalov and his ally on the central committee, party secretary Nikola Kharlakov, protested, defending the right of individual expression and accusing Blagoev of "bureaucratic centralism" and seeking to establish a "dictatorship" over the party. They were supported by a number of party intellectuals, whom Blagoev promptly labeled "anarcho-liberals" because of their defense of individualism. At the twelfth party congress in 1905, Bakalov and Kharlakov were ousted from the central committee in the name of "genuine socialist discipline," and Blagoev's press reform was adopted. Bakalov, Kharlakov, and their followers refused to recant and abandoned the Narrow Socialist Party at the end of the year to form the Liberal Socialist Party. Although its membership was small, about four hundred, its influence with the trade unions was probably equal to that of either the Broad or the Narrow Socialists.[35]

During 1908 a new group of "Progressives," Nikola Sakarov, Genko Krŭstev, and Koika Tineva, influenced by the Second International's calls for socialist unity, began to demand negotiations with the Broad Socialists. They were condemned at the fifteenth congress in 1908, and, when they failed to admit their errors, they were expelled from the party. At the end of 1908 the Progressives, Liberal Socialists, and Broad Socialists all merged to form the Bulgarian Social Democratic Workers' Party (united), which, however, was still known as the Broad Socialist Party.

The Narrow Socialist Party had purged itself three times within five years. It retained its doctrinal purity, but at the cost of popular support. Indeed, there is justification for refusing to view it as a political party at all, rather than as a sect or propaganda society. But a mass following was to come, the product not of the party's work or the growth of capitalism, but of the disastrous blunders of the country's leaders.

THE NATIONAL QUESTION AND THE BALKAN WARS

In June 1908 the revolt of the Young Turks upset the precarious equilibrium in the Near East and set in motion a train of events that was to involve Bulgaria in three major wars. The international situation, especially concerns about the future of the Ottoman empire and the Balkans, now began to dominate Bulgaria's domestic politics and perforce the attention of the socialists.

On 5 October 1908, in conjunction with the Austrian annexation of Bosnia-Herzegovina, Prince Ferdinand proclaimed the complete independence of Bulgaria from the Ottoman empire and appropriated for himself the title of tsar. This declaration, and Ferdinand's refusal to compensate the Porte for the annual tribute that Bulgaria had customarily paid, raised the possibility of war. Russian diplomacy intervened to negotiate a compromise. Bulgaria paid £5,000,000 for her independence—£1,720,000 of which was contributed by Russia.

The Narrow Socialist Party condemned Ferdinand's diplomacy. In an editorial, Blagoev wrote that the party could agree with the bourgeoisie in supporting the idea of uniting all Bulgarians in a single state. This would create a larger market and foster the development of the economy and therefore the socialist movement. But the party could not support the means chosen by the bourgeoisie, which both strengthened the monarchy at home and increased the threat of international war.[36]

In January 1910 a Narrow Socialist Party delegation consisting of Blagoev, Kirkov, Kolarov, Dimitrov, and Kabakchiev attended the first Balkan Social Democratic Congress in Belgrade. There the Bulgarians met with representatives of socialist groups from Serbia, Croatia, Slovenia, Romania, Bosnia-Herzegovina, Macedonia, Turkey, and Montenegro. Blagoev presided over the congress, which adopted a resolution condemning the interference of the great powers in the Balkans and the efforts of the rulers of the various Balkan states to achieve hegemony at the expense of their neighbors. The congress supported the idea of a Balkan federal republic, and the socialist parties agreed to fight for peace and Balkan unity. The movement for unity among the socialists was hampered, however, by the Narrow Socialist Party's objection to inviting the Broad Socialist Party to join. The congress's unwillingness to reject the Broad Socialists altogether caused the Narrow Socialist Party to cancel plans for a second congress in Sofia the following year. Instead it invited the Balkan and other Slavic socialist parties to send delegates to the Narrow Socialist Party's seventeenth congress in July, which was proclaimed a pansocialist conference (in contrast to a pan-Slav congress held in Sofia a few weeks earlier). Trotsky, on the mission of reconciliation described above, spoke on behalf of Russian Social Democracy.

Early in 1911 the Malinov government dissolved the National Assembly and announced that elections would be held in June for a Grand National Assembly to amend the constitution.[37] The proposed amendments called for changing the words *prince* and *principality* to *tsar* and *tsardom* wherever appropriate, thus ratifying Ferdinand's adoption of the tsarist title in 1908, raising Ferdinand's civil list, and allowing the tsar to conclude secret treaties without the knowledge or approval of the assembly. Both socialist parties, the Agrarian Union and the Radical Democratic Party, saw these amendments as a threat to peace and campaigned vigorously against them. In the elections the Narrow Socialist Party received 12,300 votes, more than ten times its previous high, although only one of its candidates was elected. The Broad Socialists received 18,351 votes, electing five deputies, but it was the Agrarian Union, polling 160,000 votes and electing over 50 deputies, that was the big winner among the opposition.[38] When the Grand National Assembly convened, it was Stamboliski who led an opposition coalition of Agrarians, Broad Socialists, and Radical Democrats to which the lone Narrow socialist deputy adhered.

The constitutional changes were passed by a large majority in spite of the opposition protests, and in the ensuing elections in September the government went out of its way to punish the opposition, exerting unusually severe pressure on the electorate and disqualifying a large number of candidates. Of the four parties that composed the opposition to Ferdinand, only the Agrarian Union succeeded in electing any of its candidates (four); both socialist parties were shut out, although Sakŭzov managed to win a by-election the following June.[39]

Shortly after the September elections, Italy declared war on the Ottoman empire, thus encouraging Balkan statesmen to seek an immediate solution to the problem of Turkey-in-Europe. Negotiations for a Serbian-Bulgarian alliance were concluded in March 1912. Greece joined the alliance a month later and Montenegro in June. Meanwhile, events in Macedonia were becoming more unsettled. In November 1911 Turks carried out a pogrom against the Bulgarian community in Shtip; another massacre in Kochana in July created a popular war fever.

Although without a voice in parliament, the Narrow Socialist Party opposed the approaching war in its press. At its nineteenth congress in August 1912, the party adopted a resolution condemning the war campaign, and it again endorsed the idea of a Balkan federation to be achieved through peaceful means.[40] During the following weeks, the party organized a series of antiwar demonstrations around the country. The antiwar campaign was independently supported by the BANU and the Broad Socialists. A few days after the announcement of mobilization on 30 September 1912, Sakŭzov denounced the impending war in a speech to the National Assembly that caused a mob to assault him upon his departure from the chamber.

Mobilization brought the suspension of the Narrow Socialist Party's press and the disruption of its organization as many of its members, including party secretary Kirkov, were called to the colors. Deprived of a forum at home, Blagoev published his analysis of the war in two articles in the *Leipziger Volkszeitung* and *Vorwärts*. He argued that the war had been brought about by a combination of Turkish misrule and the diplomacy of the great powers, particularly Russia. The Balkan League was a military-monarchic alliance, not a popular one, and it was directed at the conquest of territory, not the free development of the Balkan peoples. Moreover, Blagoev wrote, the Bulgarian ruling class was guilty of inconsistency since for three decades it had proclaimed the Bulgarian character of all of Macedonia, but now it had acquiesced in the division of the region with Serbia and Greece.[41]

Later, in the spring of 1913, Blagoev wrote that the Balkan bourgeoisie had appeared on the historical scene as a latecomer, at a time when the bourgeoisie in general had lost its revolutionary, democratic drive and was capable of approaching the Balkan question only through militarism and reactionary, monarchic, political institutions. This could only lead to perpetual conflict among the Balkan dynasties. The only way out of this impasse, Blagoev continued, was through the long-term economic development of the peninsula, the growth of Social Democracy, and the eventual birth of a Balkan federative republic.[42] Blagoev's analysis of the weakness of the Balkan League was accurate, but the call for Balkan federation, however noble in the abstract, was a utopian formula with no practical relevance. It was a means of avoiding an actual confrontation with the problem. The growth of Social Democracy in the Balkan setting was a matter for the distant future. And it is significant that at no point did Blagoev suggest a revolutionary approach to the war. When the party took action, it was limited to organizing measures for the relief of casualties and their families.

Nor was the Second International able to give much guidance. It organized an extraordinary congress at Basel on 24–25 November 1912, at which the Bulgarian socialist parties were represented by Kabakchiev and Sakŭzov. Adopting a resolution calling for the socialist parties to work for a speedy end to the war, the congress did not state in any explicit terms what should be done.[43]

Blagoev's prediction of future Balkan conflict was fulfilled on 16 June 1913, when Tsar Ferdinand ordered Bulgarian forces to attack the Serbian and Greek armies in Macedonia. This act of folly brought Bulgaria's quick defeat, the stripping of most of its gains from the first war, and the loss of the southern Dobruja to Romania.

The national humiliation suffered by Bulgaria undermined the hold of the country's traditional rulers and provided a powerful impetus to the radicalization of the electorate. The National and Progressive Liberal parties of Geshov and Danev were permanently discredited. In the first postwar elections the governing Liberal coalition was able to poll barely 38 percent of the votes and fell short of a parliamentary majority. As Table 2 shows, the antiwar parties greatly increased their following.

When the assembly convened, the Narrow Socialist deputies staged a demonstration against the tsar and then introduced legislation calling for the punishment of those responsible for the war. So tumultuous were the assembly sessions that parliament was dissolved after only twelve days. In the elections for a new assembly on 8 March 1914, the government managed a slim victory, but the Narrow Socialists still received 43,766 votes and eleven mandates.[44]

THE PARTY AND THE FIRST WORLD WAR

When the First World War began, Blagoev attributed it not to the assassination at Sarajevo but to "the relations between the European powers created by the development of capitalism," and he predicted, echoing the resolution of the Basel socialist conference, that it would lead to the collapse of the capitalist order.

> After the general war in Europe will come general revolution. What is more, at the height of the war, at the height of mutual annihilation, we can expect the outbreak of revolution. We are still at the beginning of the insane annihilation of peoples that capitalism has brought about, but already we hear the rumblings of revolution, the beginning of the social revolution, the salvation of mankind from the barbarian butchers, toward which the present capitalist society is leading. And there is no doubt that the only victor in the present general European war will be the inevitable general European revolution.[45]

TABLE 2   ELECTIONS FOR THE SIXTEENTH NATIONAL ASSEMBLY,
24 NOVEMBER 1913

Party	Deputies	Votes	Percentage of Votes
Liberal Coalition	95	207,763	38.2
BANU	48	113,761	20.9
Broad Socialist	17	55,171	10.2
Narrow Socialist	18	54,217	10.0
Democratic	15	42,971	7.9
National	5	24,344	4.5
Radical Democratic	5	24,007	4.4
Progressive Liberal	1	11,863	2.2
Others	0	9,333	1.7
Total	204	543,430	100.0

SOURCE: *Statisticheski godishnik na bŭlgarskoto tsarstvo: Godini X–XIV, 1913–1922* (Sofia, 1924), sec. 30, p. 57.

But Blagoev expected the revolution to begin in Germany, France, or England, and it came as a tremendous shock and disappointment to him that the leaders of the great European socialist parties succumbed to war fever, voted for war credits, and took positions in war cabinets. If his reaction was less immediate and decisive than Lenin's, he still unequivocally rejected the path of social chauvinism.

Blagoev was particularly disturbed by Plekhanov's joining the patriotic camp. At the end of October 1914, Plekhanov sent Blagoev a letter for publication in *Novo vreme* that explained his position and asked the Narrow Socialists to throw their influence to the side of the Entente. Blagoev published this letter but accompanied it with his own article, "Magister dixit," which rebutted Plekhanov's arguments and rejected his "nationalist outlook" in favor of "international proletarian solidarity." [46] Early in 1915 Blagoev similarly rebuffed an attempt by Parvus to persuade the Narrow Socialist Party to back the German side.

Blagoev interpreted the failures of European socialism in terms of his own struggle with the Broad Socialists, attributing them to opportunism and the influence of nonproletarian elements. He was not ready, however, to break with the Second International, nor was he yet able to grasp Lenin's strategy of converting the international war into a revolutionary civil war. At the Zimmerwald conference in September 1915, the Narrow Socialist Party's delegate, Vasil Kolarov, voted against Lenin's plan to create a new, revolutionary International and in favor of the majority resolution that simply condemned the war. [47] This resolution was printed in *Rabotnicheski vestnik* on the day of Bulgarian mobilization. With Bulgaria's entry into the war, travel restrictions isolated the Narrow Socialist Party from international socialism until late in 1917.

It is a source of pride to Bulgarian Communists that the Narrow Socialist Party never wavered in its opposition to Bulgarian intervention and that, when Tsar Ferdinand and the Radoslavov government brought Bulgaria in on the side of the Central Powers, the Narrow Socialist Party was the only one to vote against the war budget. The Broad Socialists abstained during votes on war credits and later accepted important posts in the government. But it is also true that the Narrow Socialist Party's opposition to the war had an abstract, theoretical character, and that Blagoev's distrust of other parties opposed to intervention and his unwillingness to cooperate with them robbed the antiwar forces of unity. What, indeed, was the significance of the party's introducing a parliamentary resolution that called for Balkan federation when Serbia was locked in combat with Austria-Hungary? Although Blagoev wrote articles predicting proletarian revolution, it was the Agrarian leader Stamboliski who threatened the tsar to his face and called for the troops to refuse to obey the mobilization order. And it was Stamboliski and the BANU that bore the brunt of government repression during the war.

The marginality of the Narrow Socialist Party in Bulgarian life, at least until 1917, was its best protection, for its predictions of inevitable revolution were unaccompanied by revolutionary acts. For most of the war, it was a tolerated opposition. *Rabotnicheski vestnik* was published continuously, although it was occasionally banned at the front, and the party's resolutions in the assembly provoked mirth rather than apprehension. As his biographers wrote: "Blagoev passed the difficult war years with his family in Sofia. He worked as a member of the central committee of the party, . . . took an active part in the work of the National Assembly as a deputy and as president of the BWSDP (n.s.) parliamentary group, sat at the regular meetings of the Sofia City Council, the school board, etc." [48] It was not until the collapse of tsarist Russia that Blagoev and the Narrow Socialist Party began to conceive of a Bulgarian socialist revolution, and even then Blagoev's analysis had little relationship to Bulgarian reality.

2

Expansion and Defeat, 1917–1923

The material and human costs of the war were greater than Bulgaria could bear. By the autumn of 1918 approximately 900,000 men, nearly 40 percent of the male population, had been conscripted. The army suffered 300,000 casualties, including 100,000 killed, the most severe per capita losses of any country involved in the war.[1] Troops at the front were poorly supplied, irregularly paid, and resentful of their German allies, who took advantage of their privileged position to loot the country. As the war dragged on, sporadic revolts and increasing desertion marked the cracking of military discipline. In the interior, bad weather and the absence of adult male labor cut grain production nearly in half, while the town population suffered from food and fuel shortages and runaway inflation. Rumors of hoarding and vast fortunes made overnight through speculation by privileged individuals helped to spark widespread antigovernment demonstrations, the "women's riots" for food that began early in 1917 and continued to the end of the war.[2] In June 1918, the replacement of Radoslavov by Alexander Malinov, a leader of the parliamentary opposition, raised hopes for an end to the war, which only increased frustration when Malinov yielded to Ferdinand's determination to fight on.

Misery created by the war and the example of the revolution in Russia raised the prestige and influence of the Narrow Socialist Party. *Rabotnicheski vestnik*, with a circulation of 30,000 by 1918, was the most widely read paper in the country. Party membership, which stood at 3,400 in 1915, had doubled and was growing rapidly.[3] And the party leadership, inspired by the victory of the Bolsheviks, began to act with greater energy. The Soviet "Decree on Peace" was widely disseminated, and during December 1917 the party organized demonstrations to demand its acceptance. Blagoev published a series of articles in *Rabotnicheski vestnik* that interpreted the war in terms of Lenin's *Imperialism: The Highest Stage of Capitalism*, and already by the spring of 1918 Blagoev was proposing to change the party name to "Communist."[4] The party began to produce and distribute illegal literature calling on the troops themselves to put an end to the war.

Increased antiwar agitation brought stiffer repression. Georgi Dimitrov was convicted of "inciting to mutiny" when he encouraged a wounded soldier to defy an officer's order to vacate a first-class railway compartment. Similar charges were brought against two other Narrow Socialist deputies, Todor Lukanov and Kosta Tsiporanov, who were arrested for distributing revolutionary leaflets.[5]

But the Narrow Socialist Pary was still far from recognizing a "revolutionary situation" in the country. Its propaganda and agitation continued to focus on the demand for peace, and it took few steps to prepare itself for actual revolutionary leadership. The party conference held on 22 September 1918, at the very time the front was collapsing, demonstrated that the Narrow Socialist leadership was still "insufficiently Bolshevized." Although it adopted a resolution hailing "with rapture" the victory of the Russian proletariat and calling it "the *avant garde* of the European socialist revolution," there was no discussion of preparing a Bulgarian revolution, for Blagoev's vision, like Lenin's, was focused on the advanced capitalist states. When one of the soldier-delegates asked Blagoev what should be done in the event of a military uprising, the Narrow Socialist leader replied: "You should take your guns and point them at Sofia to seize power."[6] When the soldiers did just that, Blagoev and his party were not equal to the test.

THE RADOMIR REBELLION

In the dome of the Buzludzha Monument, erected in 1981 to commemorate the ninetieth anniversary of the founding of the Bulgarian Social Democratic Party, important dates in the history of Bulgarian communism are cast in concrete. Among them is 1918, marking the Soldiers' Uprising and the "revolutionary upsurge" of the Bulgarian masses. In fact, insofar as the uprising had political leadership and organization, they were provided by the Agrarian Union, above all by Alexander Stamboliski, who became convinced after the February Revolution in Russia that Ferdinand's regime would not survive the war. From his cell in Sofia's Central Prison Stamboliski strove to orient the BANU toward the assumption of power. His first attempt to translate this strategy into action was the Radomir Rebellion.

Briefly stated, the sequence of events was as follows.[7] On 15 September 1918 the Allied Expeditionary Force on the Macedonian front broke through the Bulgarian lines at Dobro Pole. Troops fell back in disorder, many deserting to return home, others determined to march on Sofia to punish Tsar Ferdinand and the politicians responsible for the war. By 24 September rebel soldiers captured the critical rail center of Kiustendil on the road to the capital. On the following morning Stamboliski was released from prison to confer with Malinov, who proposed that he join a government of national unity aimed at preserving domestic order and military discipline until an armistice could be negotiated. Stamboliski refused this offer to board a sinking ship, but in an audience with Ferdinand later in the day he agreed to use his influence to calm the troops in return for the tsar's promise to seek an immediate armistice. Arriving at Radomir, the advance point of the rebellion, about 35 miles southwest of Sofia, Stamboliski placed himself at its head, declared the monarchy overthrown, and proclaimed Bulgaria a republic with himself as president of the provisional government and his colleague Raiko Daskalov as commander in chief. The Radomir Republic was short-lived and failed for three reasons: the signing of an armistice on 29 September satisfied many of the rebels, who laid down their arms and returned home; German and die-hard Macedonian units successfully repulsed Daskalov's badly organized assault on Sofia; and the rebellion received no support from inside the capital.

What was the attitude of the Narrow Socialist Party to the rebellion? On 25 September, shortly after his meeting with Malinov, Stamboliski sought out Blagoev and found him at home in bed recovering from an illness. He proposed that the Agrarians and Narrow Socialists ally to overthrow Ferdinand. "You are strong in the towns," he told the Narrow Socialist leader, "we are strong in the villages; together we can take power." Blagoev, who later confessed to having been taken by surprise, demurred, citing "irreconcilable differences" between the two parties. Stamboliski denied their significance and offered to accept the Narrow Socialists' entire program with the exception of its stand on private property for peasants. But Blagoev still refused, and, despite the fact that many Narrow Socialists took part in some phase of the rebellion, the party officially remained aloof from it. Blagoev and his allies in the party leadership later justified their decision on the grounds that the party was still poorly organized and without experience in guiding the masses, that the international situation was unfavorable, and that the peasantry would not in fact be a reliable ally in a genuinely revolutionary situation.[8] Later experience was to show that the last consideration was the strongest factor. Having fought for years to preserve the proletarian purity of the party, Blagoev could not rapidly jettison this Narrow Socialist heritage in favor of accepting a subordinate role in an Agrarian-led uprising.

Today party historians criticize Blagoev's inflexibilty and take this decision as evidence that the Narrow Socialist Party had not yet absorbed the lessons of Leninism.[9] But two things at least can be said in Blagoev's defense. He was undoubtedly correct about the international situation. Bulgaria soon submitted to Allied occupation, and it was hardly likely that the Allies would have permitted Narrow Socialist participation in a Bulgarian government, particularly one that had come to power through illegal means. Moreover, Lenin's tactics vis-à-vis the peasantry were not simply transferable to the Bulgarian scene. If Blagoev was no Lenin, Stamboliski was no Chernov or Kerenski. Given the BANU's superior numbers, organization, and drive for power, the Narrow Socialists' role would inevitably have been limited and secondary. Blagoev, who, like Lenin himself, was still looking for the spread of socialist revolution to industrial Europe, can hardly be faulted for choosing to husband the party's resources in expectation of a more favorable moment.

THE BULGARIAN COMMUNIST PARTY

In the months after the defeat of the Radomir Rebellion, events seemed to confirm Blagoev's belief that a revolutionary tide was running that would in time bring his party to power. Outside Bulgaria, between January and April 1919, the Red Army reached the Black Sea, installing Bulgarian-born Krŭstiu Rakovski as master of the Soviet Ukraine; the proclamation of Bela Kun's Hungarian Soviet Republic in March was quickly followed by the communist seizure of power in Bavaria. Against the background of these events, Lenin founded the new Communist International.

Inside Bulgaria, politics shifted steadily leftward, seeming to repeat the Russian experience after the February Revolution. In October 1918 Tsar Ferdinand was compelled by the Allies to leave the country after abdicating in favor of his 22-year-old son Boris. Later in the month, Malinov reorganized his cabinet, admitting one representative each from the Broad Socialist Party and the BANU. Before a month had passed, this government, too, had fallen, to be replaced by a coalition that included two Broad Socialists and two Agrarians. In January 1919 the National Assembly amnestied the participants in the Radomir Rebellion, and Stamboliski came out of hiding both to enter the government and to purge the BANU of its conservative wing.

When the Sofia Workers' Choir sang the "Internationale" to open the twenty-second congress of the Narrow Socialist Party on 25 May, circumstances had never appeared more favorable. The 636 delegates crowded into the Crown Cinema heard Blagoev describe the party's tremendous growth. Table 3, compiled from his central committee report, shows the party's recovery from the war and its postwar expansion.

If anything these figures understate the extent of the party's growing influence. The party-controlled GFTU had 13,000 members, and the party-affiliated unions of teachers and civil servants added another 2,000. To administer these larger bodies the congress approved a new party structure that created two levels of provincial and district committees. A Higher Party Council, composed of the central committee, the control commission, and delegates from the provincial committees, was to coordinate party activities.[10]

Two months before the Narrow Socialist congress, the Comintern was founded in Moscow. Because the Narrow Socialist Party's invitation was not received until shortly before the founding congress was held, and because travel between Sofia and Moscow was then next to impossible, the party was represented by Rakovski, who performed a similar duty for the Romanians. By May, however, the Narrow Socialist leadership was well informed about the Comintern, and its principles were clearly reflected at the Narrow Socialist Party congress. The Narrow Socialists voted unanimously to join the Comintern, the only party other than the Bolsheviks to do so. At the same time, the party name was changed to Bulgarian Communist Party (n.s.), so that the twenty-second Narrow Socialist congress became simultaneously the first congress of the BCP. The program established as the party's goal the dictatorship of the proletariat, "the sole means of bringing genuine freedom to the laboring masses," and it endorsed "new forms of revolutionary struggle—from mass demonstrations and the mass political strike to the armed uprising." But these brave words were not easily translated into action. Blagoev maintained that socialist revolution in Bulgaria depended "three-quarters on the external situation, one-quarter on the internal," and no concrete preparations for illegal actions were contemplated. On the one hand, a group of "leftists," who demanded that the party quit the National Assembly and turn to "direct action," were sharply criticized by Kolarov, and their proposals were rejected. On the other hand, the congress also turned down the offer of Nikola Kharlakov to rejoin the party if it would depoliticize the trade unions. Finally, the congress elected a new central committee consisting of Blagoev, Kirkov, Kolarov, Kabakchiev, Dimitrov, Lukanov, and Nikola Penev.[11]

After the congress, the BCP sought to test its strength in the mines, factories, and streets by organizing a series of strikes and demonstrations in protest against unemployment, the cost of living, and food shortages. The

Table 3   Party Membership, 1915–1919

Year	Groups and Organizations	Members
1915 (before mobilization)	134	3,435
1915 (after mobilization)	19	650
1916	31	830
1917	57	1,623
1918 (before armistice)	70	2,041
1918 (end of December)	109	6,000
1919 (beginning of February)	239	10,000
1919 (end of April)	582	21,577
1919 (May 20)	636	22,533

Source: Petko Boev, *Kongres istoricheski* (Sofia, 1980), p. 14.

most serious clash came on 27 July when the party's plan for nationwide demonstrations was ruthlessly met by Krŭstiu Pastukhov, the Broad Socialist minister of the interior, who imposed martial law and enlisted the help of Allied occupation troops. An estimated 100 people were killed in the fighting. Although Pastukhov won this battle, the BCP succeeded in pinning the label "police socialists" on his party and won over much of the Broad Socialists' following among the working class.

New reason for optimism came with Bulgaria's first postwar elections on 17 August 1919, whose results, shown in Table 4, were clear evidence of the leftward swing of the electorate.

When these elections were held, Stamboliski was in Paris as a member of Bulgaria's peace delegation. When he returned to Sofia at the end of September, he followed parliamentary tradition by making a pro forma offer to the BCP to enter a coalition government.[12] After Blagoev declined to join hands with the "petite bourgeoisie," Stamboliski turned to the party he really wanted, the Broad Socialists. The Broad Socialists, however, were torn between fear and ambition. They had clearly lost working-class support to the Communists; their solid 13 percent of the vote in August was not so impressive when it is recalled that they controlled the Interior Ministry, always a heavy advantage on Bulgarian election days. But because the Broad Socialists had learned the uses of power and still possessed a committed following in the government bureaucracy and among the railroad workers, they hoped to emerge as the respectable leftist alternative to both Agrarians and Communists. Consequently, they agreed to form a coalition with the BANU, but, as a price, demanded the ministries of the interior; war; commerce; and rails, post, and telegraph—in effect a request for control of the police, army, and a critical segment of the working class. Stamboliski, who suspected the Broad Socialists of trying to set the stage for a coup, rejected the proposal, and when the Broad Socialists refused to settle for less, he turned to two conservative parties, the National Party and the Progressive Liberal Party, to form a government.[13]

The failure of the Agrarians and Broad Socialists to come to terms was a misfortune for them and for the country. Such an alliance could have brought Stamboliski's government badly needed cadres with administrative skills and experience, and it could have established a firm niche for the Broad Socialists in Bulgarian political life. It was doubly unfortunate in that the tradition of Broad Socialism had been to reach out to the countryside for allies. Unhappily, the Broad Socialists had always seen themselves as directors of the worker-peasant movement, and they could not be reconciled to a subordinate place. They paid a high price for their decision, since it led to political isolation. During the following years, the BCP dealt the Broad Socialists [henceforth referred to simply as "Socialists"] another blow by inviting the secession of those willing to accept the Comintern's Twenty-one Conditions. This cost the Socialists about a fifth of their membership.[14]

The General Strike

The question of who had real power in Bulgaria was not settled by the formation of Stamboliski's coalition. During their negotiations with the Agrarians, the Socialists had raised the threat of strikes. And the BCP had

TABLE 4   NATIONAL ASSEMBLY ELECTIONS, 17 AUGUST 1919

Party	Deputies Elected	Votes	Percentage of Votes
BANU	85	180,648	28
BCP	47	118,671	18
Broad Socialists	36	82,826	13
Democrats	28	65,267	10
Nationals	19	54,556	8
Progressive Liberals	8	52,722	8
Liberals	2	42,024	6
Radicals	8	33,343	5
Others	0	26,258	4
Total	233	656,315	100

SOURCE: *Statisticheski godishnik na bŭlgarskoto tsarstvo: Godini V–XIV, 1913-1922* (Sofia, 1924), p. C59.

shown at its congress that it was moving toward more revolutionary tactics. In November the party organized a new series of demonstrations directed against the Treaty of Neuilly, and in town and village council elections on 7 December the BCP polled 20,000 more votes than it had won in August.[15] Although the BANU swept the rural localities, the BCP did very well in the towns, winning absolute majorities in Plovdiv, Varna, Ruse, Shumen, Pleven, Sliven, Burgas, and Dupnitsa (Stanke Dimitrov).[16] For its part, the Agrarian Union prepared for the coming trial by turning to its village organizations, or *druzhbi*, to form the Orange Guard, composed of able-bodied peasants, some with firearms and others with clubs, under the command of local *druzhba* leaders.

The BCP decided to test its strength by holding nationwide demonstrations to coincide with the opening of the National Assembly on 24 December. Because the government proclaimed martial law and brought Orange Guards into the towns, most of the demonstrations failed to take place, but there was some fighting in Pleven, Stara Zagora, and other towns, and in Dupnitsa the workers actually seized control of the town for several hours. The next day a wildcat strike broke out among the transport workers. It seems to have taken the leaders of both unions and political parties by surprise, but the BCP was quick to react, calling for a general strike. The Socialists, frightened of falling behind, joined in. The general strike began officially at noon on 28 December.[17]

Although aware of the deprivations suffered by the workers, Stamboliski was convinced that the stike had been called for political reasons. The Orange Guard was mobilized, and peasants who had served in transport battalions during the war were put to work on the railroads. The Allied occupation authorities lent troops, expertise, and moral support to the government.

Stamboliski attacked the Communists in their stronghold, the Pernik coal mines. Half the Sofia garrison was sent to the mines, where hundreds of strikers were arrested; Orange Guards put the mines back into production.[18] The government also militarized the transportation and communications industries. Workers were mobilized, and those who failed to report were evicted from their state-owned apartments, deprived of food-ration cards, and threatened with military courts. Several party leaders were arrested, and others directly involved with the strike committees went underground. In the face of this decisive counterattack, the party leadership faltered and broke, calling an end to the general strike on 5 January. The transport and communications workers and the Pernik miners continued to hold out, but by 19 February the entire strike effort had collapsed.

Stamboliski wanted to defeat the Communists, not crush them. He recognized the BCP as the legitimate political representative of the Bulgarian proletariat, with which some accommodation would have to be reached to restore social and political stability. Moreover, he knew that fear of the Communists would make the right-wing parties more willing to accept the BANU as a lesser evil. Consequently, when the strike formally ended, the government dropped its countermeasures and scheduled new elections for 28 March. As Table 5 shows, the BCP won 66,000 more votes than it had in August 1919, but the BANU nearly doubled its total and came close to an absolute majority in parliament.

Rather than form another coalition, Stamboliski invoked rarely used provisions in the electoral law to quash the election of thirteen deputies, nine of whom were Communists. With a narrow majority of four votes, he proceeded to form a one-party, Agrarian cabinet.

THE BCP AND THE STAMBOLISKI GOVERNMENT

The Agrarian government rapidly enacted a sweeping reform program to implement its ideological vision. Its principal measures included land reform, setting a maximum of 30 hectares of arable land per household; the encouragement of cooperative organizations in the countryside; the vast expansion of the country's educational system; and the introduction of compulsory labor service, requiring young men to devote a year of work to state enterprises and construction projects in place of the compulsory military service that had been abolished by the Treaty of Neuilly. Because Stamboliski had long identified militarism and jingoistic nationalism as false ideals with which Bulgaria's traditional leaders had manipulated the people, he renounced the "national goal" of uniting all Bulgarians in a single state, accepted the peace settlement (including the incorporation of the bulk of Macedonia in the Serb-Croat-Slovene Kingdom), and sought to develop good relations with Bulgaria's neighbors, seeing in Balkan cooperation if not a federation then at least a solution to the longstanding conflicts on the peninsula.[19]

Communist historians now hold that the emergence of the Agrarian government was "lawful" (that is, in conformity with the laws of history), that the Agrarian reforms were progressive and reflected the genuine aspirations of the peasant masses, and that the coup d'état of 9 June 1923 was a tragedy both for the Bulgarian people and for Bulgarian communism.[20] This interpretation is far removed from the contemporary views of the BCP, for in 1923 the party retained Narrow Socialism's traditional antipathy toward the peasant and applied, or, more accurately, misapplied the Russian analogy to the Bulgarian environment to arrive at the conclusion that the Agrarian regime was the major counterrevolutionary force in the

TABLE 5   NATIONAL ASSEMBLY ELECTIONS, 28 MARCH 1920

Party	Deputies Elected	Votes	Percentage of Votes
BANU	110	349,212	38.2
BCP	51	184,616	20.2
Democrats	23	91,177	10.0
Nationals	15	61,647	6.7
Broad Socialists	7	55,542	6.1
Progressive Liberals	9	46,930	5.1
Radical Democrats	8	41,930	4.6
National Liberals	6	39,537	4.2
Others	0	44,581	4.9
Total	229	915,172	100.0

SOURCES: Iaroslav Iotsov, "Upravlenieto na Zemedelskiia sŭiuz, 1919–1923 g.," *Istoricheski pregled* 3 (1950): 324, 3 (1951): 249; and *Statisticheski godishnik na bŭlgarskoto tsarstvo: Godini V–XIV, 1913–1922* (Sofia, 1924), p. C60.

country. The party line on Stamboliski and the Agrarian government was spelled out in a report from Bulgaria published in the Comintern journal.

> The rural bourgeoisie grew rich during the war through speculation and rising agricultural prices. Its members moved to the cities where they took over commercial outlets and began to participate in the founding of banks and joint stock companies. Through this they learned the importance of political power for furthering their interests, and their appetite for power grew. After the collapse of the bourgeois parties, their only means to this end was the Agrarian Union. Because it had not yet been in power, it was still not discredited in the eyes of the masses, and because it was an *Agrarian* union it guaranteed the rural bourgeoisie complete authority [against the urban bourgeoisie]. Stamboliski . . . better than anyone embodies the drive to power of the ignorant, rural bourgeoisie and kulak class. And he is able to appeal to the unenlightened, unclassconscious peasantry with his demagogy.[21]

The report went on to argue that the Bulgarian countryside—even before the land reform one of the most egalitarian in Europe—was rife with class conflict that would soon lead to the BCP's predominance. In its press and in the National Assembly the party leveled a constant barrage of criticism at the Agrarian government and its reform program and denounced its "repression," such as the prohibition of celebrating "Red Week" in the public schools.

That the BCP was considerably overstating the government's severity can be seen in even a cursory examination of the party's growth and activities during the years before the 9 June coup. According to information presented at the annual party congresses, membership continued to grow steadily, if slowly, after the rapid immediate postwar expansion.

The party also did well in local politics. By 1922 it claimed majorities on 113 town and village councils; 3,623 elected party members sat on these councils, and an additional 115 served at the provincial level. At the same time, the GFTU had about 29,000 members, and the newly formed Communist Youth League had 15,000. Borrowing an idea from the BANU, the party founded a network of cooperative enterprises with over 35,000 subscribers. The party press, flourishing in the absence of censorship, published thirteen newspapers and periodicals and about 1.5 million books and pamphlets.[22]

Bulgarian party leaders also acquired prominence on the international scene. Kabakchiev accompanied Zinoviev when he split the USPD in Halle in October 1920, and three months later Kabakchiev used this experience when he and the Hungarian Matyas Rakosi split the Italian Socialists at their Livorno congress. Vasil Kolarov played a similar role with regard to the Norwegian and Mongolian parties, and he served as secretary general of ECCI, the Comintern's executive committee, between the fourth and fifth Comintern congresses. Georgi Dimitrov became a member of the central committee of the Profintern.

The party also championed Soviet interests at home. During 1921, in cooperation with a delegation from the Soviet Red Cross, it organized an extensive relief campaign for the victims of famine in the Volga region. Blagoev set a personal example by foregoing a marker for his wife's grave—Vela Blagoeva died on 21 July—to contribute 1,000 leva to this effort, which collected 1,200 boxcars of grain for shipment to Saratov.[23] The party was even more active in opposing the resettlement of White Guard refugees in Bulgaria. Bulgaria had been pressured by the Allies to accept some 36,000 refugees, including 15,000 veterans of Baron Wrangel's army—who

TABLE 6   PARTY MEMBERSHIP, 1919–1923

Year	Members	Number of "Wage Workers"
1919	21,577	9,281
1920	35,478	11,177
1921	37,191	10,654
1922	38,036	12,546
1923	39,000	12,000

SOURCE: Joseph Rothschild, *The Communist Party of Bulgaria: Origins and Development, 1883–1936* (New York, 1959; reprinted by AMS Press, New York, 1976), p. 106.

retained their arms and remained a part of Wrangel's military organization. Their arrival was met with protest demonstrations organized by the BCP, and at the Genoa Conference Rakovski prodded Stamboliski to disarm the Whites. In fact, while the conference was in progress, one of Wrangel's commanders was arrested in Sofia in possession of files containing detailed information on the Bulgarian police and military and records of secret meetings with the leaders of Bulgaria's conservative parties. When the government ordered the arrest of several other White Guard officers, Wrangel threatened armed resistance. In response Stamboliski ordered the immediate deportation of some 150 White officers and the disarming of their troops. He further permitted the BCP and the Soviet Union to organize a "Union for Return to the Homeland" in Bulgaria to send agents to campaign among the refugees. Many were recruited for the Red Army, and several thousand were repatriated.[24]

THE 9 JUNE COUP

By the end of 1921, Bulgarian conservatives had begun to recover from their postwar demoralization and to mount a more effective opposition to the Agrarian government. The National Progressive, Democratic, and Radical Democratic parties allied to contest local elections in February 1922 and gained one-third of the vote. A few months later they merged to form the "Constitutional Bloc." A more ominous threat appeared with the formation of *Naroden sgovor* (National Alliance), inspired by the example of Mussolini's Fascists in Italy. *Naroden sgovor* represented itself as a nonpartisan organization of citizens, whose members came from commercial, industrial, and military circles. Alexander Tsankov, *Naroden sgovor*'s moving figure, later became Bulgaria's principal apologist for fascism. Tsankov wanted the organization to serve as a catalyst to bring together the various elements in the country that were opposed to the Agrarian government's domestic reforms and its policy of rapprochement with Belgrade. *Naroden sgovor* counted on the support of Tsar Boris, the Constitutional Bloc, the Military League (a secret organization of active-duty and retired officers), and the Internal Macedonian Revolutionary Organization (IMRO), whose bands employed terrorist tactics against the authorities in Macedonia and against Bulgarian politicians who failed to champion the Macedonian cause. At the beginning of August, Constitutional Bloc spokesman Atanas Burov announced that the time of legal struggle had ended, and that the Bloc would take to the streets to drive out of power "that garbage from the Bulgarian village." Advocating the tactics that were then bringing the Blackshirts to power in Italy, he announced that the Bloc would hold three mass meetings: in Tŭrnovo on 17 September, in Plovdiv on 1 November, and culminating in Sofia on 15 November.

The mobilization of the right caused the BCP to moderate a little its hostility to the Agrarians. In April 1922, during the developing crisis over the White Guards, the party council met secretly in Sofia to discuss tactics. It adopted a resolution stating that "Any bourgeois attempt at a coup, even if directed against the Agrarian government, represents a direct threat to the Communist Party as well," and the BCP pledged to resist a coup with armed force.[25] The significance of this resolution, however, was vitiated by qualifications ruling out anything except "technical cooperation" with the BANU and by the fact that the pledge was kept secret. At the fourth party congress in June, party leaders continued to inveigh against Agrarian "repression and demagogy."

The Agrarians met the Constitutional Bloc head on at Tŭrnovo on 17 September. Even before the train carrying the Bloc leaders reached Bulgaria's ancient capital, crowds of aroused peasants had taken them into custody. The government also ordered the arrest of all former members of the Geshov, Danev, and Malinov-Kosturkov cabinets (these included nearly all the leaders of Bulgaria's traditional parties) to stand trial for involving Bulgaria in the Balkan wars or for failing to extricate the country from the First World War. The BCP belatedly offered its help. Kolarov approached Raiko Daskalov, the Agrarian minister of the interior, with a request that the BCP be given arms to defend the government against the right. Daskalov, who must have been amused at the transparent attempt to repeat the Russian experience of the Kornilov Affair, dismissed Kolarov with the advice that if the government ever needed help from the Communists, he would notify them fifteen minutes in advance.[26]

Both Agrarians and Communists assumed that the right had been crushed by the debacle at Tŭrnovo and by the arrest of the former ministers, and the BCP promptly returned to the line it had proclaimed during the Radomir Rebellion, namely, that the differences between the BANU and the right-wing parties were simply a quarrel between the rural and urban bourgeoisie in which the working class had no interest. Even after the fourth congress of the Comintern turned to the tactics of the united front, adopting the slogan "Workers' and Peasants' Government," the BCP remained unmoved. At a council meeting held to discuss the Comintern resolutions on 21–22 January, the party stated that no worker-peasant government could be achieved in Bulgaria through coalition between the BCP and the BANU, and that the party understood the Comintern resolution as calling for greater efforts to win the peasantry away from the Agrarian Union.[27]

For his part, Stamboliski moved to consolidate the Tŭrnovo victory by

TABLE 7   NATIONAL ASSEMBLY ELECTIONS, 27 APRIL 1923

Party	Deputies Elected	Votes	Percentage of Votes
BANU	212	569,139	53.9
BCP	16	203,972	19.4
Constitutional Bloc	15	198,647	18.8
National Liberals	0	55,963	5.3
Broad Socialists	2	27,816	2.6
Total	245	1,055,537	100.0

SOURCE: *Statisticheski godishnik na bŭlgarskoto tsarstvo: Godini V–XIV, 1912–1922* (Sofia, 1924), pp. C49–50.

signing the Treaty of Niš with Belgrade, which provided for cooperation against IMRO terrorism, and by purging the moderate wing of the Union and scheduling new elections for April 1923.

The BCP maintained its voting strength, but, because the government had replaced proportional representation with single-member constituencies, the BANU achieved complete domination of the National Assembly.

The coup began at 3:00 A.M. on 9 June.[28] Military units occupied key locations in Sofia and the provincial centers. Most of the Agrarian ministers, members of parliament, and BANU leaders in the capital were placed under arrest. Later in the morning Tsar Boris signed an edict recognizing the new government with Alexander Tsankov as prime minister.

The country was not immediately pacified. In many areas the Orange Guards attempted to implement their defense plans, and some Agrarian leaders raised substantial resistance around Plovdiv, Pleven, and Orkhanie (Botevgrad). Most important, the detachment sent to capture Stamboliski, who was at his villa in Slavovitsa near Pazardzhik, was repulsed by loyal troops. In addition to trying to mobilize his own supporters, Stamboliski appealed to the Communists for help. He sent a directive to Anastas Bŭrzakov, the district BCP organizer in the nearby village of Tserovo and a former officer, appointing him commander in chief of a "new people's army" and instructing him to prepare an assault on Pazardzhik.[29]

During the morning of 9 June, the BCP's central committee issued a proclamation announcing the overthrow of the government of the "peasant bourgeoisie" and ordering party members "not to come to the aid of this government." Todor Lukanov, acting as party secretary in Kolarov's absence, dispatched telegrams and couriers to inform local party leaders of the central committee's decision, and Khristo Kabakchiev reported to the Comintern that the toiling masses had met the coup "with indifference and even a certain amount of relief."[30] Bŭrzakov, who had mobilized a considerable force from the surrounding region, disbanded it after a courier reached him with the central committee's directive. In other areas, local Communists who had instinctively sided with the Agrarians were also persuaded to abandon the struggle. Stamboliski's assault on Pazardzhik was defeated and the Agrarian leader was captured. Several officers and IMRO fighters beheaded him after prolonged torture. By 14 June the country was completely pacified.

THE SEPTEMBER UPRISING

News of the Bulgarian coup reached Moscow on 12 June, while Zinoviev was in the course of delivering the presidential address to the enlarged plenum of the ECCI. Interrupting his speech to inform the delegates of the news from Bulgaria, he repeated the unconfirmed report that the BCP had declared neutrality, adding that he hoped this report was mistaken. He compared the situation in Bulgaria to the Kornilov Affair, and stated that resistance was the only correct policy.[31] Two days later Kolarov delivered a longer report, describing the BCP's conduct as a serious blunder, although he reminded the delegates that the party had been persecuted by the Agrarians.[32] On 23 June Karl Radek delivered a more thoroughgoing critique of the BCP's passivity. Calling the 9 June coup "the greatest defeat ever suffered by a communist party," he accused the Bulgarian Communists of narrow sectarianism for failing to recognize that "the peasant government of Bulgaria was the one foreign organism among the bourgeois governments of the Balkans." Radek added that the BCP's inactivity was proof that the party was in need of a thorough reorganization, and the plenum unanimously demanded that the Bulgarian party make an alliance "from above" with the BANU and prepare for battle with the Tsankov regime.[33] Zinoviev had already dispatched Kolarov to Bulgaria with instructions to implement the Comintern line, but he was arrested soon after landing and was held on charges of illegal entry. It was a measure of the party's good relations with the Tsankov regime that it was able to gain Kolarov's release.

On 1–6 July, a month before Kolarov's arrival in Sofia, the party council met to discuss the Comintern's criticism. By a vote of 42 to 2 it rejected the Comintern position and defended the policy of neutrality.[34] Since Blagoev was in ill health and was recuperating outside of Sofia, Kabakchiev undertook to explain the party's stand to the ECCI. Repeating the old arguments that the BANU represented only the upper stratum of the peasantry and was strongly anticommunist, Kabakchiev denied the validity of the Kornilov analogy. Since no revolutionary situation existed, and since there was no landlord class in Bulgaria to be overthrown, he argued, the two cases were not parallel. Moreover, he concluded, with Stamboliski overthrown, the peasantry would perforce have to turn to the BCP, so that in fact the party occupied a stronger position than it had before the coup. These arguments only provoked a fresh outburst of scorn from Soviet and other Communist Party leaders.[35]

When he arrived in Sofia, Kolarov convened an emergency meeting of the central committee on 5–7 August. With the authority of the Comintern behind him, he prevailed on a majority of its members to reverse the neutralist line and to adopt a resolution stating: "The 9 June coup has created a crisis on the issue of power that may be resolved in no other way than through an armed uprising of the masses in the name of a worker-peasant government." That substantial opposition to this new direction remained is indicated by the fact that four new members were co-opted into the central committee. Later testimony revealed that Todor Lukanov was unmoved by Kolarov's arguments, and that Blagoev also did not believe a successful uprising was possible.[36] The aged founder, however, was too ill to attend the meeting and had no further influence over the course of events. He died on 7 May the following year.

The central committee set up a military-technical committee to direct preparations for the uprising, tentatively scheduled for October or November.[37] Kolarov also approached the remnants of the Agrarian Union, the Socialists, and even elements of IMRO to appeal for their participation in a united front against Tsankov. Only a handful of left-wing Agrarians responded favorably. The Socialists rejected the proposal with contempt, and officially endorsed the participation of Dimo Kazasov, who had privately joined the conspiracy of 9 June, in Tsankov's government.

Tsankov was hardly unaware of the Communists' preparations, and on 12 September the police carried out a mass roundup of some 2,000 party functionaries. Kabakchiev and Blagoev were placed under arrest, although Kolarov and most of the central committee evaded capture. Those members who remained at large met on 15 September and decided to send out scouts to assess the situation in the provinces. The decision whether or not to proceed with the uprising was given to a committee whose members were Kolarov, Dimitrov, Lukanov, and Todor Petrov. Two days later, only Kolarov and Dimitrov were able to reach the site of the planned meeting, and they decided to launch the uprising during the night of 22–23 September. On 20 September, when the central committee gathered secretly to ratify this decision, Lukanov opposed it altogether. He was outvoted, and the central committee placed the direction of the uprising in the hands of a Supreme Revolutionary Committee composed of Kolarov, Dimitrov, and Gavril Genov. The next day this committee prudently shifted its headquarters to Ferdinand (Mikhailovgrad) near the Serbian and Romanian borders.

The September Uprising has become one of the heroic myths of BCP history, proclaimed as the "world's first antifascist uprising" and said to mark the transformation of the BCP itself into a "bolshevik, revolutionary party."[38] In fact, it is hard to see the uprising as anything other than a catastrophe. In some localities where the BCP had a strong organization and numerous followers (such as Ruse, Burgas, and Sofia itself), party leaders disobeyed the central committee's order to rise. Scattered revolts in the countryside were put down with considerable bloodshed by government troops supported by IMRO detachments, and these incidents provided an excuse for the government to officially outlaw the party.[39] On 28 September Kolarov, Dimitrov, and between one and two thousand of their followers escaped across the border into Yugoslavia, where they were given asylum. Kolarov and Dimitrov moved on to Vienna, where they constituted themselves as the Foreign Bureau of the central committee and began to publish an exile edition of *Rabotnicheski vestnik* in mid-October.

At best, the September Uprising was a blood sacrifice through which the party gained expiation for its past sins in the eyes of the Comintern, and it provided its survivors with reputations as revolutionary heroes. The fifth Comintern congress in 1924 paid tribute to the courage of the BCP and held it up as an example to other communist parties.

3

In the Wilderness,
1923–1939

The tracks of the BCP become much harder to follow after the September Uprising, for the party leadership was dispersed and its organization was forced underground. Moreover, the history of the post-September era was rewritten many times to reflect shifts in the party line or the changing fortunes of particular party leaders.

TERRORIST INTERLUDE

With the defeat of the uprising, the Tsankov regime moved to legitimize itself by holding new parliamentary elections on 18 November. Tsankov's coalition, which the Socialist Party joined, took 202 of the assembly seats.[1] In spite of government pressure and electoral finagling, the BCP won 8 seats and the BANU 31. Seven of the Communists, however, belonged to a group led by Nikola Sakarov, who had brought a faction of the (Broad) Socialist Party into the BCP in 1920. These seven now disavowed the September Uprising and severed relations with the Comintern. The emigré central committee promptly excommunicated them. In January the National Assembly adopted a "Law for the Defense of the State" that formally suppressed the BCP and dissolved the GFTU and other party front organizations.[2]

On 17–18 May a clandestine party conference convened on Mount Vitosha outside Sofia to discuss the new situation. Its guiding spirit was

Stanke Dimitrov (his underground name was Marek), a close associate of Kolarov and Dimitrov, who also sent two delegates from the Vienna Bureau to uphold the Comintern line. The Vitosha conference not only endorsed the September Uprising over the objections of Lukanov and his supporters, but also resolved that the country was still in a revolutionary situation that demanded continued preparations for armed struggle against the Tsankov regime. An eleven-member central committee, composed of both domestic and exile leaders, was chosen to carry out this decision. Kolarov and Dimitrov were named to head what was now called the party's Foreign Bureau, and Dimitrov-Marek, Ivan Manev, and Kosta Yankov were made the Internal Executive Bureau. Dimitrov-Marek and Manev were charged with political and organizational affairs, and Yankov, a lieutenant colonel in the army, became head of the party's Military Organization.[3]

Preparations for a second armed uprising involved two components: attempts to reach agreement with elements of the Agrarian Union and IMRO and the strengthening of the party's own fighting organization. Refugees from the Agrarian leadership established an Exile Bureau in Prague and were trying to organize their own armed groups in Yugoslavia. Accounts of their negotiations with the BCP and with the Comintern are confused and contradictory, but the talks were clearly marked by cynicism on both sides. By the spring of 1925 they were broken off, and in any case the Yugoslav government disarmed the groups on its territory.[4]

IMRO had long harbored some members who looked to Marxism for the solution to the Macedonian question. During the Stamboliski era, mutual antipathy toward the Agrarian government led the BCP and representatives of the Macedonian organization into more direct contact. Moreover, the June coup did not bring the changes in Bulgaria's foreign policy that IMRO desired, for the Tsankov government was afraid to repudiate the Treaty of Niš. When Italy and Yugoslavia signed the Pact of Rome in January 1924, Italian subsidies for IMRO temporarily dried up, creating an opportunity for the BCP and the Comintern to attempt to detach the Macedonians from the Sofia government. This effort seemed to bear fruit in the spring of 1924 when, after secret negotiations in Vienna in which the Macedonian Communists Dimitŭr Vlakhov and Dimo Hadzhi Dimov played a central role, IMRO issued its "May Manifesto" to the Macedonian people. Condemning the great powers for their neglect of the Macedonian cause, and accusing the Tsankov government of practicing an anti-Macedonian, Serbophile policy, the manifesto stated that IMRO would continue its fight only with the help of "the extreme progressive and revolutionary movements of Europe." The Bulgarian government and conservative elements in IMRO reacted quickly. Ivan Mikhailov, an IMRO leader loyal to the Tsankov regime, organized the massacre of those who had dealt with the Communists and kept IMRO closely tied to the Bulgarian government. Similar attempts by the BCP to enlist the support of nationalist groups in the Dobruja and Thrace also came to nothing.[5]

Official histories speak of an "ultraleft deviation" among some party members, who after the Vitosha conference turned to terrorist tactics against the advice of more experienced leaders such as Kolarov and Dimitrov. Supposedly, the BCP's underground Military Organization became isolated from the party as a whole and was infected with a dangerous spirit of adventurism.[6] The denunciation of these tactics, however, came only after their failure was apparent and renunciation became expedient for the party. In fact, the militarization of the party underground was the logical consequence of the decisions taken at the Vitosha conference. There is no reason to believe that the party leadership, or the Comintern, was either ignorant of it or disapproved it.

During 1924 the party's Military Organization established a network of local organizations that perpetrated sporadic acts of terror against police and local officials.[7] On 14 April 1925 General Kosta Georgiev, a prominent member of the Democratic Alliance, was gunned down in a church courtyard by a group of Communist guerrillas. Two days later Sveta Nedelya Cathedral, where political and military leaders had gathered for the funeral services, was ripped by an explosion that killed 128 people and wounded over 300 more. The dead included three National Assembly deputies, fourteen generals, the chief of police, and the mayor of the capital. By a quirk of fate, Tsar Boris and the leading members of the cabinet had been delayed in arriving and so escaped harm.[8]

The BCP at first denied any involvement in the bombing; Georgi Dimitrov called it a police provocation. He later changed this story to call it "an ultraleft deviation . . . an act of desperation committed by the leadership of the Military Organization of the party."[9] A different version of this story is given by Petŭr Semerjeev (Semerdzhiev), a former member of the central committee now residing in Israel, who appears to have had access to material in party and state archives that has never been made public. According to his account, orders to carry out the plan were given by Georgi Dimitrov himself, and therefore presumably came from the Comintern. Dimitrov gave them to Stanke Dimitrov-Marek during the latter's visit to Vienna early in 1925. Dimitrov-Marek in turn passed the decision on to the central committee in Sofia in March, at the time of his departure for Moscow to attend a plenum of the ECCI. Semerjeev gives as his principal source the confession extracted by the police from Tsola Dragoicheva after her arrest in 1925. Dragoicheva's own memoirs contain a great deal of information on the activities of the Military Organization, but she passed over the cathedral bombing in silence.[10]

The Tsankov government had no doubt of the BCP's responsibility for the bombing and exacted a bloody retribution. Kosta Yankov and Ivan Minkov were killed in battle with the police. Marko Fridman, Lieutenant General K. Koev, and cathedral sacristan Petŭr Zadgorski, who were charged with planting the explosives, were condemned and publicly hanged. Hundreds of party members and sympathizers were never brought to trial but perished in the cellars of police headquarters or at the hands of IMRO bands. Among them were Todor Dimitrov, Georgi Dimitrov's brother, and Zheko Dimitrov, Georgi Dimitrov's successor as head of the GFTU. Traicho Kostov, the future general secretary of the party, leaped from the fourth floor of Sofia police headquarters during interrogation and was left with a permanently twisted spine. Tsola Dragoicheva, another future party leader, was condemned to death for her conspiratorial work in Plovdiv and survived only because she became pregnant in prison.[11]

A new wave of exiles joined the political emigration, either immediately or after some years in prison or the underground. They usually made their way to the Soviet Union, where they were frequently absorbed in the Comintern or Soviet bureaucracies. Many received training in the Communist University for the National Minorities of the West, in which a Bulgarian section was established under the direction of Dimitrov-Marek. Bulgaria's future "Little Stalin," Vŭlko Chervenkov, attended the OGPU Academy in Moscow and became a lecturer in the Lenin International School. Party veteran Khristo Kabakchiev earned a doctorate in history and became a candidate member of the Soviet Academy of Sciences. Todor Pavlov, later the party's principal theoretician, rose to be dean of the Faculty of Philosophy at the Moscow Institute. The full scope of the Bulgarian emigration in the USSR has never been fully described. Nissan Oren estimated that it included between two and three thousand people, making the Bulgarians second only to the Poles among the foreign Communists domiciled in the USSR.[12]

THE RISE OF LEFT SECTARIANISM

Following the defeats suffered by the Communist and Agrarian opposition between 1923 and 1925, Bulgarian political life began a slow recovery. The widespread hatred for "Bloody Tsankov," the murderer of Stamboliski and so many others, rendered the prime minister unsuitable as a spokesman for the ruling Democratic Alliance. In January 1926 he relinquished the premiership to Andrei Liapchev, who pledged to moderate the reign of terror. A gradual and qualified return to a free press and parliamentary politics marked his five-year tenure. The relaxation of the police regime prompted the BCP in early 1927 to establish the Workers' Party as a legal front for participation in the new parliamentary elections set for 29 May. Although it won only 29,210 votes and 4 seats (from a total of 1.2 million votes and 273 seats), this was nonetheless a significant recovery. This election also saw the revival of the Agrarian Union and other opposition parties; the Democratic Alliance managed to poll only 39 percent of the vote, although its manipulation of the electoral process did give it 167 seats and a majority in the assembly.[13] Four years later the government was actually defeated by the People's Bloc, a coalition of the Democratic, Liberal, and Radical parties and the Agrarian Union. The People's Bloc made the Democratic leader Alexander Malinov prime minister.

Although the Workers' Party won 166,000 votes and elected 31 deputies to the assembly in the 1931 elections, it was not genuinely admitted to political life. The People's Bloc government, like its predecessor, exerted considerable pressure to limit activities of the Worker's Party, and of course the underground BCP remained subject to direct persecution. In October 1931 party secretary Nikola Kofardzhiev, who had secretly returned to Bulgaria from Moscow, was shot down in Sofia by the police. Repeated trials of communist conspirators in the army frequently led to death sentences or long prison terms.[14] When the Workers' Party won the Sofia municipal elections in September 1932, the government petitioned the courts to invalidate the result on the grounds that the party was actually a front for the BCP. Following the court's ruling, 29 deputies of the Workers' Party were expelled from the assembly. The remaining 2 signed pledges stating that they had abandoned their ties to the BCP.[15]

The People's Bloc government came to power during a period of economic crisis brought on by the world depression. Its inability to alleviate the economic situation—Bulgaria's GNP fell by more than one-third between 1929 and 1934—led to further political instability and a rising tide of labor unrest.[16] On 19 May 1934 the Military League carried out a peaceful coup d'etat organized by Kimon Georgiev and Damian Velchev. The coup installed Georgiev as prime minister. The ideology of the new regime was supplied by Zveno, an elitist group drawing its membership from intellectual, commercial, and military circles. Inspired by Dimo Kazasov, who had left the Socialist Party in 1926, Zveno advocated "national restoration" through an authoritarian, technocratic regime.[17] The "divisive forces" associated with parliamentary politics were eliminated by the suspension of the constitution and the suppression of all political parties. A new assembly was created, composed of individuals without party affiliation and elected from approved government lists. To its credit, the new regime suppressed IMRO gangsterism, restored the government's authority over Pirin Macedonia, and opened diplomatic relations with the USSR. Its political base, however, was too narrow to allow it to consolidate power firmly. The chief beneficiary of the 1934 coup was Tsar Boris III, who relied on his own clique in the army to unseat Georgiev. By the end of 1935, Tsar Boris had installed a subservient government under Georgi Kioseivanov, purged the Military League, and jailed Georgiev. Bulgaria thus ended the 1930s as a royal-military dictatorship, the form of government that had become nearly universal in Eastern Europe.

Although the BCP, through the Workers' Party, was a limited participant in these events, they were largely peripheral to the party's own history, for the crucial issues for Bulgarian communism in this era were internal, involving the party's leadership and orientation and its relationship to the Comintern and to Stalin's Russia.

Since the end of the world war there had been an undercurrent of "leftist" opposition to the course set by Blagoev and the party leadership. The so-called ultraleft (or "Iskra-ites" after their short-lived journal *Rabotnicheska iskra* [Workers' Spark]) had criticized the Narrow Party's aloofness from the Radomir Rebellion, its timidity at the time of the transport strike, and its emphasis on parliamentary politics over revolutionary action. Advocating "bold deeds," the ultraleftists had appealed to the Comintern, but were never given a serious hearing.[18] The shattering blows of 1923–1925, Blagoev's death, and the flight of the party leadership led to the re-emergence of a more militant outlook, embodied now in a younger group of party activists, the so-called left sectarians. The movement's principal figures came out of the Komsomol after 1923. Men like Petŭr Iskrov, Georgi Lambrev, Ivan Vasilev (Boiko), Ivan Pavlov (Encho), and Nikola Kofardzhiev mounted a strong attack on the party traditions and leadership, successfully pushing aside Kolarov and Dimitrov.[19]

According to the left-sectarian critique, the BCP had inherited from its Narrow past a tradition of opportunism and compromise that blunted its revolutionary edge. Narrow Socialism had been "Social Democracy on Bulgarian soil," fatally infected with parliamentary and united-front illusions. It would have been better if the leadership had been purged at the time of the party's entry into the Comintern, for Blagoev and the rest of the so-called Old Guard had never learned or understood the lessons of Bolshevism. The pressing task of the party now was to rid itself of its Narrow heritage and to prepare for the next inevitable revolutionary upsurge.

The left-sectarian position was voiced at the second party conference, held in Berlin from 8 December 1927 to 15 January 1928. Here, Kolarov and Dimitrov sought to deflect criticism to the party's right wing. Todor Lukanov and his ally Georgi Popov, who had never endorsed the insurrectionary line imposed on the party in 1923, were expelled, and Khristo Kabakchiev was dropped from the central committee. The left sectarians still attacked

Kolarov and Dimitrov for their links to the Narrow past, neutrality in the face of the 9 June coup, and bungling of the September Uprising and declared the two generally unfit for positions of leadership. Although Kolarov and Dimitrov escaped direct condemnation and remained on the party's Foreign Bureau, Petŭr Iskrov was added to that body and the left prevailed in the new central committee chosen to supervise the party at home.[20]

The decisive factor in the victory of the the the left sectarians was the change in the policy of the Comintern, which late in 1927 and 1928 abandoned the idea of the united front in favor of the tactic of "class against class." Such prominent functionaries as Bela Kun, Osip Piatnitski, and Henryk Waletski, who held Kolarov and Dimitrov in low regard in any case, took advantage of the switch in the Comintern line to throw their support to the left sectarians, promoting many of them to important positions in the machinery of international communism.[21] Kolarov and Dimitrov, however, were well connected with the Soviet leadership and possessed impressive records of Comintern service, so that they could not easily be dismissed. Instead, during 1928 Dimitrov was assigned to the Comintern's newly created Western European Bureau (he became its head in April 1929) to coordinate relations between Moscow and other Comintern sections in Europe. Kolarov was assigned to Moscow to head the Soviet Agrarian Institute, and other supporters of the Old Guard were given jobs that removed them from direct involvement with the Bulgarian party.

At the second plenum of the BCP, which met from 15 August to 23 October 1929 in Berlin, the left sectarians were in a solid majority. Iskrov replaced Kolarov as chief editor of the party's *Kommunistichesko zname* (Communist Banner), and soon afterward the headquarters of the Foreign Bureau was shifted from Berlin to Moscow, making it impossible for Dimitrov to remain a member. He was demoted to candidate membership, and his place was taken by Bela Kun. In February 1930 Dimitrov complained to the ECCI that the BCP was being taken over by youths whose inexperience in practical affairs was leading to the alienation of the masses from the party, but he was not permitted to attend the ECCI discussion of the problems in the Bulgarian party that took place in Moscow in August.[22] The ECCI's political secretariat adopted a resolution that praised the past achievements of Narrow Socialism but held that the party had not been truly Leninist. The resolution also endorsed the left sectarians' militant tactics. In December, at its third plenum, held illegally in Sofia, the central committee interpreted the resolution as approving the left-sectarian course.[23]

At home the left sectarians echoed the current Comintern slogans, calling on the workers to "control the streets" and condemning the "Social Fascists" and "Agrarian Fascists" of the noncommunist left. The left sectarians spurred a new wave of labor militancy, sought to infiltrate the army, and fought with courage in frequent battles against government authorities. The inability of the People's Bloc government to suppress them was one of the factors motivating the 1934 coup. But events in Germany and Russia, not Bulgaria, settled the fate of the left sectarians. Hitler's triumph revealed the bankruptcy of the "class against class" tactic, leading to a new Comintern reversal. And Georgi Dimitrov's arrest by the Gestapo set the stage for the rise of the Bulgarian exile to world fame and to a position that would allow him to take vengeance on his former detractors.

THE APOTHEOSIS OF GEORGI DIMITROV

From 1929 until his arrest in 1933 Georgi Dimitrov headed the West European Bureau (WEB) of the Comintern and was also secretary of the executive committee of the Balkan Communist Federation (BCF). Both these positions held more prestige than power; the WEB, although it allowed Dimitrov to develop contacts with a large number of communist parties, was primarily a communications center, and the BCF was an empty shell. Dimitrov bitterly resented his enforced separation from his native party, and he devoted enormous effort to acquiring information about its internal affairs and to intriguing against its current leaders. Tsola Dragoicheva, still a relatively minor party functionary, passed through Berlin in late 1932 after her release from prison. At Dimitrov's request, she wrote over 100 pages of notes on the situation inside the party, which Dimitrov then used for the basis of a long interrogation.[24] He constantly sent criticism of the left sectarians to the ECCI, and in 1931 he formally asked to be relieved of his duties in order to devote more attention to the BCP. The Comintern, however, still backed Iskrov and the left and so kept Dimitrov in Berlin. As a counterweight to Dimitrov's tactics, the BCP assigned Georgi Lambrev, one of the prominent left sectarians, as its resident in Berlin. When Lambrev was arrested in 1932, he was replaced by Blagoi Popov, another of Dimitrov's critics.[25]

On the night of 27 February 1933, the German Reichstag went up in flames. The young, apparently feeble-minded Dutch Communist, Marius Van der Lubbe, was arrested on the scene, but Hitler quickly charged that the fire was the product of a larger, Bolshevik conspiracy. On 9 March, Dimitrov, Blagoi Popov, and another Bulgarian Communist, Vasil Khadzhitanev, were taken into custody and charged, along with Ernst Torgler, the head of the KPD Reichstag delegation, with responsibility for the crime. By the time the trial was held in Leipzig, from 21 September to 23 December, the policies and tactics of the Nazi regime were provoking revulsion and alarm among broad sectors of Western public opinion. The

Leipzig trial became a cause célèbre, the focus of worldwide attention and protest. It pointed the way toward the policy of the popular front, the antifascist coalition that the Comintern soon officially launched. Dimitrov greatly aided his cause by conducting his own defense and turning the trial into an indictment of the Nazi regime. His skill in poking holes in the prosecution's case, bold defiance of Göring, and expressions of pride in both his Communist affiliation and Bulgarian nationality made him an international hero. "There is only one brave man in Germany," went the popular saying, "and he's a Bulgarian."[26]

The court, which had not yet been Nazified, convicted Van der Lubbe and sentenced him to death, but it acquitted the other four defendants for lack of evidence. The three Bulgarians (Torgler remained in custody and was later sent to a concentration camp) were granted Soviet citizenship and went from Germany to the USSR.

Dimitrov received a hero's welcome when he arrived in Moscow. *Pravda* hailed him as "the symbol of the struggle of the proletarian masses in all countries" and credited him with bringing more than a million new workers into the Comintern fold.[27] On 7 April Dimitrov addressed a session of the Soviet Politburo and called for a new approach in the Comintern's relations with European workers' movements. Afterward Stalin apparently recommended that Dimitrov head the Comintern and promised him the politburo's support. Two weeks later Dimitrov was appointed to the ECCI's political secretariat as head of its Central European section. Shortly after this, he joined the ECCI presidium and was placed in charge of the preparations for the upcoming seventh Comintern congress. When the congress met from 25 July to 20 August 1935, Dimitrov was very much the man of the hour. He delivered the keynote address on "The Offensive of Fascism and the Tasks of the Comintern in the Struggle for the Unity of the Working Class Against Fascism," which marked the formal abandonment of the line of "class against class" in favor of the "popular front against fascism." In the discussions that followed, speaker after speaker rose to eulogize the "hero of Leipzig." It was only a formality when after the congress the new ECCI raised Dimitrov to the post of secretary general, a position he retained until the Comintern's dissolution in 1943.[28]

Although the congress lauded Dimitrov's courage and wisdom, these were not, of course, the qualities that were decisive in his success (namely, his history of loyalty and obedience). A cipher in matters in theory but a tireless and effective organizer, Dimitrov was a communist functionary in the Stalinist mold and the ideal agent to cement Stalin's control over international communism. One indication of his true position is that he was made general secretary rather than president, the title that Zinoviev and Bukharin had held; that is, Dimitrov was chief executive of a council composed of

Stalin's appointees. Moreover, throughout his tenure, Dimitrov was surrounded by a group of "ideological advisers" that watched over his work.[29] There is no indication that during the time of his leadership he had either the inclination or authority to moderate the victimization of thousands of Communists by Stalin's terror. But if his position as Comintern general secretary was that of a figurehead, Dimitrov's power over the BCP became real, and it was precisely by Stalinist methods that he consolidated it.

THE PURGE

Leipzig made Dimitrov a hero to everyone but his own party. His arrest in Germany was initially seen by the left-sectarian leadership at home as one more instance of his blundering. Even as his defense drew world attention, the Bulgarian party paid it little regard. A measure of the enmity the left sectarians felt toward the Old Guard is indicated by the fact that the central committee turned down the appeal of Dimitrov's mother for money to travel to Leipzig. She was eventually aided by Kosta Todorov from Agrarian Union funds and by Pastor Vasil Ziapkov on behalf of the Bulgarian Protestant churches. According to the account given by Kolarov, during 1933 the left sectarians sought to liquidate the Foreign Bureau and to convene a party congress inside Bulgaria to remove both Dimitrov and himself from the party hierarchy.[30] The plan came to nothing in view of Dimitrov's rapidly mounting prestige.

By the end of 1933, the tide in the Bulgarian party was clearly turning. At the thirteenth ECCI plenum (November–December), Iskrov praised Dimitrov as an outstanding revolutionary, although he dwelt even more on the achievements of the party at home, claiming that Dimitrov's experience in Germany demonstrated the correctness of the line against "social fascism." By the time of Dimitrov's arrival in Moscow, *Pravda* already referred to him as the leader (*vozhd'*) of the Bulgarian Communists, and this term was quickly adopted by his supporters. On 17 May Dimitrov addressed a gathering of Bulgarian Communists in Moscow on the occasion of the tenth anniversary of the death of Blagoev. The occasion provided him with an opportunity to discuss again the Narrow Socialist heritage of the party. Although party leaders in the past had been guilty of some serious errors, Dimitrov said, they had created a priceless fund of Marxist experience that was the party's most valuable asset.[31]

Dimitrov's speech preceded by exactly two days the Military League's coup d'etat in Bulgaria, which threw the left sectarians still further on the defensive. Their analysis—that the coup was the replacement of one band of fascists by another and so without real significance—was fatuous and flew in the face of the Comintern's emerging popular-front line. The central committee's political secretary, Ivan Pavlov-Encho, was summoned to Moscow, where the BCP's tactics were subjected to sharp criticism by the ECCI's political secretariat. Pavlov-Encho was given a resolution, "The BCP and the Events of May 19, 1934," that condemned the party's mistakes in rejecting the possibility of cooperation with the nonfascist "bourgeois democratic" elements, specifically, the Agrarian Union and the Socialists. The central committee was also directed to prepare for a party plenum to be held in Moscow, where it could be dominated by Kolarov and Dimitrov. The left-sectarian leadership formally accepted the ECCI resolution in October but protested against Moscow as the site of the plenum. As a compromise, the ECCI insisted on the immediate removal of Pavlov-Encho as political secretary but allowed the plenum to be held in Sofia, sending Traicho Kostov as the Foreign Bureau's emissary. Meeting at the end of January 1935, the plenum did drop Pavlov-Encho but did not allow Kostov to participate. It enlarged the Foreign Bureau, adding to it a number of the Old Guard, but kept control of the key positions at home. Kostov reported with some understatement that "a turnabout in the party will not easily be forthcoming," and Dimitrov moved to step up the Comintern's pressure.[32]

On the eve of the Comintern's seventh congress, a meeting of Bulgarian Communists was held in Moscow. Here Kolarov demanded a thorough cleansing of the party organization, and a few of the left sectarians began to recant their past mistakes. Among them were Blagoi Popov and Vasil Khadzhitanev, Dimitrov's codefendants at Leipzig, who were condemned for their conduct at the trial because they had concentrated on proving their personal innocence rather than launching a counterattack against fascism. At the congress Kolarov stated that the BCP provided an object lesson in how the struggle against fascism ought not to be conducted, but it was another delegate, named Krumov, who provided a long denunciation of the left sectarians, employing such terms as "disloyalty and treachery." After the congress, the Foreign Bureau dispatched Stanke Dimitrov-Marek and Georgi Damianov to Bulgaria to join Kostov in completing the purge of the home leadership. This was accomplished by the time of the sixth party plenum, held in Sofia in February 1936. The plenum denounced the left-sectarian course, installed the popular front as the party's new line, expelled the remaining left sectarians from the central committee, and elected a new politburo of Dimitrov's supporters.[33]

The sixth party plenum marked the political liquidation of the left sectarians. Their physical liquidation soon followed. In September 1936, shortly after the trial of Zinoviev, Kolarov issued a brochure linking left sectarianism to Trotskyism. During the summer he delivered a speech making the connection even more explicit, and it was followed by the arrests of hundreds of Bulgarians who were either resident in or recently recalled to the USSR. Charges against them focused on two broad conspiracies. One, involving exiles settled in the southern regions of the USSR, accused the victims of plotting to annex the Ukraine to Bulgaria. The second, striking mainly at the left sectarians, made the more usual accusation of spying for Nazi Germany or another foreign power. Until the publication of Blagoi Popov's memoirs by an emigré Bulgarian press in 1981, no direct information about these events was available, for they were never publicly discussed by Bulgarian historians or party leaders. Tsola Dragoicheva's memoirs are absolutely silent on this question, although her brother Tseniu Ninchev was one of the victims of the liquidation of the "Ukrainian conspiracy." Nissan Oren, who has made the most thorough investigation to date, estimated the total number of victims to have been between four hundred and six hundred.[34] According to Blagoi Popov:

> More than a thousand Bulgarian emigrés were imprisoned. I don't know the exact number of those who died, but it was not less than six hundred. Some of them were shot, others died in prison, but the largest number of them perished from hunger and disease in the labor camps of Kolyma and elsewhere.[35]

The victims included nearly all of the left-sectarian leadership (Iskrov, Vasilev-Boiko, Pavlov-Encho, Lambrev, and others) as well as Bulgarian emigrés in various positions in the Soviet government or Comintern. Only a handful ever returned.

At least some members of the old rightist opposition fared better. Todor Lukanov, who had joined the CPSU after his expulsion from the BCP in 1928, survived until 1946, although his circumstances are not known. His son Karlo broadcast to Bulgaria from Soviet territory during World War II and held the post of foreign minister from 1956 to 1962. His grandson Andrei is currently a candidate member of the politburo. Khristo Kabakchiev was arrested and then freed, apparently after Dimitrov interceded for him, although his health was broken in the Lubianka. Party members jailed in Bulgaria were also largely beyond the reach of Soviet terror. After the Second World War, the BCP's pressing need for cadres frequently caused past associations with left sectarianism to be overlooked, at least for a time.

Among foreign Communists who lived through the great terror, there arose the myth of a "Bulgarian exception." As Milovan Djilas put it: "The Bulgarian emigrés were lucky that Dimitrov was Secretary of the Comintern and a person with such authority. He saved many of them."[36] Dimitrov is believed to have intervened on behalf of Kabakchiev and Vŭlko Chervenkov, his brother-in-law, but Stalin, too, is known to have plucked certain individuals from the terror. There is no evidence that Bulgarian emigrés as a whole benefited from Dimitrov's influence. On the contrary, Kolarov's accusations of Trotskyism probably intensified the persecution. Before his arrest, Blagoi Popov heard that Kolarov and Dimitrov already referred to him as a prisoner. His appeals to Dimitrov and to Dimitrov-Marek went unanswered, and at least one of them was later found among Dimitrov's papers. In his address to the fifth congress of the BCP in 1948 Dimitrov repeated the charges that the left sectarians were both Trotskyites and spies, and he called them the "best allies" of the Bulgarian fascist dictatorship.[37]

THE POPULAR FRONT

One of the problems that remained after the defeat of the left sectarians was the question of the Workers' Party, which had been the legal front of the BCP until the 1934 coup. Arguing that there was no need for two illegal parties, the left sectarians had sought the dissolution of the Workers' Party. This was overruled at the sixth party plenum, which decided to preserve the Workers' Party against the day when parties might be legalized and to use it as a vehicle for united-front negotiations with other political formations. There was a further practical consideration, for, although all Bulgarian political parties were illegal, some were more illegal than others. Penalties for membership in the BCP were considerably more severe than those imposed for membership in the Workers' Party. Some even argued that it was the BCP that should be dissolved, but this idea was rejected by Dimitrov and the ECCI. Consequently both parties were kept in existence. In theory, the Workers' Party concentrated on recruiting membership and building contacts with other groups, whereas the BCP consisted of more professional cadres working deeper underground. In practice, the result was more often confusion, overlapping authority, and disagreement. At the end of 1939, the Foreign Bureau authorized the merger of the two under the name Workers' Party. This remained the official name of the party until 1948, when the BCP designation was restored at the party's fifth congress.[38]

Although the regime of Tsar Boris had suppressed political parties, it had not deprived them of all significance. The prestige of elder statesmen among the opposition, such as Alexander Malinov of the Democrats or Krŭstiu Pastukhov of the Socialists, kept the hopes of their followers alive. In 1932 the Agrarian Union had split between the followers of Dimitŭr Gichev and a more radical group organized around exiles Alexander Obbov and Kosta Todorov and some younger domestic activists. Gichev's BANU-Vrabcha 1 (after the address of his headquarters at 1 Vrabcha Street) retained most of the Agrarian Union's organization, but the more radical Pladne (or Noon, the name taken from the faction's newspaper) possessed more dynamic leadership in such figures as Dr. G. M. Dimitrov and Nikola Petkov.[39]

In 1936 five leaders of the democratic opposition, Gichev, Pastukhov, Georgi Genov, Boian Smilov, and Grigor Vasilev, petitioned the tsar for a restoration of the constitution and new elections, a request that Pladne and the Democrats supported later in the year. None of these groups was warm to the Communists' popular-front proposals, so the party issued an independent endorsement. The result was the formation of what was referred to as the People's Constitutional Bloc, an extremely loose alliance of opposition forces mainly concerned with electoral cooperation on the local level.

Tsar Boris did permit town and village council elections in April 1937, but under so restrictive a system that the members of the Bloc boycotted them. Encouraged by the results, the tsar announced new parliamentary elections for the following year. Again, an extremely restrictive electoral system was used to ensure a government majority. Candidates had to be certified by government commissions and could not run as members of a party, districts were gerrymandered, and election dates were staggered to allow the government to concentrate its forces. The other members of the Bloc would make no formal agreement with the Communists, but on the local level were willing to arrange combined support for particular candidates. The result was a minor victory for the opposition, which won more than a million votes and elected 67 of the 160 deputies, including 5 with some links to the Communists. Boris's regime, however, quickly expelled the most vocal members of the opposition from the assembly.[40]

Local cooperation in the 1938 elections represented the high point of the party's popular-front line inside Bulgaria, for the signing of the Hitler-Stalin pact brought the party at least temporarily into the government camp.

The primary manifestation of Bulgarian communism's adoption of the popular front outside the country was the participation of approximately 460 Bulgarians in the Spanish Civil War. The majority of these came from Bulgaria itself, although about 100 had been living in exile in the USSR. Although not organized into a single fighting brigade, many of the Bulgarians played significant roles in the units to which they were assigned. Sŭbi Dimitrov, former head of the party's parliamentary delegation, was the Bulgarian political commissar in Spain; Boris Stepanov-Minev, Dimo Dichev, and Ruben Avramov-Levi were prominent in the political-ideological organization of the republican forces; Tsviatko Radoinov-Rodionov, Karlo Lukanov, Anton Ivanov, Vlado Trichkov, and others held prominent military commands; and Dr. Tsvetan Kristanov and Dr. Petŭr Kolarov, Vasil Kolarov's son, directed the organization of medical services for the International Brigades. When the Soviet effort in Spain ended, most of the Bulgarians who had come from the USSR returned there, some to suffer in Soviet purges. Other Bulgarians were held in French internment camps until allowed to return to Bulgaria in 1940.[41]

4

World War II, 1939–1944

The Hitler-Stalin Pact brought an abrupt end to the Communists' united-front efforts. Overnight, the leaders of the democratic opposition were transformed in party propaganda from sought-after allies to agents of Anglo-French imperialism. Todor Pavlov, the party's philosopher-theoretician, produced a pamphlet extolling the pact as a contribution to peace and justifying the Soviet intervention in Poland. With the dialectical gymnastics customary in such exercises, he argued that since the Polish state had ceased to exist, the USSR could not have attacked it; Soviet military forces were engaged in maintaining order and protecting a fellow Slavic people from the dangers of anarchy.[1]

The pact also brought an improvement in Bulgaria's relations with the USSR. Although the Bulgarian government rejected the Soviet offer of a mutual assistance treaty in September, a number of commercial and cultural agreements were negotiated. Soviet films and printed works were distributed legally, direct air communications between Moscow and Sofia were established, and Moscow's Spartak soccer team toured the country to enthusiastic demonstrations. Because of this rapprochement and because its line now corresponded to government policy, the Workers' Party found itself in a substantially improved position. It enjoyed a quasi-legality not extended to the pro-Western parties or even, after the assassination of Romanian prime minister Calinescu by the Iron Guard, to the formations of the far right. In December and January 1940, the government conducted new parliamentary elections in which the communist-affiliated candidates increased their representation from five to ten, the same number achieved by the rest of the opposition. The communist deputies fraternized with the tsar, and party propaganda advocated the arrest of the pro-Western political leaders.[2] But this era of good feelings rested on the fiction of genuine German-Soviet partnership and on the fact that neither Germany nor the Soviet Union wanted a disturbance in the Balkans. As relations between the two great powers worsened and as Bulgaria became a focus of their rivalry, the party and the regime resumed their mutual hostility.

When the war began, Bulgaria proclaimed neutrality, but it moved steadily closer to the German orbit in succeeding months. After the parliamentary elections, Tsar Boris replaced Prime Minister Kioseivanov with Bogdan Filov, a notorious Germanophile. The successes of German arms and Soviet setbacks in Finland clearly influenced the Bulgarians; the fate of Belgium demonstrated that a small country could not rely on its own resources to preserve neutrality. During the summer of 1940 the tsar took advantage of the constellation of forces in Eastern Europe to press for the return of the southern Dobruja from Romania. And when the Romanians yielded at the end of August, he gave full credit to Hitler and Mussolini, although the USSR and Great Britain had also supported the Bulgarian claims.

In August the Bulgarian Communists launched a propaganda counter-offensive aimed at stopping or slowing Bulgaria's drift into the German camp. The party denounced Boris's regime as a "fascist dictatorship" and called the Nazis a threat to the country's independence. In concentrating their fire on the Germans, the Communists were in advance of Soviet diplomacy, a fact noted by the British, who used the BBC to suggest that the party's declaration indicated the real attitude of the USSR toward Germany. Tsola Dragoicheva was summoned to Moscow for consultations with the Foreign Bureau, during which Georgi Dimitrov told her that the Bulgarian party's orientation was causing difficulties for Soviet diplomacy and that the "highest quarters" of the Soviet government were concerned. The Foreign Bureau instructed the Bulgarian party to reduce its anti-Nazi campaign and to stress instead the importance of Bulgarian-Soviet friendship. It also constituted Kostov, Radenko Vidinski, and Dragoicheva as a special inner circle within the central committee to supervise party activity and to prepare for a new party plenum. Dragoicheva was also told that Anton Ivanov, a member of the Foreign Bureau, would be dispatched to Bulgaria within a few months to take part in the group.[3]

Having properly oriented the Bulgarian party, the Soviet Union launched a new initiative to keep Bulgaria out of the German camp. On 18 November Molotov informed the Bulgarian ambassador that the Soviet

Union could not tolerate Bulgaria's becoming a "Legionnaire state" like Romania, and he renewed the proposal for a mutual assistance pact. If Bulgaria agreed, the USSR was prepared to support Bulgaria's territorial aspirations in Thrace and European Turkey and to render assistance in the form of loans, food, or arms. A written version of this proposal was delivered to Sofia on 25 November by Arkadi Sobolev, the general secretary of the Soviet commissariat for foreign affairs. The Bulgarian government, after informing the Germans, rejected the proposal.[4]

The Bulgarian public was not informed of the Soviet approach. Since secret diplomacy had failed, the Soviet Union now ordered the Workers' Party to undertake a massive campaign to inform the people of the Soviet offer and to urge its acceptance. Hundreds of thousands of leaflets describing the proposal were distributed, and a petition and letter-writing campaign generated more than a million signatures and a deluge of telegrams and letters, impressive evidence of the Bulgarian public's reluctance to commit to the German side.[5] While this effort was in progress, Anton Ivanov arrived secretly and published an article comparing Boris's regime to the government of Colonel Beck in Poland, which had paid a high price for ignoring Soviet offers of friendship. After Ivanov's return the party held its seventh plenum secretly in Sofia. It elected a politburo composed of Kostov, Ivanov, Dragoicheva, Vlado Georgiev, and Radenko Vidinski, and it confirmed a Foreign Bureau composed of Dimitrov, Kolarov, Dimitrov-Marek, and Georgi Damianov.[6]

The Italian debacle in Greece and the establishment of British bases on Greek soil forced Hitler to turn his attention to the Balkans, leading to stepped-up pressure on the Bulgarian government. Already in November 1940 Tsar Boris had agreed to allow German forces to operate from Bulgarian territory, and by the end of December there were several thousand German troops—albeit disguised as civilians—engaged in preparing military installations. Filov met with Hitler and von Ribbentrop at Obersalzburg on 2 January and won a promise that Bulgaria would receive Aegean Thrace in return for a pledge to sign the Tripartite Pact. Large German forces crossed the Danube on 20 February, and on 1 March Bulgaria formally joined the Axis. Coinciding with the entry of German troops, the government struck at the pro-British opposition, placing those who did not manage to escape the police nets in newly formed concentration camps.

Bulgaria's commitment to the Germans sparked the first acts of armed resistance. These came not from the Communists, whose policy while the German-Soviet alliance lasted was to oppose the Germans with propaganda rather than deeds, but from the Anglophile Pladne Agrarians. Pladne had been in contact with the British Special Operations Executive, which had established a few small underground resistance centers. Dr. Georgi M. Dimitrov had evaded arrest and had been smuggled into Yugoslavia in the baggage of the British diplomatic mission. There he organized armed bands to cross into Bulgaria, but they were intercepted by invading German forces.[7]

Armed Resistance: The First Phase

It was 7:00 a.m. on 22 June 1941 when Radio Sofia broadcast the news of Germany's attack on the Soviet Union. Later that morning, the three members of the politburo in the capital, Kostov, Ivanov, and Dragoicheva, gathered in the party's secret headquarters. There they listened to Radio Moscow's broadcast of Molotov's address to the Soviet people, Kostov taking down the words in shorthand while Ivanov paced and chain-smoked.[8] The three then drafted a ringing manifesto condemning the attack and the pro-German Filov government.

> History does not know a more criminal, more imperialist, more counter-revolutionary war than the one fascism has launched against the USSR. And there has never been a more just or progressive war than that which the Soviet people is waging against fascist aggression, and on whose outcome the fate of all peoples depends . . . .
> Before us stands the colossal task of not allowing our land or our army to be used for the criminal purposes of German fascism. Before us stands the task of helping, however we can, the Soviet people in its difficult struggle.
> Not one grain of wheat, not one crust of Bulgarian bread for the German fascists and plunderers. Not one Bulgarian in their service! . . .
> Everyone to his post![9]

During the night the first radiogram from Georgi Dimitrov arrived, directing the party "to take every measure to aid the struggle of the Soviet people, to oppose the anti-Soviet plans of the Bulgarian reaction, to consolidate a united, popular front in the struggle against fascism."[10]

Meeting on the evening of 24 June, an enlarged conference of the politburo established the fundamental goal of overthrowing the "monarcho-fascist" regime through armed struggle. Recalling the experience of 1923–1925, it established a Central Military Commission, composed initially of Khristo Mikhailov, Georgi Minchev, Dimo Dichev, Gocho Grozev, and Ivan Maslarov, with Tsola Dragoicheva (later in July she was replaced by Yugov) as liaison with the politburo.[11] The tasks assigned to the commission were ambitious:

First, . . . diversionary actions along the roads, telephone and telegraph lines serving the Hitlerites; blowing up railroad lines, tunnels, and bridges to disorganize the German rear and interfere with the transport of troops and materiel to the Eastern Front. It was also necessary to organize economic sabotage, especially in those branches of industry whose products were exported to Germany . . . Resistance activity also had to extend into the countryside to ignite mass opposition to the confiscation of livestock and crops for the Hitlerite forces; where it couldn't be stopped, the crops would have to be destroyed, the sheaves burned in the fields, mowing machines and threshers broken, dairy production destroyed.[12]

Such acts were easier to visualize than to perform, and from the beginning the party's resistance efforts encountered serious difficulties. Dragoicheva pointed out in her memoirs that in Yugoslavia and some other countries the barbarous policies of German occupation became themselves a powerful stimulus to popular resistance. Bulgaria, however, lacked this "advantage," since it was an allied rather than an occupied country, and German forces generally kept to themselves. Bulgaria never joined the war against the USSR and its declaration of war on Great Britain and the United States in December 1941 had little real meaning for the population, at least until Allied bombings began in the summer of 1943. The crushing defeats inflicted on the Red Army in the first months of the war also had a demoralizing effect, and many party functionaries rejected the call for armed resistance on the grounds that it was hopeless and that it would be better to husband resources until a more favorable time.[13] The Bulgarian police also took energetic and effective measures to break the party's organization and will.

To aid their comrades at home, the Foreign Bureau set up "Radio Khristo Botev." Under Chervenkov's management, it directed broadcasts to Bulgaria from Soviet territory throughout the war. During the summer, Soviet military forces transported groups of Bulgarian emigrés, many with military training or experience from the Spanish Civil War, to Bulgarian territory. In all, 58 men were either parachuted into the country or landed by submarine. Betrayed by at least one of the Soviet radio operators that accompanied them, they were nearly all killed or captured soon after arrival, although one, Tsviatko Radoinov, managed to reach Sofia, where he briefly took command of the Central Military Commission.[14]

The destruction of this mission was only the first in a series of crushing blows inflicted by Nikola Geshev, chief of Division A, the political section of the police. This "diabolically cunning butcher," as Dragoicheva described him with grudging admiration, made use of three disloyal party officials to penetrate the party apparatus. They led him to Georgi Minchev of the Central Military Commission, whom Geshev kept under constant surveillance, noting his contacts and party safe houses. After some weeks

Minchev was arrested, and he broke under torture. The information he supplied, combined with what was already known, permitted the police to round up the Communist underground.[15] On 4 March they captured 46 of the party's leading functionaries, including several members of the central committee and the Central Military Commission. Tsviatko Radoinov was arrested on 24 April, and Anton Ivanov on the following day. According to Petŭr Semerjeev, both men broke during interrogation and provided information that led to the arrest of Traicho Kostov a few days later.[16] The police also struck successfully at the party provincial organizations.

During the summer the regime organized two mass trials of communist conspirators. The first, the Trial of the Parachutists (as it was described in the press), included 27 of the emigrés that had been sent to Bulgaria, with Radoinov as the chief defendant. Their defense lawyers vainly sought to establish that these men were members of the Red Army and should be considered prisoners of war. Nine of the defendants, who were minors, were given prison terms. The remaining 18 were sentenced to death and executed the same day. The second trial, the Trial of the Sixty-two, involved members of the party apparatus and the Central Military Commission. The court handed down death sentences for Anton Ivanov, Nikola Vaptsarov, Atanas Romanov, Petŭr Bogdanov, Georgi Minchev, and Anton Popov. Hours after the verdict, they were shot in the tunnels beneath the Sofia garrison. Six of the defendants, including Traicho Kostov, were sentenced to life in prison; 20 to fifteen-year terms; and the rest to lesser terms. The court also handed down six death sentences in absentia for Dragoicheva, Yugov, Khristo Mikhailov, Avram Stoianov, Diko Dimov, and Boris Kopchev, who had so far eluded the police.[17]

The failure of Traicho Kostov to receive a death sentence has been the subject of considerable speculation. In 1949, at the hands of a communist court, he was charged with having bought his life by betraying his comrades. Semerjeev, however, argued that Kostov held out through interrogation, not permitting the police to build an ironclad case. But this, too, is unlikely, since sufficient evidence against him was available from other sources and an ironclad case was hardly necessary. More likely is the story reported by Nissan Oren, to the effect that Tsar Boris intervened personally to spare Kostov's life after an appeal from one of his advisers, whose son was Kostov's friend.[18]

In the spring of 1942 the Bulgarian police, aided by the Gestapo, also broke up a spy center linked to Soviet intelligence. Headed by former General Vladimir Zaimov, who had once led the Military League, it had transmitted military intelligence to the USSR by clandestine radio. Zaimov was sentenced to death and shot on 1 June.

During 1942 the police captured and brought to trial slightly over a thousand party functionaries and members of the Workers' Youth.[19] Those members of the party who remained outside prison were preoccupied with survival. The end of 1942, with most of the party leadership dead or in prison and the Germans at the gates of Stalingrad, marked the low point of party morale.

Still, the party slowly regrouped. Cut off from contact with the Foreign Bureau, Dragoicheva and Yugov co-opted two new members for the politburo, Iordan Katrandzhiev and Dimitŭr Ganev. The former had supervised the party's illegal press, and the latter had been involved with the work of the Romanian Communist Party. Jailed in Romania in 1935, Ganev was freed in 1940 and had just then recovered his health sufficiently to resume party work. The Central Military Commission was also re-established under the command of Emil Markov.[20]

Operating with limited means and inspired by the broadcasts of Radio Khristo Botev, the Central Military Commission turned to the tactics of political assassination that the party had adopted after the defeat of the September Uprising in 1923. Markov authorized the creation of a "fighting group with special assignment," whose leaders were Metodi Shatorov and Slavcho Radomirski. Composed of fifteen of the "bravest and best" young men and women, the group was subdivided into smaller squads that were given intensive training in terrorist methods. A list of targets was prepared by the Central Military Commission and approved by the politburo. It included leading pro-German political figures, police commander Geshev, and party members identified as police agents. The first victim was Nikola Khristov-Kutuza, one of the informers who had betrayed Minchev. He was shot on 8 February 1943. Five days later, former General Khristo Lukov, a leading figure in the fascist Legionnaires and an advocate of war with Russia, was gunned down. Because the assassins escaped without a trace, suspicion fell for a time on the court, since it was rumored that Tsar Boris feared that the Germans intended to replace him with a more pliable regime under Lukov's dictatorship. During the next six weeks terrorist squads wounded Lukov's secretary, Nikolai Tsonkov, himself a Legionnaire leader; shot and killed in his office the chairman of the National Assembly's committee on foreign relations; and killed Colonel Atanas Pantev, chairman of the Military Court for the Sofia Region and a former police commander.

After the assassination of Pantev the tide began to turn. On 10 May an attempt was made on the life of an electronics specialist who had implemented an effective means of locating illegal radio transmitters. The attempt failed and led to the capture of two squad members. An attack on the editor of the semiofficial newspaper *Zora* resulted in the deaths of the would-be assassins. A second attempt, carried out without higher approval, saw the four-man squad wiped out. The death squads had gotten out of effective party control and were alienating potential noncommunist allies and provoking extensive police countermeasures that led to the arrests of a large number of underground party members. Hence, the party leadership decided to abandon political murder, at least in the capital. Sporadic acts of terror continued in the countryside throughout the war, but these were often the product of local vendettas rather than a larger strategy.[21]

ARMED RESISTANCE: THE SECOND PHASE

During March and April 1943, the party leadership approved a new operational plan prepared by Emil Markov that revised overall strategy and broadened the scope of armed resistance. The partisans were renamed the People's Liberation Insurgent Army (*Narodoosvoboditelna vŭstanicheska armiia*), or NOVA, and the country was divided into twelve insurgent operational zones (*Vŭstanicheska operativna zona*), or VOZ, each with its own leadership composed of a commander, political commisar, and chief of staff. The first two positions were assigned to the most eminent local party leaders, while the third was intended for party members with military experience, preferably retired or active-duty officers. The Central Military Commission became the NOVA general staff and retained its former membership with one exception. Spas Georgiev, who had fallen into the hands of the police, was replaced by Petŭr Iliev.[22]

The changes in nomenclature were accompanied by a change in tactics. Until this time the basic unit of the resistance was the "fighting group," composed of a small number of members who maintained legal existence and committed acts of sabotage or gathered information. The party now proposed to add to this form of struggle permanent groups of partisans in the mountains. At least one such group had been organized in Pirin Macedonia under the command of Nikola Papapunov as early as 1941. By the summer of 1943, the police estimated that there were about 47 partisan bands with approximately 650 members. These included some larger formations such as the Anton Ivanov Detachment, with about 100 members operating in the Rhodope Mountains in central Bulgaria, and the Trŭnski Detachment, led by Slavcho Trŭnski, which operated along the Bulgarian-Yugoslavian border and could rely, as did the detachment in the Pirin, on the help of Tito's partisans and havens in liberated Yugoslav territory.[23]

The attempt to broaden the scope and impact of the resistance was not without setbacks. Partisan groups suffered heavy casualties in engagements with the police or military units. On 13 July the police discovered the hiding place of Emil Markov in Sofia, and the NOVA chief of staff was killed in the ensuing gun battle. His place was taken by Khristo Mikhailov, who had headed the Central Military Commission before the return of Radoinov. He was aided by Dobri Terpeshev, who had escaped from a concentration camp and became NOVA's political commissar. Both Mikhailov and Terpeshev were added to the politburo. Two other escapees, Vlado Trichkov and Georgi Chankov, brought valuable military experience that was employed in organizing the Sofia VOZ. Chankov was also added to the politburo in 1944, as was Iordanka Nikolova, general secretary of the *Rabotnicheski mladezhskisŭiuz* (Workers' Youth Union), the party's youth organization. Nikolova was killed fighting in Trŭnski's detachment during the summer. Mikhailov was also killed in February 1944, after which Terpeshev became both commander in chief and political commissar of NOVA.[24]

At the end of 1943 the first limited contacts were established between the Bulgarian resistance and the Allies. The British Special Operations Executive parachuted a team under the command of Major Mostyn Davies into Albania in September. After a two-month journey north, it made contact with Slavcho Trŭnski's group, and in January Vlado Trichkov arrived as emissary of NOVA's general staff. A second British team, under Captain Frank Thompson, also arrived in January. Although Davies and Trichkov reached an understanding calling for the dropping of British arms and supplies to the Bulgarian partisans, poor communications, bad weather, and the low priority assigned to the effort by the British kept substantial amounts of arms from being provided. In March Davies and most of the British mission were killed in an engagement with Bulgarian troops, and in June an effort by Thompson to penetrate deeper into Bulgarian territory also met with disaster. Trichkov and most of the partisans were killed, and Thompson was captured, court-martialed, and shot. Little thus resulted from the Bulgarian-British contacts except a legacy of distrust.[25]

The strength of the armed resistance grew as the military fortunes of Germany declined, and during the summer of 1944, in particular, partisan groups mushroomed. After the war, it was claimed that the resistance movement numbered 30,000 fighters, aided by 200,000 helpers (*iatatsi*) who provided food and shelter. A more reasonable estimate is that, in all, during the war there were about 10,000 partisans and 20,000 helpers.[26] There is no doubt that the vast majority of those engaged in armed resistance were Communists, the bulk coming from the party's youth organization, although individuals from other political parties did participate.[27] The actual military contribution of the Bulgarian resistance was slight, and, until the last months of Bulgaria's participation in the war, it had primarily a nuisance value. Nonetheless, it was the largest resistance movement to appear in any of Germany's East European satellites.

It is probably fair to say that the armed resistance was more important after the war than during it. The party's leading role in the armed struggle helped to legitimize its claims to postwar political power; it provided cadres to supplant the official police and military forces; and the alliances and loyalties formed in the struggle were often strong and enduring, remaining important in Bulgarian political life down to the present time.

RELATIONS WITH THE YUGOSLAV COMMUNISTS

Macedonia proved to be as much an apple of discord for the Balkan Communist parties as it had been for the Balkan governments. Immediately after the German conquest of Yugoslavia and Greece, Bulgarian forces occupied most of historic Macedonia and set up a Bulgarian administration of "the new lands." Although not officially annexed—that issue was to be settled upon conclusion of the war—for all practical purposes the Vardar and Aegean regions of Macedonia became Bulgarian territory.

Macedonia was one of the most primitive, underdeveloped regions of Yugoslavia. Its communist party was small and had only ephemeral ties with the Yugoslav party. From the spring of 1940 its secretary, appointed on the recommendation of Georgi Dimitrov and the Comintern, had been Metodi Shatorov, whose past activities had been mainly with the Bulgarian party. After Yugoslavia's defeat and the establishment of a Bulgarian administration, Shatorov made contact with Traicho Kostov and the Bulgarian Communists.[28] On 10 May Kostov and Anton Ivanov drafted a report to Dimitrov and the Foreign Bureau stating that the party organization in "former Yugoslav Macedonia" would henceforth operate under Bulgarian direction.[29]

The transfer of the Macedonian party organization to Bulgarian control was not acceptable to the Communist Party of Yugoslavia (CPY). The German attack on the USSR and the Soviet call for general European resistance provided Tito with an opportunity to reopen the question. Denouncing Shatorov as a counterrevolutionary and an impediment to the organization of an effective Macedonian resistance, the CPY leadership expelled him and dispatched Mara Natseva and Lazar Kolishevski to reassert CPY authority over the Macedonian organization. Shatorov and the local leadership were not moved—they in fact expelled Kolishevski for "factional activity"—and in August Kolishevski made his way to Sofia to confront the Bulgarian party leaders directly. According to Dragoicheva, who represented the politburo in the discussions, Kolishevski took a "crude and condescending tone," accusing the Bulgarian Communists of opportunism because they did not support an immediate, large-scale resistance effort; calling Shatorov a "traitor, enemy, and saboteur"; and demanding that he be sent to Yugoslavia to be shot.[30]

At this point the Comintern intervened on the side of the Yugoslavs. It may be assumed, in fact, that the decision was made by Stalin, since Dimitrov had supported the Bulgarian party's position up to this point, and the Comintern directive was carefully worded to leave open the ultimate fate of Macedonia. Making no statement on the nationality of the Macedonians, the directive assigned Macedonia to CPY control "for reasons of practicality and expediency" (a recognition of the importance of the partisan resistance to German and Italian forces being organized on Yugoslav territory). Furthermore, it directed the Bulgarian and Yugoslav parties to cooperate. Since contact between the CPY and the USSR had not yet been established, the Bulgarian party sent a copy of the directive to Tito along with its own letter accepting the decision "without reservation." Shatorov, who was informed of the decision by the courier passing through Skoplje, left Macedonia and arrived in Sofia in December, becoming head of the Sofia regional organization.[31] His creation of terrorist squads has already been recounted. He was killed in the resistance on 4 September 1944, only days before Soviet troops entered Bulgaria.

Kolishevski returned to Macedonia to set up a new party committee and to organize partisan detachments. In October 1941 the Bulgarian party wrote to the CPY opposing this course on the grounds that conditions in Macedonia, as in Bulgaria, did not favor large-scale resistance. "It must not be forgotten," the letter said, "that in Yugoslavia the Macedonian people suffered the most from Great Serb chauvinism, and that they were the most deprived of rights, and that this has certain consequences. Among them exists a certain hatred for old Yugoslavia." And the letter warned that there would be little popular support for armed resistance to Bulgarian occupation.[32] In this the Bulgarians were proved correct, for in the first engagements with Bulgarian forces Kolishevski's partisans were destroyed. Soon afterward, Kolishevski and a number of his colleagues were captured and imprisoned. The remaining Macedonian Communists were less hostile to the Bulgarian party and developed good relations with Boian Bŭlgaranov, the party's delegate to the Macedonian organization, a fact that led the CPY to purge some of them for "Shatorovism" later on. During 1942 it was in fact the Bulgarian strategy of small-scale resistance that was followed in Bulgarian-occupied Macedonia.

The situation changed in February 1943 with the arrival of Svetozar Vukmanović-Tempo. Making his headquarters in western Macedonia, the region under Albanian and Italian occupation, he succeeded in organizing large-scale partisan detachments that tipped the military balance toward the CPY as the prospect of an Allied victory drew nearer. The conduct of Bulgarian occupation authorities had also by this time alienated much of the previously sympathetic population.

At the second session of the Antifascist Council of National Liberation of Yugoslavia (AVNOJ) in Jajce in November 1943, the CPY leadership decided to include Macedonia (that is, the entire region, not just the portion belonging to prewar Yugoslavia) within a future Yugoslav federation. Two Bulgarians of Macedonian origin, Vladimir Poptomov and Dmitŭr Vlakhov, were named to the AVNOJ presidium as representatives of Bulgarian and Greek Macedonia, respectively. Neither man was present nor knew of this decision. Poptomov later refused to participate, but Vlakhov sided with the Yugoslav party and later made his career in the Yugoslav Macedonian Republic. The decisions of the second session of AVNOJ were not fully communicated to the Bulgarians or to the USSR for several months, and it was not until the spring of 1944 that the Bulgarian party learned of Tito's plans. By this time the tide had clearly turned in the Yugoslav's favor. For Tito the issue was closed. According to Djilas, Tito said that he would not yield on this issue for Stalin himself.[33] Thus, as the end of the war neared, the Bulgarian Communists were on the defensive, reduced to trying to save their minimum objective, Bulgarian retention of the Pirin region.

THE FATHERLAND FRONT

The initiative for creating an antifascist, political front in Bulgaria came from Georgi Dimitrov. On 15 December 1941, Radio Khristo Botev broadcast his appeal for a revival of the united front.[34] Later broadcasts specifically called for cooperation with the Agrarians, in view of the BANU's pro-Western orientation. Quiet soundings of Agrarian leaders, however, led to nothing. Dimitŭr Gichev, head of Vrabcha-1, stated that he could have no faith in a party that had so recently been "with the Germans," and Pladne leaders still at large were both strongly Anglophile and skeptical of the prospects of armed resistance.[35] In any case, the capture of the "parachutists" and the arrest of most of the party leadership in April brought a halt to discussions.

On 17 July Karlo Lukanov broadcast, on behalf of the Foreign Bureau, a new appeal with more specific proposals. Warning that Bulgaria's salvation could be achieved only by the entry of "the people, the army, and the patriotic intelligentsia into a mighty Fatherland Front," the broadcast advocated a slate of twelve points that could be supported by all antifascist groups or parties. These included Bulgarian noninvolvement in the war, the breaking of ties with the Axis powers, the withdrawal of Bulgarian forces sent to fight "the fraternal Serbian people," amnesty for political prisoners, and the restoration of political freedoms. This was to be accomplished by the replacement of the present regime by a "genuine national government" that would prepare for a Grand National Assembly to decide Bulgaria's future.[36] The text of the broadcast, now called the program of the Fatherland Front, was printed in the first issue of the party's *Rabotnichesko delo* when it began illegal publication on 1 September. It was accompanied by an appeal to "the Agrarian Union, Workers' Party, Social Democrats, Democrats, Radicals, and others" to join in making the front a reality. The party pledged to consider any additions or modifications to the program that came from groups or individuals in general sympathy with its goals.

During August the politburo instructed Tsola Dragoicheva to set up a commission to negotiate with the noncommunist opposition. The commission was headed by Dr. Kiril Dramaliev, a philologist and long-time party member who had led the procommunist Teachers' Union in the 1930s, and it included Boris Bogdanov, brother of the Petür Bogdanov who had been executed in June; Petür Münzelov, a leading figure in the General Union of Bulgarian Agricultural Cooperatives; Dimitür Khalov, who had been active in a number of mass organizations; and Dr. Liuben Gerasimov, a veterinarian with wide contacts among Sofia intellectuals. At various times it was assisted by Dr. Racho Angelov, a physician well known in Sofia society; Dr. Ivan Pashov; Dr. Mincho Neichev; and other communist intellectuals. These men were chosen because of their contacts among the opposition and because they could operate legally; only Dramaliev was at that time in the underground.[37]

The Communists hoped most of all to win the support of Nikola Mushanov, the most respected leader of the legal opposition, who had inherited the leadership of the Democratic Party after the death of Malinov in 1938. Possessed of considerable civic courage, Mushanov was one of the few in the assembly to speak out consistently against the tsar's German orientation and the government's measures of internal repression. During the fall of 1942 he met several times with Dimitür Khalov to discuss the Fatherland Front program. Although he was convinced that Germany would lose the war, Mushanov was not ready to join the front, for he objected to the program's unclear stand on the Macedonian question and to the Communists' advocacy of illegal armed struggle. Above all, he would not accept the antimonarchist implications of the program or its characterization of Boris's regime as "monarcho-fascist." Like many other Bulgarian statesmen, Mushanov had great faith in Boris's acumen. When the time is right, he told Khalov, the tsar will appoint a new government of "genuine democrats," extricate Bulgaria from the war, and restore the constitution. Mushanov's rejection of the front carried great weight with other figures in the legal opposition, most of whom, when appealed to, immediately asked about his stand.[38]

Next to Mushanov, the most important figure in the opposition was

Dimitŭr Gichev, the leader of the conservative wing of the Agrarian Union, Vrabcha-1, which still enjoyed broad support in the countryside. But Gichev, like Mushanov, expected at some point to be called on by the tsar to "save Bulgaria." He was even more hostile to the idea of the front than the Democratic leader, and during his meeting with Dramaliev he even declined to discuss the front program, saying that for him the fact that it originated with the Communists was sufficient grounds to reject it.[39] Atanas Burov, leader of the National Party, the most conservative of the opposition groups, would not meet with the commission's representative. Stoian Kosturkov of the Radicals expected Germany to win the war or at least to make a separate peace with the Western powers. The "independent democrat" Professor Petko Stoianov called the front program "extremist." Professor Petko Stainov, long known as a Russophile, believed it "premature," and he echoed Mushanov's "wisdom" that the tsar would know when to change sides.[40]

The party's negotiating commission was not entirely without success in recruiting potential members for the front. Social Democrat Grigor Cheshmedzhiev, a lawyer who had defended Radoinov and his group at the trial of the parachutists, agreed to join, as did his colleague Dimitŭr Neikov. Khrŭstiu Pastukhov, however, the aged leader of the party's conservative wing, declined. Kimon Georgiev and Damian Velchev of Zveno were also prepared to join. Although they had no popular following, they did possess valuable contacts in military circles. Dimo Kazasov, a former member of Zveno but in 1942 an independent, accepted the commission's invitation with alacrity. Most important, Nikola Petkov, of the Pladne faction of the BANU, added his support. In some respects this came as a surprise, since the principal figures in Pladne, Dr. G. M. Dimitrov and Kosta Todorov, had little trust in the Communists and had established a Bulgarian National Committee in the Middle East that broadcast to Bulgaria under the aegis of the British. Petkov, however, was more sympathetic to the Soviet Union and admired the Communists' skill in underground organization and their resistance effort.[41] Pladne's adherence was significant, for it brought a degree of grass-roots support for local front committees that were being secretly organized in various parts of the country. By the end of 1942 these numbered 136 and, by the summer of 1943, over 500.[42] Still, because the major figures in the opposition remained aloof, the Communists decided to wait before creating a formal Fatherland Front organization.

During the spring of 1943 the issue of Jewish deportations evoked spontaneous cooperation between the Communists, the legal opposition, and even some members of the government camp. In February the Bulgarian commissar of Jewish affairs signed an agreement with the Germans calling for the deportation of 20,000 Jews. Slightly more than 11,000 of these came from the Macedonian and Thracian territories under Bulgarian occupation. They were placed under arrest and deported in early March; all but a handful perished at Treblinka. This provoked an unprecedented storm of opposition led by Dimitŭr Peshev, the vice-president of the National Assembly. Peshev and 42 other deputies sent a letter of protest to the tsar, halting temporarily the plans to deport Jews from Bulgaria proper. Still under strong German presssure, the government decided to resettle the Jews in the interior as a preliminary to deportation. The announcement of this plan provoked a much broader protest from opposition and government politicians, intellectuals, and the church. The Communists' contribution was the organization of a mass demonstration in Sofia on 24 May that ended in a violent confrontation with the police.[43] Shaken by the scope of the protests, the government decided against any further deportations, and the Bulgarian Jewish community survived the war. To their credit, the Communists had from the beginning protested the government's anti-Semitic measures, and party historians recall that the per capita contribution of the Jews to the armed resistance movement was higher than that of any other group.[44]

Because the leaders of the legal opposition kept their distance from the Communists in spite of their mutual opposition to the Jewish deportations, the party decided to proceed with the formal organization of the Fatherland Front with only the groups that had welcomed its advances. On 10 August a National Council of the Fatherland Front was established that included Kiril Dramaliev, Nikola Petkov, Kimon Georgiev, Grigor Cheshmedzhiev, Dimo Kazasov, and Petŭr Mŭnzelov. There were no officers; all of the members in theory had equal voice.[45]

The formal organization of the Front Council was hardly a significant step forward. Its members did not agree on a common strategy beyond the broad outline of the front program, nor could they even agree to issue a manifesto to the population. Its significance, therefore, at least until the approach of the Red Army, remained more symbolic than real.

The members of Bulgaria's legal opposition rested their hopes on Tsar Boris. They believed, as do many Bulgarians to this day, that he was planning to turn on the Germans at the first favorable opportunity. Certainly Boris had no ideological commitment to fascism, and up to the summer of 1943 he had satisfied Bulgaria's territorial aspirations while fending off German demands for a greater degree of cooperation. Despite his complaint that "My army is pro-German, my wife is Italian, my people are pro-Russian; I am the only pro-Bulgarian in the country," Boris was in fact in command of the political situation and had the means to act decisively. On 15 August he had a strained meeting with Hitler in East Prussia. On his return, he went on a mountain-climbing expedition and three days later suffered a heart attack. He died on 28 August.[46]

Simeon II, Boris's son and successor, was six years old at the time of his father's death. The constitution required that royal authority be exercised by a regency council chosen by a Grand National Assembly. In these circumstances, the legal opposition addressed a letter to Prime Minister Filov demanding that elections for a Grand National Assembly be held and that the government be broadened by the inclusion of "popular elements" to strengthen public confidence. Alternatively, the opposition proposed to accept the election of a regency council by the existing assembly, provided that the council included at least one figure from the opposition. The letter was signed by ten leaders of the opposition, including Nikola Petkov and Kimon Georgiev.[47] Filov saw no need to compromise, and on 9 September the assembly named him, Boris's brother Prince Kiril, and the war minister, General Nikola Mikhov, as regents. Five days later the regents named Filov's man, Finance Minister Dobri Bozhilov, as prime minister. The opposition remained shut out.

That Petkov and Georgiev had signed the opposition letter demonstrated that these men saw the Fatherland Front as only one possible political avenue. They had not ruled out accommodation with the rest of the opposition or even with the government.[48] For the Communists, "this fact was a signal to us to increase by all means and at all levels our efforts to unite the healthy national and antifascist forces around the saving program of the Fatherland Front." [49] On 16 September Georgi Dimitrov also published an article in *Pravda*, that urged greater efforts to separate Bulgaria from the Axis. Members of the front's negotiating commission again approached the main figures in the legal opposition, but again were rebuffed.

Allied bombers made their first raid on Sofia on 14 November. In the panic that followed, as Bulgaria's "symbolic war" became suddenly real, the Communists tried again to win over Mushanov and Gichev. On behalf of the party central committee, Dragoicheva sent Mushanov a letter pressing on him the need for action.

> We understand your position [it read in part], your age, social position, etc., and we do not ask you to take the hard and difficult course of illegality as we have done, but we do ask from you a firm, clear, and consistent stand against the antinational policy of the court and government . . . We ask you to take an active part in the National Council of the Fatherland Front . . . And we ask this because we still regard you as a popular, democratic leader.

But this letter and a similar one to Gichev went unanswered. Moreover, the party's allies in the front did not adhere to it unreservedly, but continued to seek their own contacts with members of the legal opposition. Nikola Petkov, especially, explored the possibilities of a coup with friends in the military "behind the backs of the other front parties." [50]

By the spring of 1944, Germany's military situation was deteriorating rapidly, and on 12 May the Allied governments warned the Nazi satellites in the Balkans that the longer they persevered in their collaboration with Germany, the harder their punishment would be. Six days later the Bozhilov government resigned, and the regency council turned to Ivan Bagrianov to form a new cabinet. An Agrarian of the far right, Bagrianov had been a member of the government camp throughout the war but had been outside its leadership. His appointment was welcomed by the Communists—first, because they had feared that the regents might turn to Alexander Tsankov or some other pro-German extremist who would open the country to complete German domination and declare war on the Soviet Union and, second, because since January Bagrianov had been involved in secret negotiations with party representatives during which he had expressed his readiness for "decisive and fundamental changes in internal and external policies." [51] The Communists were further encouraged by the fact that Bagrianov named Professor Doncho Kostov to his cabinet as minister of agriculture. Kostov was a Soviet-trained agricultural biologist who had only recently returned from the USSR, and he was also head of the underground Soviet-Bulgarian Friendship Society.[52]

At the time of Bagrianov's appointment, the party central committee was in Plovdiv, having relocated there after the heavy Allied bombings of the capital early in the year. Dobri Terpeshev was sent to Sofia to reopen contacts with Bagrianov. He received a package of proposals from the prime minister in which Bagrianov promised "at the appropriate moment" to break off relations with Germany, demand the evacuation of German troops, name new police officials acceptable to the party, and broaden the cabinet with representatives of the Fatherland Front. In return the party would have to halt all resistance activities and use its influence with the USSR to prevent a Soviet attack on Bulgaria's Black Sea coast. Terpeshev countered with a demand that the government halt all operations against Bulgarian and Yugoslav partisans and undertake military preparations for declaring war on Germany. When Bagrianov said that these conditions were acceptable (although he asked for time to persuade the regents), Terpeshev ordered NOVA to refrain from further armed attacks on government authorities.

According to Dragoicheva's account, Terpeshev had drastically exceeded his instructions and was not supported by the rest of the politburo, which sought more extensive and concrete proofs of Bagrianov's intentions. Terpeshev, however, was not easily dissuaded and was reluctant to admit his error. The result was a period of confusion during which party members received contradictory orders from the NOVA commander in chief and the central committee. But it soon became obvious that Bagrianov had promised more than he was willing or able to deliver. The police and military continued operations against the partisans, and on 12 June Doncho Kostov was summarily dropped from the cabinet.[53]

At the end of July, in a new attempt to gain the cooperation of the legal opposition, the front's national committee prepared a manifesto to the government. The manifesto warned that Bulgaria was faced with disaster and called for a break in relations with Germany, political amnesty, and the withdrawal of Bulgarian forces from "Serbia, Bosnia, Montenegro, and Greece," a formulation that implied the retention of Macedonia. Signed by 33 representatives of the Workers' Party, Pladne, the Social Democrats, and Zveno, the manifesto marked the emergence of the front into the open, since it believed (correctly) that the government was not in a position to prosecute its members.[54] Representatives of the legal opposition were also invited to sign, and for the first time the Communists received a positive response. Gichev and Vergil Dimov of Vrabcha-1 informed the front that they now accepted not only the idea of cooperation against the Bagrianov regime but also joint participation in a future government. They did not, however, add their names to the front's manifesto, but invited front representatives to take part in the preparation of a protest letter being drawn up by the legal opposition. The result was a note to the government, dated 6 August and known as the "Declaration of the Thirteen." The declaration was signed by nine members of the legal opposition and four representatives of the Fatherland Front: Mincho Neichev and Ivan Pashov of the Workers' Party, Nikola Petkov, and Kimon Georgiev.[55] Although in substance it differed little from the front's manifesto, it reflected a different balance of forces, since the dominant figures were from the legal opposition. Potentially, it provided the outline of both the policy and the composition of a new government, one in which the front occupied a secondary and subordinate position. It was probably for this reason that the communist leadership soon reconsidered and required Neichev and Pashov to withdraw their signatures.

In response to the pressure from the opposition and the worsening military situation, the Bagrianov government at last began to move toward the "decisive and fundamental changes" it had earlier promised. Bagrianov dispatched Stoicho Moshanov, a former president of the National Assembly, to Ankara to open negotiations with the British. On 17 August 1944 he called the assembly into session, announcing to it that Bulgaria would adopt a position of "strict neutrality" and promising a full political amnesty. Moshanov had presented his credentials to the British ambassador in Ankara the previous day, informing him that Bulgaria desired to leave the war but pleading for time to prepare the country against possible German reprisals and to bring in the harvest.[56] But time had run out, and it was the Communists who reaped the harvest.

THE FINAL PHASE

In retrospect it can be argued that there were two unforseeable events that had a decisive effect on Bulgaria's fate in the war. The first was the sudden death of Tsar Boris. The second was the coup d'état in Bucharest on 23 August that opened the Romanian frontier and brought the Red Army to the Bulgarian front months before it had been expected. If Bagrianov had intended to negotiate a relatively painless surrender to the Western powers, this rapidly became an empty hope.

The turnabout in Bucharest led to panic in Sofia, and Bagrianov quickly accepted Dimo Kazasov's proposal that the prime minister meet with representatives of the Fatherland Front's national council. At this meeting, which took place on 24 August, Dr. Ivan Pashov told Bagrianov that he must step aside to give power to the front, "which alone can save Bulgaria from a national catastrophe." Bagrianov replied that he would not cling to power, but that the decision on a new government rested with the regency council. He invited the front's representatives to meet with the regents, but the lattter declined to receive them on the grounds that there was "no ministerial crisis." Three days later, however, the regents proposed to consult with all former prime ministers and the leaders of all parties that had in the past participated in the government of the country. This formula was designed to exclude the Communists, who alone had never belonged to a governing coalition, although Bagrianov did inform Pashov that the party might well be assigned a ministry in a new cabinet. Under these circumstances, the Communist's allies in the front refused to meet with the regents. Only Kimon Georgiev, in his capacity as a former prime minister, participated, and he insisted that any new government should be composed only of elements from the Fatherland Front.[57] On the same day Bagrianov issued a new statement of neutrality, including an announcement that his government had ordered the disarming of German troops on Bulgarian soil. Stoicho Moshanov was also dispatched to Cairo for new negotiations with the Allies.

In the meantime, the Communists and their partners in the front reacted quickly to the new situation. On 25 August the front's national council issued a manifesto appealing to the people and the army to prepare to assume power. In addition to the original front program, the manifesto called for "people's courts" to punish those responsible for the national catastrophe, the confiscation of illegally acquired wealth, and other social reforms. On the following day the party central committee issued Circular No. 4, which called for the establishment of a front government, directed local party organizations to engage in strikes and demonstrations, and instructed partisan units to concentrate at strategically important points.[58]

The sudden change on the battlefield was also reflected in Soviet policy and in the acts of the Bulgarian party's Foreign Bureau. Three days after the Romanian coup, Stanke Dimitrov-Marek and a group of Bulgarian emigrés took off for their homeland from Briansk, but their aircraft crashed on Soviet territory, killing Dimitrov-Marek and all but one of his companions.[59] Soviet diplomacy at first appeared to favor Bagrianov's declaration of neutrality and the decision to disarm German troops. This aroused concern among the British, who, apparently thinking in nineteenth-century categories, recalled the aftermath of the Russo-Turkish war, when tsarist Russia had tried to use Bulgaria as its foothold in the Balkans. Bulgaria's borders, including the occupied territories, were close to those of the 1878 San Stefano treaty. Was there a possibility that the USSR might seek to take a "big Bulgaria" under its wing to increase its leverage in the Balkans and the Middle East? The British apparently thought so, for on 29 August their ambassador to Moscow asked Molotov to take a firm stand against Bulgarian neutrality. The Soviets quickly complied. On 30 August TASS published a statement denying that the Soviet government recognized Bulgarian neutrality and calling Bagrianov's declaration "completely inadequate." Plans for an invasion of Bulgarian territory were hastily drawn up in preparation for a declaration of war.[60]

The TASS announcement dashed Bagrianov's last hope, and he resigned the following day. The regents at last turned to the legal opposition, appointing Konstantin Muraviev of Vrabcha-1 as prime minister.[61] The choice of Muraviev was surprising, since Gichev and Mushanov had been more likely candidates. Still, Muraviev was the nephew of Stamboliski, and the fact that he was half Russian may also have influenced the regents' decision. Muraviev sought to include the Fatherland Front in his government, but met with categorical refusal. Consequently, his cabinet was composed exclusively of members of the legal opposition. Gichev, Mushanov, and Burov became ministers without portfolio, Girginov was minister of finance, and Vergil Dimov was minister of the interior. Three ministries were left open for the front. Special mention should be made of Muraviev's minister of war, the "nonparty" General Ivan Marinov, who was in secret contact with the front through his associates in Zveno. A Trojan horse in the Muraviev government, he became chief of the army's general staff after the 9 September coup.[62]

The Muraviev government reiterated Bagrianov's pledge of neutrality and promised to withdraw Bulgarian troops from Serbia and to negotiate an armistice with the Allies. On 5 September, with only a half-hour's notice to the British and Americans, the USSR declared war on Bulgaria. Muraviev still hoped to avert Soviet occupation. The cabinet ordered the military not to resist any Red Army penetration and decided to declare war on Germany. General Marinov, however, persuaded the cabinet to delay the official announcement on the pretext that the army needed time to prepare for possible German reprisals. It was not until 8 September, with the Red Army already entering Bulgarian territory, that the government officially declared war on the Germans. Consequently, in its last hours the Muraviev government was simultaneously at war with both sides.

During the night of 2 September the BCP politburo began its preparations for a coup. It envisioned a series of strikes, demonstrations, and military revolts throughout the country that would culminate in a final assault on the capital. The national committee of the Fatherland Front was also reorganized, both to broaden its representation by the inclusion of new allies—such as the "independent intellectuals"—Tsviatko Boboshevski, Venelin Ganev, and Petko Stoianov—and to link it more closely with Terpeshev's partisan staff. During the week of 1–8 September, more than 120 new front committees were formed to take power from local authorities.[63]

Following the announcement of the Soviet declaration of war, the politburo and the general staff of NOVA set the night of 8–9 September for the seizure of power in Sofia. Credit for planning the coup has traditionally been assigned to Dobri Terpeshev, whose role was undoubtedly large, but it is also not difficult to see the experienced hand of Zveno, whose leaders organized the active or at least passive complicity of numerous military officers and police officials. In any case, the authority of the Muraviev government was rapidly crumbling. Strikes of transport and factory workers broke out in Sofia, Plovdiv, and other towns. On 7 September a crowd stormed the prison in Pleven, freeing the prisoners, one of whom was Traicho Kostov. On the same day the coal miners of Pernik seized the mines and fought with police. The Chavdar Brigade of partisans infiltrated the capital, where it came under Todor Zhivkov's command. Soviet troops entered the country on 8 September, meeting no resistance. Bulgarian troops in Varna joined the partisans; the garrison in Burgas mutinied and arrested its officers.

At 4:00 in the afternoon the national council of the Fatherland Front assembled in the home of Kimon Georgiev to decide the composition of the future government. It was not a calm meeting. The main bone of contention was control of the Interior Ministry. Zveno and Pladne leaders wanted it to go to Damian Velchev, but "in the end they yielded to realism." The new government had the following composition:

Communists	Dobri Terpeshev (minister without portfolio)
	Anton Yugov (minister of the interior)
	Dr. Mincho Neichev (minister of justice)
	Dr. Racho Angelov (minister of health)
Zveno members	Kimon Georgiev (prime minister)
	Damian Velchev (minister of war)
	Professor Petko Stainov (minister of foreign affairs)
	Professor Stancho Cholakov (minister of education)
Pladne members	Nikola Petkov (minister without portfolio)
	Angel Derzhanski (minister of transportation)
	Asen Pavlov (minister of agriculture)
	Boris Bumbarov (minister of public works)
Social Democrats	Grigor Cheshmedzhiev (minister of social welfare)
	Dimitŭr Neikov (minister of trade and industry)
Independents	Dimo Kazasov (minister of propaganda)
	Professor Petko Stoianov (minister of finance)

The national council also decided against the immediate abolition of the monarchy and appointed a new regency council composed of communist theoretician Todor Pavlov and "independent intellectuals" Tsviatko Boboshevski and Professor Venelin Ganev.[64]

At midnight, in accordance with an agreement that the Communists had negotiated with the Sofia police commandant, all police patrols were withdrawn from the streets, permitting the front's forces to take up positions around the city. At 2:15 A.M. officers in the War Ministry, where the Muraviev government made its headquarters, opened the doors to allow a front unit to enter. The building was taken and the government was arrested without firing a shot. General Marinov cooperated by ordering military units near the capital not to interfere. Other ministries, the post office, telephone exchanges, the National Bank, and Radio Sofia were captured with similar ease. At 6:25 A.M. Prime Minister Kimon Georgiev broadcast the announcement that the Fatherland Front had taken control of the country. There was little resistance in the provinces.[65] As one of its first acts the new regime made contact with Soviet Commander Marshal Fedor Tolbukhin, who agreed to an immediate cessation of hostilities.

5

The Consolidation of the Communist Regime, 1944–1948

The consolidation of communist power in Bulgaria was accomplished by the beginning of 1948, coinciding in time with completion of the peace treaty with the Allies and the presence of Soviet occupation forces. Only months after the Fatherland Front's coup, Stalin told Tito and Milovan Djilas that "whoever occupies a territory also imposes on it his own social system." [1] Just as the approach of the Red Army had triggered the 9 September coup, the Soviet military occupation both largely determined Bulgaria's place in interallied negotiations and precluded any resort to armed resistance on the part of the domestic opposition. But the communization of Bulgaria was neither instantaneous nor simply the product of Soviet bayonets. Two other factors were of primary importance: the ability of the Communists to gain a monopoly over the instruments of state power and the low priority of Bulgaria on the agenda of the Western democracies.

BULGARIA IN ALLIED NEGOTIATIONS

A precedent for Soviet pre-eminence in the administration of occupied Bulgaria had been established in the terms of the Italian armistice. That agreement gave full control to Great Britain and the United States, whose forces were on the scene, and provided for only token Soviet participation. [2] It was invoked in the cases of Romania and Finland, where the Western powers agreed to accept formal representation on the Allied Control Commission while leaving actual power with the Soviet military commanders. The Soviet Union proposed the identical formula for Bulgaria, but encountered American and British opposition. In Moscow Churchill and Stalin discussed the question in the context of the general situation in the Balkans. On 9 October Churchill made his famous "percentages" proposal to Stalin, which provided for a 90 percent role for the USSR in Romania in return for a similar British preponderance in Greece. With regard to Bulgaria, Churchill suggested a 75 percent preponderance in favor of the Russians, which implied a larger role for Britain in Bulgaria than in Romania. In the discussions between Molotov and Eden that followed, the British foreign secretary continued to insist on a significant British influence in Bulgaria, and Molotov held out for the 90 percent/10 percent mix applied to Romania.

What prompted British concern for Bulgaria? The principal factor seems to have been the continuing presence of Bulgarian forces in Macedonia and Thrace. The Fatherland Front government had complied with the Allied demand to withdraw its occupation forces from these regions, but had done so by converting some of them into combat units and placing them under Soviet command. The British feared that these troops might be used to aid the communist resistance in Greece or, alternatively, that Bulgaria might keep Thracian territory to regain a coastline on the Aegean. On 11 October Molotov agreed to a complete evacuation of Bulgarian troops from the occupied territories, whereupon Eden accepted the Soviet formula for representation on the Bulgarian Allied Control Commission. This varied slightly from the terms of the Romanian armistice, since it provided for the "participation of British and American representatives," but this was a cosmetic difference only. When informed of this agreement, the State Department expressed displeasure and sought to have it revised. Molotov was obdurate, and American diplomacy was content with reserving the right to reopen the question later.

According to the armistice terms, the Allied Control Commission in Bulgaria was under the formal chairmanship of Marshal Tolbukhin, commander of the Third Ukrainian Front. Tolbukhin delegated actual authority to his deputy, Colonel General Sergei S. Biriuzov, who represented him in Bulgaria through April 1946. Biriuzov's conception of his duty is revealed in the following excerpt from his memoirs.

> I had somehow to pick out the main theme of my work. This I perceived to be the rigorous struggle against the fascist proclivities of the reactionary bourgeois circles. They incessantly called attention to themselves: they conspired to bring back the fascist regime, opposed the punishment of war criminals, supported links to Hitlerite Germany and other members of the

notorious fascist "Axis." We did not have the right to withhold our help from the Bulgarian people in crushing this foul beast. Still, we had to take account of the fact that representatives of the USA and England were included in the Allied Control Commission. We had no doubt that they would try to interfere with the establishment of a democratic order in Bulgaria. We had to strike from our "partners' " hand the spoke they were constantly trying to throw in the wheel of history.[3]

Biriuzov kept close watch on Bulgarian events for Moscow and frequently acted with the authority of all the allies without informing the British or American representatives. In the early stages of the occupation, the latter could not even move outside the city limits of Sofia unless accompanied by a Soviet officer. Even though relations gradually improved, Biriuzov's freedom of action was never significantly impaired.

PARTY LEADERSHIP, EXPANSION, AND REORGANIZATION

Immediately after 9 September the party began a process of reorganization and expansion to adapt to the new situation in the country. On 12 September the politburo was reorganized on a provisional basis. Its members were as follows: Traicho Kostov, first secretary of the central committee and head of the party's agitation and propaganda section; Georgi Chankov, in charge of organizational affairs; Tsola Dragoicheva, liaison with the Fatherland Front; Dimitŭr Ganev, liaison with mass organizations; Raiko Damianov, liaison with the trade unions; Petko Kunin, head of the party commission on administration; and Ivan Vinarov, head of the military section. Yugov and Terpeshev, as ministers in the Fatherland Front government, were not formally included, although they and the other communist ministers and Regent Todor Pavlov usually attended politburo meetings. Iordan Katrandzhiev was dropped from the politburo but was named to a newly created Central Control Commission along with Nikola Pavlov, who had been in a concentration camp since early in the war, and Georgi Damianov, who was still in the Soviet Union. The commission's task was to examine the records of party members and to assign them to appropriate jobs. Three days later, in accordance with instructions from Georgi Dimitrov, the Foreign Bureau of the party was dissolved and Dimitrov and Kolarov were added to the politburo. Vŭlko Chervenkov and Georgi Damianov were named candidate members, and Vinarov was reduced from full to candidate status. Vinarov's demotion was probably connected with the impending return of Georgi Damianov, who was to take control of the party's military section. Damianov had emigrated to the Soviet Union after the 1923 uprising, graduated from the Frunze Military Academy, and held the rank of commander in the Red Army.[4]

Dimitrov and Kolarov remained in Moscow until November 1945, presumably because Stalin believed that their return to Bulgaria might complicate relations with the Western powers. Although Dimitrov regularly sent extensive instructions to the Bulgarian party by radiogram, the chief figure on the scene was Traicho Kostov. Was there resentment of Kostov's resumption of party leadership? According to material that has recently appeared, Dobri Terpeshev, Georgi Damianov, "and some others" opposed Kostov for the post of first secretary. They advanced Kolarov's name instead, on the grounds that Kostov lacked "public recognition and authority" of the sort presumably acquired by wartime partisan leaders. In this case Dimitrov backed Kostov. In a radiogram dated 13 October he stated his support for Kostov as first secretary, adding: "We must decide such questions in the interest of the party, in the Bolshevik manner, and we must not be guided by considerations of personal prestige or other similar considerations." And he directed the leadership to popularize Kostov both within the party and among the general public.[5]

Party structure and leadership were formalized at the eighth enlarged plenum of the central committee (27 February–1 March 1945) that followed Kostov's visit to Moscow for discussions with Dimitrov, Molotov, and Stalin. The new central committee, now composed of 39 full and 15 candidate members, was expanded to allow the co-option particularly at the candidate level, of younger leaders who had distinguished themselves in the partisan movement. Dimitrov was named president of the central committee, and a three-man secretariat composed of Kostov, Chankov, and Chervenkov was established with Kostov as first secretary. The politburo was also expanded, to 13 full and 3 candidate members. Full members were Georgi Dimitrov, Vasil Kolarov, Traicho Kostov, Georgi Chankov, Vŭlko Chervenkov, Dobri Terpeshev, Anton Yugov, Tsola Dragoicheva, Dimitŭr Ganev, Raiko Damianov, Georgi Damianov, Petko Kunin, and Vladimir Poptomov; candidate members were Dimitŭr Dimov, Gocho Grozev, and Titko Chernokolev.

On the eve of 9 September the party had approximately 13,700 members. Not all of them, however, could be utilized by the leadership, for there was strong feeling among former partisans and political prisoners that party members who had remained aloof from active struggle during the war should not share in the fruits of victory. In a radiogram to the politburo on 4 November Dimitrov stressed the party's need for cadres and warned against the tendency to make a cult of a prison record or membership in a partisan unit. He advised that the party make use of those members who had been inactive during the war but suggested that they not be placed in leading or highly visible positions.[6]

Three days after the seizure of power, the central committee sent out its first directive to local party units with instructions for transforming the illegal, underground organization into "a mighty, mass party of industrial workers and laborers in town and country."[7] The new party structure was generally based on existing political boundaries, although some exceptions were made for large-scale enterprises. Party committees for the nine regions (*oblasti*) were in place by late September. They in turn oversaw the formation of approximately 90 district (*okoliia*) committees during the next six weeks. On 18 September the party found its voice with the appearance of the first legal issue of *Rabotnichesko delo*, which, with its advantages in access to newsprint and publishing facilities, quickly developed the widest circulation of any Bulgarian newspaper (60,000 copies, rising to 250,000 by March 1945). A theoretical journal, *Sǔvremennik* (Contemporary), also began to appear in January 1945, and a Central Party School for the training of cadres opened in the same month.[8]

During the first 40 days of the Fatherland Front regime, party membership doubled and doubled again. By mid-January 1945 it numbered over 250,000. A similar expansion occurred in the party's youth organization, which grew from 15,000 to 225,000 between 9 September and the end of 1944.[9] Information on the social composition of the party given at the eighth plenum is presented in Table 8.

Although this growth in numbers was impressive, it was also uneven. Some local party committees, under the influence of "left-sectarian tendencies," refused to admit even industrial workers who lacked the proper party

TABLE 8   SOCIAL COMPOSITION OF PARTY MEMBERSHIP, JANUARY 1945

Category	Number	Percentage
Workers	53,090	21.4
Peasants	100,915	40.7
Intelligentsia	16,424	6.6
Artisans	11,393	4.6
Unreported	65,905	26.6
Men	172,020	67.9
Women	15,597	6.2
Unreported	65,905	25.9

SOURCE: Petŭr Avramov, "Organizatsionno izgrazhdane na BKP sled izlizaneto i ot nelegalnost, 9 septemvri 1944 g.–fevruari 1945 g.," *Istoricheski pregled* 2 (1965): 19.

consciousness or admitted them only to a candidate stage, a measure that the central committee had outlawed. Other less demanding committees conducted door-to-door recruitment campaigns or group enrollments, with little or no regard for the recruits' quality, class background, or sometimes even of their desire to join the party.

Given the rapidity of party expansion, it is not surprising that the new membership was not a reliable tool for the consolidation of communist power. During the struggle with the opposition, repeated efforts were made to organize grass-roots campaigns, build strong local organizations, and win an ever-larger following. These efforts were repeatedly judged failures. And it could hardly have been otherwise, one Bulgarian historian has written, when 95 percent of the party had joined only after 9 September.

> Careerist and other elements who wormed their way into party organizations ruined party and state discipline, stole property just like their opponents, speculated in the black market, set up internal group conflicts, [and] were guilty of intrigue and factionalism, moral and political degeneration, and carrying out illegal acts against the working population.

The party committee in Vratsa *oblast* attributed the continuing strength of the opposition to "the irresponsible, lunatic acts of our own insolent comrades, who disgust the honest citizens . . . by their hooliganism, larceny, drunkenness, moral degeneration, abuse of ration cards and so on." Similar reports reproduced from party archives indicate that this state of affairs on the local level was widespread.[10]

Coinciding with the rapid expansion of party membership was the mushrooming of Fatherland Front committees outside the formal apparatus of government. Although they nominally represented all of the parties in the Fatherland Front coalition, they were in fact weighted in favor of the Communists. According to government statistics, by the end of 1944 there were 7,292 committees with 26,255 members. Of the members, 14,120 (54 percent) were Communists, 8,682 (33 percent) were Agrarians, 854 (3 percent) were Socialists, 410 (2 percent) belonged to Zveno, and 2,179 (8 percent) were unaffiliated.[11]

Some historians have seen the Fatherland Front committees as the principal engine in the consolidation of communist power on the local level, playing a role analogous to the soviets during the Russian Revolution.[12] More recent studies have shown this view to be highly romanticized. Despite the Communists' preponderance, there were numerous committees that were not under their control, nor were the communist cadres sufficiently experienced and disciplined to carry out a coordinated policy. Moreover, the committees were often amorphously organized and without clearly defined authority. For the purposes of the communist leadership, they had at best a nuisance value, interfering with noncommunist local authorities, but even this was of doubtful utility. By the end of the year, the Ministry of the Interior issued directives aimed at curbing the committee and ordering them not to interfere with the legal representatives of authority.[13]

On a higher level, however, the national council of the Fatherland Front, of which Tsola Dragoicheva became chairman after 9 September, played a more significant role. It concealed what was fast becoming a one-party dictatorship and provided the Communists with a means of intervening in the internal affairs of their partners. It became a sort of prison for the noncommunist parties until the fall of 1945, when political organization outside the front became legal.

THE INSTRUMENTS OF POWER

According to one historian of Bulgaria's revolution,

> The regime of people's democracy, as a nonsoviet form of the dictatorship of the proletariat, of necessity rested on the most important organs of state power: the Ministry of the Interior, the Ministry of Justice, and the Ministry of War, the first two of which were held by Communists and the third by a minister from Zveno. The two ministries in the hands of the Communists gave the party the commanding positions in the administration, which was of decisive significance for carrying out the fundamental measures for the internal security of the country.[14]

Within a few weeks after the seizure of power, the Ministry of the Interior, under Yugov's control, discharged nearly 30,000 officials. The police were replaced by a state militia, whose creation proceeded entirely under communist direction. Composed primarily of "partisans, former political prisoners, members of the party and the party youth organization," the new militia received the arms and authority of the old police apparatus, and used them to settle scores with their old enemies or any "reactionaries" who got in their way.[15] Within the Interior Ministry, Dimo Dichev supervised the organization of a political police, the future state security police, relying on the "rich experience" of Soviet advisers from the NKVD.

By the end of the year Yugov had brought about an almost complete turnover in the personnel of local administration. Table 9, based on statistics compiled by the Interior Ministry for 81 of the country's 92 districts, shows the distribution of power in local administration as of 31 December 1944. If anything, it understates the communist domination of

TABLE 9   DISTRIBUTION OF LOCAL OFFICES,
31 DECEMBER 1944

Office	Communist	BANU	Socialist	Zveno	Nonparty
Town Mayors	63	11	2	2	6
Town Vice-mayors	17	13	7	2	—
Village Mayors	879	137	8	2	32
Village Vice-mayors	1,763	540	3	5	260

SOURCE: Petŭr Ostoich, *BKP i izgrazhdaneto na narodnodemokraticheskata dŭrzhava, 9 septemvri 1944–dekemvri 1947*, (Sofia, 1967), pp. 76–77.

local government, since the noncommunists appointed to these positions were likely to be those most inclined to cooperate with the party.

The legal appointment of large numbers of Communists to positions in local administration was made possible by the Interior Ministry's elimination of the educational requirements for officeholders that had existed in the past. The ministry established training schools to provide crash courses in administrative law and accounting for its new functionaries, although this hardly satisfied the noncommunists' complaints that Yugov was "beheading" local administration.

The need for expertise forced the Ministry of Justice to retain a larger proportion of its personnel. Nonetheless, by the end of 1944 it had replaced 200 of its 628 officials, including 121 judges and prosecutors in the district courts.[16] But the main work of the Justice Ministry lay in the establishment of the people's courts.

The concept of people's courts was not new in Bulgaria. After World War I the Agrarian government had put on trial "those responsible for the national catastrophe," but in that case the defendants were limited to 22 former ministers and high military officials, not one of whom, the Communists complained, received the death sentence. Moreover, the demand for the punishment of the fascists had been included, although in an imprecise way, in the original program of the Fatherland Front, and the prosecution of war criminals was also required by the terms of Bulgaria's armistice with the Allies. But it quickly became apparent that the Communists intended to define "fascist" and "war criminal" as broadly as possible. As the Communists initially proposed, the people's courts would be empowered to try anyone charged with fascist acts after 1923. In response to the objections from other parties in the front, particularly Zveno, this was modified to apply only to crimes committed after 1 January 1941. Even so, the people's courts had a very broad scope.

As the extent of the prosecutions became apparent, the noncommunist ministers in the government tried to intervene. War Minister Velchev, especially, used the full extent of his powers in an effort to shield military officers from the courts. On 23 November, at a meeting of the Council of Ministers that for some reason the Communists did not attend, Velchev persuaded his colleagues to issue Decree No. 4, which provided a blanket amnesty for all military personnel who served with honor in the war against Germany. The Communists immediately organized demonstrations against the decree and, more effectively, enlisted the aid of Biriuzov. According to the general's memoirs:

> The conduct of the Soviet representatives of the Allied Control Commission was always based on the firm, Leninist principles of Soviet foreign policy: we did not permit ourselves to interfere in Bulgaria's internal affairs, and still less to put any kind of pressure on her government. But when the reaction became insolent and its hostile action went beyond the limits permitted by the armistice agreement, our duty was to waste no time in coming to the aid of the Bulgarian working people.[17]

Biriuzov insisted that the decree be withdrawn and faced down the noncommunist ministers who tried to protest.

The work of the people's courts got under way with the mass trial of former political leaders that was held in Sofia from 20 December 1944 to 1 February 1945. The defendants included the three former regents, Filov, Prince Kiril, and General Mikhov, the ministers of the five wartime cabinets, 130 National Assembly deputies, and a number of advisers to the late tsar. When the trial began, some of the chief defendants were missing, having been sent to the Soviet Union "for interrogation" and possible trial before an international war crimes tribunal. They were returned to Bulgaria, however, owing to the Soviet Union's "great confidence in the people's court." This confidence was not misplaced, since the court went beyond even the demands of the prosecution in handing down an even 100 death sentences. The former regents, 28 former ministers, 68 deputies, and adviser to the tsar Pavel Gruev were all executed the next day. Even the members of the anti-German Muraviev government received lengthy prison sentences combined with the confiscation of their possessions. The people's courts in the provinces followed the example of the Sofia trial. By the time they completed their work in April 1945, according to official statistics, they had tried 11,122 people. Of these, 2,730 were condemned to death, 1,305 to life imprisonment, 5,119 to terms up to twenty years, and 1,516 were acquitted; the fates of 452 defendants could not be determined.[18]

The purge of the military was slower to develop, both because War Minister Velchev fought skillfully within the limits of his authority to protect the professional officer corps and because the Soviet Union wanted to use the Bulgarian army in the campaign against Germany. Nevertheless, several measures were rapidly adopted to raise the party's influence in the military. An initial purge of approximately 1,100 officers, supposedly the most notorious Germanophiles, was completed by the end of 1944. At the same time, 718 Communists with military or partisan experience were given commissions, and an additional 334 members of the party or of the party youth organization were enrolled in the military academy. Upon graduation in 1945 they were appointed to ranks as high as colonel. At the army and divisional levels, Communists were appointed to the newly created post of deputy commander, where they functioned as political commissars. They were responsible to the Institute for Deputy Commanders, which was directed by Georgi Damianov, head of the central committee's military department. A number of Bulgarian emigrés with experience in the Red Army were thus placed in key military positions. The party also persuaded the Fatherland Front government to approve the creation of a National Guard, organized around the partisan units, which brought 28,581 reliable troops into the regular army.

Bulgarian forces fought well in the concluding stages of World War II, helping to clear Macedonia and southern Serbia of Germans and advancing along with the Red Army into Hungary and Austria.[19] Approximately 30,000 troops were killed. With the conclusion of hostilities, the struggle for control of the army resumed. Velchev ordered the demobilization of all officers who did not meet minimum education requirements and tried to limit the number of political officers. The Communists' response was to secure the transfer of the control of military personnel from the Ministry of War to the full ministerial council. This permitted a hastily organized government investigating committee to purge 1,940 officers. The political police also "unmasked" a number of clandestine organizations with ties to the military or to former officers, and this provided grounds for further arrests and intimidation. Control of the army was fully secured by September 1946 when Velchev was replaced as war minister by Georgi Damianov.[20]

Propaganda Minister Dimo Kazasov was not a member of the party, but he rendered loyal service to it by placing control of the press and radio in the hands of communist functionaries. The university and Academy of Sciences were also subjected to a purge. Although some noncommunist ministers offered some resistance and in fact carried out counterpurges to limit communist influence and to provide refuge for their constituents, they had only minor success. Communist-led unions fought vigorously for "fair play" in those branches of government under opposition control, and in any case these were far less important politically than the instruments of power in communist hands.

The Opposition

Given the rapid capture of the key instruments of state power by the Communists, it is possible to agree with Georgi Dimitrov's statement to the party's fifth congress in 1948 that the "people's democracy" created on 9 September had from the beginning been a form of the dictatorship of the proletariat. But this was not so obvious, even to Dimitrov, in the early stage of the new regime.[21] The initial program of the Fatherland Front government was relatively moderate, resembling most of all the program of Stamboliski's Agrarian government after World War I. From Moscow, Dimitrov advised the party leadership not to antagonize the other front parties and to avoid premature conflicts over such issues as the separation of church and state or even the future of the monarchy.[22] Among the noncommunist parties this inspired the belief that genuine cooperation with the Communists was a real possibility. In addition, they could hope that an eventual restoration of democracy would allow them to undermine the communist domination of the state through the ballot box. Ultimately, therefore, their hopes rested on the influence that the Western democracies could or would bring to bear on the Soviet Union and its Bulgarian clients.

In the first months after 9 September, political activity was permitted only to the Communists and their partners in the Fatherland Front. As these noncommunist parties sought to adapt to the new situation in their country, they remained remarkably true to their traditions.[23] Zveno attempted to transform itself into a political party, the National Alliance Zveno, at a national conference on 1 October. Its spokesmen vowed to abandon their past elitism, and adopted a program based on that of the Fatherland Front. Although it attracted some new members from the Bulgarian middle class that had in the past adhered to the "bourgeois" parties, Zveno never became a real party in its own right. As the product of an undemocratic tradition, it consisted of a corps of elite, often highly capable individuals, who conceived of politics in terms of putschism and behind-the-scenes maneuvers. Lacking both strong ideological commitments and a popular constituency, Zveno's leaders saw no role for themselves in a democratic order and were highly susceptible to the Communists' threats and blandishments. To be sure, Damian Velchev fought to prevent the communist takeover of the army, but most of the Zveno leadership followed the example of Kimon Georgiev, who chose the path of collaboration and was well rewarded.

The constituency of the Social Democratic Party was also narrow, since the party had drawn most of its support from teachers, civil servants, and a small segment of the working class that had traditionally adhered to socialist trade unions. Moreover, from the beginning it was deeply divided over the issue of its cooperation with the Communists. On the right, party doyen Krŭstiu Pastukhov had never wanted the party to enter the Fatherland Front, and he continued to inveigh against the Communists, whom he accused of trying to run Bulgaria with "rifles and political commissars." On the left, Dimitŭr Neikov advocated the closest possible collaboration between Bulgaria's two working-class parties. Grigor Cheshmedzhiev and Kosta Lulchev attempted to find a middle ground that would preserve the party's independence by agreeing to drop Pastukhov and his allies from the central committee. But their efforts foundered under incessant pressure from Neikov and the left. During the spring and summer of 1945, a series of factional congresses led to Neikov's capture of the official party machinery, and Cheshmedzhiev and Lulchev formed a new Social Democratic Workers' Party (united).

The heart of the democratic opposition was the Agrarian Union. Immediately after 9 September, the Agrarian ministers in the front government appealed to the peasantry, still 75 percent of the country's population, to form village units, the *druzhbi*, and to merge the Pladne and Vrabcha-1 factions to reconstitute the BANU as a "mighty, united, and creative organization, the exclusive representative of the Bulgarian village." The Agrarian Union's growth matched, and in fact probably far exceeded, that of the Communists, and under less favorable conditions.[24] On 23 September Dr. Georgi M. Dimitrov returned from exile, and his progress by train from Svilengrad on the Turkish border to Sofia occasioned mass demonstrations all along the route. At the BANU's national conference on 14–15 October he was acclaimed as the Agrarian Union's general secretary.[25]

From the beginning, Dr. Dimitrov believed that the Communists planned to take full control of the country. Nikola Petkov confided to him that he had misread their intentions and had blundered in conceding them control of the police and judiciary. Similar warnings came from the two noncommunists on the regency council. Dr. Dimitrov consequently rejected proposals that he join the Fatherland Front government, even though Traicho Kostov held open the possibility of his becoming prime minister. Instead, Dr. Dimitrov chose to devote his full effort to preparing the Agrarian Union for an independent struggle. In a series of impressively large meetings around the country, he reminded the Agrarian Union's constituents that he had advocated a united front against fascism when the Communists still backed the Soviet-German pact, and that from the time of Stamboliski it had been the BANU that had spearheaded the cause of democracy in Bulgaria.

Inspired by Dr. Dimitrov's firmness, the Agrarians began to move away from the official positions of the Fatherland Front. At political meetings and in the press they revived the traditional Agrarian slogan "Bread, Peace, and Democracy," which implied criticism not only of the front government's economic and political policies but also of the continued participation of the Bulgarian army in the war. In meetings with the Communists and other leaders of the Fatherland Front, Dr. Dimitrov protested the conduct of the people's militia and the sweeping powers of the people's courts, and he was backed by the Agrarian ministers, who threatened resignation.

At the end of October Nikola Petkov returned from Moscow, where he had been part of the government delegation sent to sign the armistice. Petkov warned Dr. Dimitrov that the Russians regarded him as a provocateur and that (communist leader) Georgi Dimitrov seemed determined to eliminate him. Dimitrov had early on ordered the Bulgarian Communists under no circumstances to allow an Agrarian political monopoly in the countryside. In December he sent a radiogram to Kostov, telling him that the time had come for an open attack on the Agrarian leader.[26]

The initial move came from General Biriuzov, who had always believed that Dr. Dimitrov had secret ties with the British. The general seized on the Agrarian call for peace to charge Dr. Dimitrov with defeatism. He threatened to use his authority to dissolve the entire Agrarian Union if Dr. Dimitrov did not step down from the leadership. Faced with this pressure and ill with pneumonia, Dr. Dimitrov resigned as general secretary on 20 January, yielding his place to Nikola Petkov. Later in the month the Communists pushed through the Council of Ministers a Law for the Defense of the People's Authority, which prohibited acts contributing to the demoralization of the army or injurious to Bulgaria's international prestige.[27] The law was intended to further intimidate critics of the regime, and it provided the grounds for Dr. Dimitrov's arrest in April.

If the Communists had hoped that Nikola Petkov would be a more pliable partner than Dr. Dimitrov—and given their past experience with him they had every reason to think so—they were soon disappointed. Petkov had lost his illusions about the Communists, and from this point on he offered firm and courageous resistance. The main area of conflict was the organization of National Assembly elections, which, according to the Yalta Declaration on Liberated Europe (11 February), were to be "free elections of governments responsible to the will of the people." At his party's eighth plenum, Kostov proposed that the four parties of the Fatherland Front present a single list of candidates with the distribution of power among them decided before the election. No party outside the front would be allowed to organize, so that opposition candidates would have to run as individuals, not as party representatives. Since this would have the effect of perpetuating the existing front government and communist control of the key instruments of power, Petkov objected and appealed to the representatives of the Western powers. At the end of March, United States Ambassador Harriman raised the issue of the Bulgarian elections in Moscow and proposed that the parties of the Fatherland Front run independently, but Molotov dismissed the subject as an internal Bulgarian matter.

Finding Petkov harder to deal with than expected, the Communists decided to employ the same splitting tactics that were succeeding with the Socialists. Late in April, coinciding with the placing of Dr. Dimitrov under house arrest, "the communist party rendered friendly assistance to the healthy forces in the BANU in order to purge the *druzhbi* and their leaders of Gemeto's followers. [Dr. G. M. Dimitrov was often referred to by his detractors as "Gemeto," that is, "the G. M."] The party also invited the other members of the Fatherland Front to cooperate in freeing the Agrarian Union of the ulcer of Gemeto-ism." [28] This assault on the local Agrarian organizations was followed by the staging of a national conference on 8–9 May that was attended only by the Agrarian Union's "healthy elements," led by Alexander Obbov.

Western historians have portrayed Obbov as the BANU's quisling, a renegade and political prostitute who sold his party to the Communists. [29] This is misleading, for Obbov's position was based at least in part on principle. As an Agrarian organizer before the First World War, minister of agriculture in the Stamboliski government, and a leader of the Union-in-exile after 1923, Obbov had a long record of sacrifice and loyalty. Undoubtedly he resented being pushed to the background by Dr. Dimitrov and Petkov, but at the same time he had consistently warned them that a policy of confrontation with the Communists and their Soviet backers would lead to the Agrarian Union's destruction. He was still convinced (and the Communists played on this conviction) that a policy of accommodation was the only one that could preserve some degree of Agrarian independence. During the May conference and after, Obbov tried to persuade Petkov to remain at the head of the BANU within the framework of the Fatherland Front. From Moscow, Georgi Dimitrov added his personal invitation to Petkov to participate in a genuine Communist-Agrarian alliance. [30] When Petkov rejected these appeals, the BANU leadership elected in May expelled him from the Agrarian Union and named Obbov general secretary. The national council of the Fatherland Front promptly recognized Obbov's faction as the genuine Agrarian Union. Deprived of access to Union funds or the Agrarian press, Petkov made his own home the headquarters for a rival Agrarian Union.

What accounted for Petkov's determination? In addition to his own civic courage, he almost certainly hoped for Western support. On 23 May Dr. Dimitrov had escaped from house arrest and had been given refuge in the residence of the American ambassador, Maynard Barnes. [31] Barnes had also consistently indicated to Petkov and to other noncommunist leaders that the United States remained committed to the principles expressed in the Yalta declaration. At the same time Petkov knew of the British intervention in Greece and, since he was not aware of the price Churchill had paid for it, he probably interpreted it as a hardening of the Western position vis-à-vis Soviet influence throughout Eastern Europe.

In early June the regency council set the date for parliamentary elections for 26 August. By the end of the month the front parties agreed on a combined list that allocated 94 seats to the Workers' Party, 94 to Obbov's Agrarians, 48 to Zveno, 32 to Neikov's Socialists, and 8 to independents. Petkov's request that his faction be recognized as an independent party with the right to publish its own newspaper was rejected. On 26 July he addressed a letter to the prime minister, the regency council, and the Allied Control Commission, which stated that conditions in the country did not permit free elections and asked for a postponement until they could be held under international control. This letter was also communicated to the British and American delegations at Potsdam, where the Western leaders refused to recognize the Bulgarian government and pressed unsuccessfully for more open election procedures.[32] The Communists and Obbov's Agrarians organized a campaign to discredit the letter, and Petkov was expelled from the cabinet. Later in August the remaining Agrarian ministers, Socialist Grigor Cheshmedzhiev, and independent Petko Stoianov also asked for a postponement of the elections on the grounds that opposition candidates were being terrorized. When their appeal was rejected, they resigned from the cabinet in protest.

The sole remaining restraint on the Bulgarian regime was the possibility that the government established by the elections would not be recognized by the Western powers. Both the British and American governments formally objected to the nature of the coming elections, but did not categorically state that they would withhold recognition. On 23 August, Maynard Barnes, acting on the logic but not the letter of his instructions from the State Department, joined his British counterpart in a meeting with General Biriuzov, during which the two diplomats pressed forcefully for a postponement. At the conclusion of the meeting Biriuzov promised to consult Moscow, and on the following day the Bulgarian government announced that the elections would in fact be postponed.

Victory in the "battle of elections" marked the high point of Western influence in postwar Bulgaria, and it had been achieved largely by accident. When Barnes reported the substance of his meeting with Biriuzov, before the announcement of the postponement, he was reprimanded by the State Department for exceeding his instructions. Apparently the earlier State Department protest had been for the record only, and was not intended to have any effect. When informed that the elections had in fact been post-poned, the State Department withdrew its reprimand and congratulated Barnes on his victory, adding the hope that it would "ensure to the Bulgarian people full freedom of choice in the establishment of a representative government." [33]

The spoke that Barnes had placed in the wheel of history did not change the outcome of the Bulgarian political struggle, but it did force the Communists to slow the pace of change and to take some measures to present at least the appearance of a more democratic system. One of the first such signs was the government's announcement that it would place no obstacle in the way of Dr. Dimitrov's departure from the country, and Barnes persuaded the reluctant Agrarian leader to take advantage of the offer. Petkov's Agrarians were recognized as a legal opposition party, the BANU-NP (for Nikola Petkov), as was the Socialist Party of Cheshme-dzhiev and Lulchev. Both were permitted to publish newspapers, although access to the radio remained a monopoly of the parties in the Fatherland Front.

The Communists also amnestied approximately 1,000 prisoners who had been convicted by the people's courts—Atanas Burov, Nikola Musha-nov, and Dimitŭr Gichev among them. [34] Mushanov was allowed to reorganize his Democratic Party, and the government also recognized the small Radical Party of Stoian Kosturkov. These measures were intended both to impress the Western powers and to fractionalize the opposition. In this respect Gichev played a useful role as an opponent of what he called Petkov's "dictatorship" of the opposition Agrarian Union. [35]

The changes described above were cosmetic and did not alter the political situation in any fundamental way. When opposition candidates continued to be harassed and intimidated, they decided to boycott the parliamentary elections now scheduled for 18 November. In September Kolarov returned to Bulgaria to rally the communist forces, and on 4 November Georgi Dimitrov returned after 22 years of exile. He had been, perhaps, more impressive from abroad than he was in the flesh. He appeared ill and aging—the British ambassador likened him to "a second-rate orchestra leader"—and he was constantly accompanied by a Soviet watchdog. Still, his first public speech was a rousing and violent denunciation of the oppositon, which must have left its hearers few illusions about the regime's intentions.

During the first meeting of the Council of Foreign Ministers in London (11 September–3 October 1945), a deadlock developed over the issue of the representative character of the Bulgarian and Romanian governments that threatened to prevent the conclusion of the European peace treaties. The American secretary of state, James Byrnes, believed that reports of communist conduct in these countries may have been based on "erroneous or prejudiced information," and he asked Mark Ethridge, editor of the *Louisville Courier-Journal*, to conduct an independent investigation.[36] Ethridge spent two weeks in Bulgaria in late October, meeting with nearly all major figures from the government, the opposition, and the representatives of Great Britain and the USSR. His report to the secretary of state concluded that the Bulgarian government was "not broadly representative of all democratic elements in the Yalta sense," and that it was "authoritarian and . . . dominated by one party," with the majority of the population "forcibly excluded from representation."[37]

The National Assembly elections held on 18 November produced the expected large majority for the Fatherland Front, which received 88.18 percent of the 3,853,097 votes cast. There were 455,425 blank ballots, an impressive statement in view of the communist control of the electoral machinery.[38] The question of international recognition remained, but conditions were becoming more and more unfavorable for effective Western pressure. Even at the London foreign ministers' conference, Molotov had tried to link the arrangements in Romania and Bulgaria with the Japanese peace settlement. By the time of the Moscow foreign ministers' conference in December, American diplomacy had apparently decided to use the Balkan countries as bargaining chips, to be traded off for the exclusion of a Soviet voice in the occupation of Japan. In meetings with Molotov and then with Stalin, Byrnes pressed for a broadening of the Bulgarian government, but without success. Stalin dismissed the Ethridge report, and Byrnes's threat to publish it, with the remark that Ilya Ehrenberg, also an "impartial journalist," had received a different impression of the Balkans and would publish his views. In the end the Ethridge report was buried in the State Department archives, and Byrnes settled for Stalin's agreement to "advise" the Bulgarian government to add two members of the opposition. When Byrnes reported on the results of the conference to the president and members of his staff, only Admiral Leahy expressed disapproval of the agreement on Bulgaria. Byrnes asked what the admiral would have done and received no reply.[39]

Stalin did in fact discuss the broadening of the government with Georgi Dimitrov by telephone on 23 December, and on the following day Dimitrov reported back that the party leadership and the other front parties agreed. Kimon Georgiev invited Petkov's Agrarians and Lulchev's Socialists (Cheshmedzhiev had died in the fall of 1945) to enter the government. The opposition leaders, however, insisted on two conditions: that they retain the right to criticize government policies and that the Communists relinquish their control of the Interior and Justice ministries. Georgiev informed Stalin of these conditions during a visit to Moscow in January, and as a result Andrei Vyshinski was dispatched to Sofia to talk directly with the opposition leaders. In very blunt terms he told them that the Moscow agreement did not provide for conditions on the part of the opposition. It called only for the addition of two members of the opposition to the government. If the opposition declined, that was their responsibility. Petkov and Lulchev remained firm.

In March the Communists made a second attempt to induce the opposition to join the regime, this time agreeing to give up the Justice Ministry and to include deputy ministers from other parties in the Ministry of the Interior. These concessions were vetoed, however, by the Soviet Union, which held that they went beyond the grounds of the Moscow agreement. After this the Bulgarian Communists began more openly to take full control of the country. A reorganization of the government in March increased the number of communist ministers at the expense of the party's allies in the front. Socialist Krŭstiu Pastukhov was arrested and charged with writing articles that contributed to disorganization and disaffection in the army. War Minister Velchev, who testified in Pastukhov's defense, was ejected from the cabinet in August, and in the same month Dr. Dimitrov was tried in absentia for treason and sentenced to death. State security also publicized the "unmasking" of secret, counterrevolutionary, terrorist organizations that supposedly had links to the opposition.[40]

On 6 June Dimitrov, Kolarov, and Kostov met with Stalin and Molotov in Moscow to discuss, among other things, "the pace at which the revolutionary transformations would come about and measures to strengthen the people's democratic power in Bulgaria." [41] After their return the politburo announced that a referendum would be held on the future of the monarchy, followed in turn by elections for a Grand National Assembly that would alter the constitution. Prime Minister Georgiev "was informed of this decision." No party defended the institution of the monarchy, and in the referendum held on 8 September 93 percent of the voters favored a republic, 4 percent a monarchy, and 3 percent of the ballots were ruled invalid. Bulgaria was proclaimed a republic one week later, and Simeon and other members of the royal family left the country. Vasil Kolarov was named president of the provisional government.

The Communists decided to use the Grand National Assembly elections, scheduled for 27 October, to undermine their allies as well as to defeat their enemies. Departing from the practice of the previous election, where the Fatherland Front presented a single list of preselected candidates, the Communists announced that voters would be allowed to vote for the front with different colored ballots indicating a preference for one of the front parties. Seats in the National Assembly and ministerial posts would then be apportioned among the front parties in accordance with the result.

TABLE 10   ELECTIONS FOR
GRAND NATIONAL ASSEMBLY,
27 OCTOBER 1946

Party or Group	Votes	Percentage of Votes	Deputies
Fatherland Front	2,988,806	70.1	366
Communists	2,264,852	53.1	275
BANU (Obbov)	564,581	13.2	69
Socialists (Neikov)	79,771	1.9	9
Zveno	70,731	1.6	8
Radicals	8,864	0.2	4
Independent	—	—	1
Opposition Bloc	1,191,455	28.0	99[a]
Democrats	22,736	0.5	—
Others	298	—	—
Blank or disqualified ballots	63,399	1.5	—
Total	4,266,694	100.0	465

SOURCE: Nikolai Genchev, "Razgromŭt na burzhoaznata opozitsiia v Bŭlgariia prez 1947–1948 godina," *Godishnik na Sofiskiia universitet (ideologichni katedri)* 56 (1962): 206.

[a]Of the opposition deputies, 89 were Agrarians, 9 were Socialists, and 1 was an independent.

Since the Socialists and Zveno had almost no popular following, and Obbov's Agrarians had only an insignificant one, this measure was obviously intended to rob the noncommunist front parties of all significance. In the preparation of a draft constitution, the Communists on the front's commission also ignored the proposals and criticisms of their partners.[42]

The major opposition parties—Petkov's Agrarians, Lulchev's Socialists, and a group of "independent intellectuals"—united their forces on the eve of the elections and bitterly protested the lack of democratic freedoms. They received some support from defectors from Zveno and Obbov's Agrarians, who had lost their illusions about the Communists' intentions.[43] Considering the conditions prevailing in the country, the opposition's showing was an amazing achievement, testimony to the courage and determination of Petkov and his allies and to the spirit of the people.

As a result of these elections, the role of the noncommunist parties in the government was downgraded. Georgi Dimitrov became prime minister; Kimon Georgiev dropped to minister of foreign affairs. The Communists took half the ministries, leaving the less significant ones to be divided among their partners. The noncommunist parties in the front reacted in different ways. Neikov's Socialists were ready for whatever role the Communists assigned them. Some members of Zveno, however, regarded their loss of positions as a communist doublecross and were in any case disturbed by the purge of the army earlier in the year. The Communists dealt with this ally by naming prominent Zveno figures as ambassadors and sending them out of the country. Damian Velchev became ambassador to Switzerland and probably saved his life later by refusing orders to return home. Alexander Obbov and a significant number of prominent Agrarians still in the front moved steadily toward the opposition. Early in 1947, Obbov worked out a secret agreement by which the rank-and-file members of the opposition were to join the official BANU and use their numerical strength to vote communist agents and sympathizers out of the leadership. As a result, the Communists engineered an internal coup that replaced Obbov with Georgi Traikov. Obbov ended his political career in the camp of the opposition, warning the people of the "communist danger" and threatening the regime with the wrath of President Truman.[44]

The hope that Western pressure would restrain the regime was fast fading. By 1947 whatever interest had existed in promoting Bulgarian democracy had given way to an impatience to conclude the peacemaking process and get on to other concerns. The treaty with Bulgaria was signed on 10 February. Soon afterward, the BCP central committee ordered the printers' unions to refuse to publish the newspapers of the opposition. The State Department issued a protest for the record, but its actual response was to try to hasten the ratification of the treaty and recognition of the Bulgarian government before the situation became so much worse that it might cause embarrassment.[45]

Deprived of all other forums, the opposition made its last stand in the Grand National Assembly. In spite of Georgi Dimitrov's threat that it would cost him his head, Nikola Petkov continued to defy the regime, to protest the conduct of its agents, and to call for a restoration of genuine democracy. On 4 June the state prosecutor's office reported to the assembly that it possessed evidence linking Petkov to underground terrorist organizations. On the following day, the same day the United States Senate ratified the peace treaty with Bulgaria, the assembly voted to deprive Petkov of his parliamentary immunity. Five days later, 23 other Agrarian deputies were expelled. Petkov's trial for treason took place on 5–16 August, accompanied by constant demonstrations demanding his blood. The court complied by handing down a death sentence, and on 26 August the assembly outlawed the entire opposition BANU and ordered the confiscation of all its assets. Again there were Western protests against Petkov's trial, but the principal concern seems to have been that it might impede the normalization of relations.[46] Petkov was executed on 23 September. On 1 October the United States extended diplomatic recognition.[47]

GLEICHSCHALTUNG

The defeat of the political opposition in part coincided with and in part was followed by the elimination of nearly all elements of pluralism in Bulgarian society. This process was accelerated after the founding congress of the Cominform on 22–27 September at Szklarska Poreba in Poland. Here Zhdanov and Malenkov emphasized the increasing aggressiveness of the imperialist camp led by the United States and the necessity for a more rapid socialist transformation in the democratic camp led by the Soviet Union. In connection with the latter, they stressed the importance of Soviet experience as a guide.[48] The Bulgarian delegates, Vŭlko Chervenkov and Vladimir Poptomov, went directly to Moscow after this conference, and on 14 October Chervenkov conveyed Moscow's further instructions to a central committee plenum. According to Chervenkov's report, the Bulgarian party had not fully recognized that 9 September had been the beginning of a socialist revolution and had proceeded too slowly in asserting and institutionalizing its leading role. In response, the plenum decided to complete the elimination of the opposition, impose new conditions on the Fatherland Front, and strengthen the socialist character of the new constitution.

The impact of this "intensification of the revolutionary process" on the noncommunist parties was immediate. The Socialists in the front applied for membership in the BCP, a request that was granted to those who could pass the screening commissions set up to test their loyalty. On 11 August 1948 the party officially merged with the BCP. At the same time, the opposition Socialists were crushed by police repression and joined their Agrarian colleagues in the prisons and concentration camps that were growing rapidly.[49] On 28–29 December, at the twenty-seventh congress of the official BANU, Georgi Traikov formally repudiated traditional Agrarian ideology and defined the Agrarian Union's new role as loyal ally and helpmeet of the Communists. In the year that followed, the Union's membership underwent a thorough purge. During the winter of 1948–49, Zveno, the Democratic Party, and the Radical Party announced their "self-liquidation" and dissolved into the Fatherland Front, which itself became a broad patriotic organization under communist control.[50]

In the Grand National Assembly, Bulgarian constitutional experts were assisted by a team of Soviet jurists.[51] The resulting Dimitrov Constitution adopted on 4 December 1947, was modeled fairly closely on the Soviet 1936 Stalin Constitution. The principle of checks and balances was rejected in favor of the "unity of state power," which gave ultimate control of all state bodies to a presidium named by the National Assembly.

The party had launched an assault on private property almost immediately after 9 September, employing a variety of legislative measures aimed at confiscating the wealth of "fascists" or "speculators." By 1946, 11.8 percent of the country's industrial capital was already in government hands. The Dimitrov Constitution provided for the large-scale nationalization of private property that soon followed its enactment.[52] Trade unions, too, were an early communist target. The party sponsored a reorganization of the structure of Bulgarian trade unionism, creating the General Workers' Trade Union and gradually persuading or forcing all workers' organizations into it. Attempts by the opposition to create independent unions collapsed along with the opposition itself.[53] Similarly, the youth organizations of the various parties were incorporated into the Dimitrov Communist Youth League.

Exarch Stefan, head of the Bulgarian Orthodox Church, made a sincere effort to coexist with the communist regime. But he was a brave, independent-minded man, whose courage had been demonstrated in his resolute anti-Nazi conduct before and during the war and in his efforts to save Bulgarian Jews from deportation. He directed the clergy to support the regime in all its "good and useful" acts, but offered firm resistance to the Communists' attempts to control internal church affairs. Stefan accepted the separation of church and state decreed in the Dimitrov Constitution and the abandonment of religious education in the schools. In 1948, however, the government's director of religious denominations issued a long communication ordering the church to halt all criticism of the state, preach love for the communist leadership from the pulpit, defend the Soviet Union, and display portraits of party leaders. The exarch refused and caused the church journal to refer to the directive as "unsent, unreceived, and invalid." This act of defiance brought the relationship between the regime and the Orthodox church to a crisis. Few details of what transpired are known, but in September Stefan suddenly resigned his office and retired to a monastery. He was replaced by the more compliant Paissy, who was himself dismissed in 1950 in favor of Kiril, who created few difficulties for the political authorities.[54]

On 1 March 1949 the government enacted a Law on Religious Denominations that subjected all religious orders to direct state control. At the time the law was adopted, fifteen pastors from evangelical Protestant churches were arrested and put on trial for treason, espionage on behalf of the United States and England, speculation in foreign currency, and conspiracy to restore capitalism.[55] During 1952 approximately 30 Catholic priests, nuns, and laymen were tried for spying for the Vatican and conducting anticommunist propaganda. The bishop of Nikopol and three others received death sentences and the rest were given prison sentences.

The nearly 50,000 Jews who remained in Bulgaria at the war's end also clashed with state authority. The government resolved this problem, however, by permitting mass emigration to Israel, in return for which "large sums" of hard currency were turned over to the Interior Ministry. By the end of 1949 only about 6,000 Jews remained in Bulgaria.[56] The regime also resorted to resettlement in an attempt to reduce Bulgaria's Muslim population. More than 150,000 ethnic Turks were forced across the Turkish border before the government in Ankara closed the frontier. Even then the Bulgarians continued to force thousands of Turks and Gypsies across in isolated areas.[57]

By the time of the party's fifth congress on 18–25 December 1948, the political aspects of Bulgaria's socialist transformation had been completed or were far advanced. The opposition was destroyed, sources of independent authority had been eliminated, and Western pressure had successfully been resisted. The fifth congress was thus a celebration of victory, of the completion of the first stage of the revolution. Few were aware of what the next stage would entail.

THE MACEDONIAN QUESTION AND RELATIONS WITH YUGOSLAVIA

The campaign against the domestic opposition represented only one front on which the Bulgarian Communists were obliged to struggle. They also faced a formidable challenge from their exuberant "comrades" in Yugoslavia, who were convinced that their victory in the partisan war entitled them to the dominant position on the peninsula. The danger from Yugoslavia took two forms. The first was the possibility that Bulgaria would be submerged in a Belgrade-dominated federation. The second involved the Yugoslav plan, prefigured in the second AVNOJ conference, to annex Pirin Macedonia to the Yugoslav Macedonian republic.

The Bulgarian Communists had long endorsed in the abstract the idea of Balkan federation. In the closing stage of the war, Georgi Dimitrov raised the idea again in a communication with Stalin, probably in an effort to prevent the immediate Soviet award of Pirin Macedonia to Yugoslavia, for which Tito had been pressing. Arguing that it was impermissible for Communists to quarrel over territory and boundary lines, Dimitrov recommended that the Macedonian problem be resolved in the context of a larger federation of southern Slavs. This idea initially had Stalin's support, but the Bulgarian and Yugoslav sides had very different conceptions of its form.[58] Dimitrov proposed a union on the basis of equality between Sofia and Belgrade. This was unacceptable to the Yugoslavs, who proposed that Bulgaria become a part of Yugoslavia as one of its constituent republics, that is, with the same status as Montenegro or Slovenia. In a letter to Kostov in January 1945, Dimitrov characterized this project as an attempt to "swallow up" Bulgaria. Neither the Yugoslavs nor the Bulgarians have revealed much about their negotiations for federation, and what has been made public treats the issue as one purely between Sofia and Belgrade, as though the desires of Moscow were not the decisive element.[59] Here, the Bulgarians were probably fortunate in that their status as a defeated country nominally under Allied control limited Soviet freedom of action. It may have been fear of unnecessarily complicating relations with the British and Americans that kept Stalin from endorsing Belgrade's project when the stock of the Yugoslavs was at its highest.

After the signing of the peace treaty between Bulgaria and the Allies, the issue of a Bulgarian-Yugoslav union was again discussed when Dimitrov met with Tito in Bled, Slovenia. The two leaders agreed to the abolition of travel barriers and pledged to establish a customs union. In a return visit to Sofia in November, Tito signed a treaty of friendship with Bulgaria that called for even closer cooperation. Dimitrov, however, seemed to view rapprochement with Yugoslavia in the context of a larger movement toward East European unity that would also involve Greece, Romania, and Albania. This, at any rate, was the thrust of his famous press conference in Bucharest in January 1948, which drew a repudiation from *Pravda* and the summoning of Bulgarian and Yugoslav delegations to Moscow. At this conference, so vividly described by Djilas, Dimitrov was treated as a fool and both sides were accused of plotting behind the back of the Soviet Union.[60] In the end Stalin told the Yugoslavs and Bulgarians to proceed with a federation, but the Yugoslavs had become suspicious of Soviet motives, and the entire project collapsed with the Soviet-Yugoslav break.

If Bulgaria avoided being swallowed up in a federation dominated by Tito, it was nonetheless forced to make significant concessions to the Yugoslav position on Macedonia. The party's tenth plenum in August 1946, in deference to the Yugoslav position, recognized the existence of a Macedonian nationality and promised "cultural autonomy" to the Pirin region. The phrase implied recognition of a Macedonian language distinct from Bulgarian and the encouragement of a "Macedonian national consciousness" linked to the Macedonian republic in Yugoslavia. A census of the region's population was taken, in which "administrative means" were used to arrive at the conclusion that 70 percent of the population was Macedonian. At his meeting with Tito in Bled, Dimitrov resisted the Yugoslav leader's demand for the immediate incorporation of the Pirin into the Macedonian republic, but he agreed to the "spiritual union" of the Pirin Macedonians with their brothers in Yugoslavia. In practice this meant the arrival of "missionaries" in the form of teachers of the "Macedonian language" and propagandists for the region's unification with Yugoslavia. This work was abruptly brought to an end with the emergence of the break between Tito and Stalin. The agents from Skoplje were sent packing, but the Bulgarian regime remained ambivalent for several years about the existence of a distinct Macedonian nationality.[61]

6

Stalinization and Destalinization, 1948–1960

By the time the Bulgarian party held its fifth congress in December 1948, the conflict between Stalin and Tito had come into the open. The countries of the Soviet bloc were under increasing pressure to demonstrate their loyalty by stepping up the pace of socialist transformation. Communist parties were called upon to complete the liquidation of political opposition and to emulate Soviet experience through the collectivization of agriculture, the introduction of comprehensive central planning, and investment in spectacular projects of heavy industrialization. But faithful adherence to the Soviet pattern was not enough, for Stalin demanded the transformation of the parties themselves to reduce them to bureaucratic extensions of the Soviet regime. The tools employed were purges, show trials, and terror.

THE PURGE OF TRAICHO KOSTOV

If Dimitrov and Kolarov were the legendary heroes of Bulgarian communism, Traicho Kostov had furnished genuine leadership. From the time he had been sent to purge the left sectarians in 1934, the BCP had relied on him for its most critical tasks. After 9 September Kostov had guided the reorganization and expansion of the party as its political secretary. As vice-president of the Council of Ministers, he headed the government during the long periods of Dimitrov's medical treatment and convalescence in the USSR, and he was deeply involved in the construction of a new political apparatus. As president of the state committee on economic and financial planning, Kostov worked out the first steps for the transition to a socialist economy. In all these tasks, and in his entire career, he had never shown himself to be anything other than a dedicated party leader of the Stalinist type, nor had he ever indicated less than complete faith in communism, the Soviet Union, or its great leader. Why, then, was he made into an archetype of heretic and traitor, the author of "Kostovism," thousands of whose alleged advocates suffered purge and worse during the Stalinist era? As yet there is no clear answer, for in spite of the fact that Kostov was rehabilitated publicly in January 1963, no complete account of the circumstances that led to his downfall has ever appeared in Bulgaria.[1]

The one believable crime that Kostov was accused of, and which he in fact admitted during his trial, was that during trade negotiations with Soviet representatives he had sought to conceal prices commanded by certain Bulgarian goods on the world market. When Kostov, Dimitrov, and Chervenkov visited Stalin in Moscow during 1948, Stalin approached Kostov, removed Kostov's glasses to stare him directly in the eyes, called him a swindler, and stormed out of the meeting cursing. Although smoothed over at the time by Dimitrov, this incident was brought to light again the following year in Bulgaria, where it helped to convince reluctant members of the central committee to concur in Kostov's expulsion.

The first outward sign that Kostov was in danger came at the Bulgarian party's fifth congress, in connection with changes in the structure of party leadership. Until this time the party central committee had recognized two leadership positions: the post of president of the central committee, held by Dimitrov, and the post of political secretary, occupied by Kostov. In conformity with structural changes being made in communist parties throughout Eastern Europe under Soviet pressure, the congress replaced these positions with the single post of general secretary, to which Dimitrov was elected at the central committee's plenum in January 1949. Kostov retained his membership in the politburo and his government position as first deputy prime minister, but he was excluded from the party secretariat. During a meeting of the politburo near the end of the month, Dimitrov introduced a discussion of "mistakes" made by Kostov, accusing him of nationalism and "intellectual individualism." Kostov denied the charges and traveled to Moscow to present his defense. Finding no sympathy there, he returned to Bulgaria, where he remained in isolation from the rest of the politburo.

Soon after leveling the accusations against Kostov, Dimitrov left Bulgaria for the last time. His health failing rapidly, he entered a sanitarium near Moscow, where he died on 2 July.[2] The case against Kostov was left in the hands of Kolarov and Chervenkov, who pursued it relentlessly.

The foundation for more serious charges was laid by the arrest of a group of party officials from a few of the economic ministries, the central figure of which was Kiril Slavov. Before the Second World War, Slavov had been a manufacturer who had given refuge and financial assistance to many party members; after the war, he became a prominent economic official. Although he died at the hands of police interrogators, the "evidence" Slavov provided became the nucleus for the charges against Kostov and his fellow victims.

On 26–27 March Kolarov delivered a report to a plenum of the central committee on "The Crude Political and Antiparty Errors of Traicho Kostov." The plenum responded by removing Kostov from the politburo and from his government posts. The official report stated that Kostov was punished for his mistakes, but that he was not an enemy and would retain his membership in the central committee.

Because there was no precedent for provincial party committees taking issue with the central party leadership, it must be assumed that the objections raised by the Plovdiv and Sofia organizations, to the effect that Kostov was indeed an enemy deserving severe punishment, were part of a prearranged intrigue. This assumption is supported by the fact that the two district secretaries who were involved advanced extremely rapidly in the party hierarchy. The Plovdiv leader was Demir Yanev, who became minister of education in the mid-1950s; the Sofia party secretary was Todor Zhivkov. At the same time that these men made their protest, state security police arrested a number of party and state officials who later were charged with participation in a Kostovite conspiracy.

In response to the demands of the Plovdiv and Sofia district organizations, the politburo reopened the Kostov case, and on 11–12 June Kolarov delivered a new report to a plenum of the central committee. It went beyond the March accusations in that it "revealed" that Kostov had long been a partisan of "left sectarianism," which Kolarov again linked to Trotskyism. Kolarov also read a letter supposedly sent by Dimitrov from Moscow.

> After I read the protocol of the [March] plenum, and especially the long speech of Traicho Kostov, I became finally convinced that we are not dealing here with just intellectual individualism and blind careerism, but with a refined, accomplished scoundrel, for whom there can be no place in a genuinely Bolshevik party, which we hope with all our heart our party will be.[3]

The plenum expelled Kostov from the party. He had been put under house arrest before the plenum opened, and he was formally placed under interrogation by state security on 20 June.

Following the death of Dimitrov, Vasil Kolarov became both prime minister and head of the politburo. He was seriously ill himself, however, so that effective power was really in the hands of Vŭlko Chervenkov, who represented the rest of the politburo both to Kolarov and to Soviet authorities. Under Chervenkov's direction, a wider and wider net was cast to gather in the "Kostovites." During the fall a large number of state and party officials were placed under arrest. These included politburo member Petko Kunin, several members of the party central committee, and a number of ministers and vice-ministers. By and large these men were home Communists and were replaced by people whose careers had primarily been in Soviet emigration.[4]

The organization of the trial as well as the interrogation of Kostov and his codefendants was supervised by Beria's aide, V. S. Abakumov, who made frequent visits to Bulgaria at this time, and by the Soviet ambassador, Mikhail Bodrov. Their methods succeeded in extracting Kostov's signed confession but did not entirely break his will to resist. The authorities proceeded with too much haste in preparing the trial, so that the indictment was flawed with inconsistencies, and the chief defendant retained sufficient inner strength to fight back when the opportunity arose in open court.

Kostov was charged with having been a police agent during the Second World War, working with British and American intelligence services, conducting economic sabotage against Bulgaria and the Soviet Union, and forming a conspiracy with "Tito and his clique" to overthrow the government. Kostov's ten codefendants, including former party functionaries, officials of the economic ministries, and three party officials of Macedonian origin, were selected to substantiate the various parts of the indictment. They and 44 witnesses did indeed follow the prosecution's script, confessing to all charges or testifying in support of them. When the charges against him were read to the court, Kostov admitted that he had tried to keep the prices of certain Bulgarian goods from Soviet officials, but he pleaded innocent to the rest of the charges and repudiated his confession. Even after the final guilty verdict was pronounced, he remained unrepentant.

"In my last words before this distinguished court," he said, "I consider it a duty to my conscience to tell the court, and through it the Bulgarian people, that I never served English intelligence, never participated in the criminal plans of Tito and his clique . . . I have always held the Soviet Union in devotion and respect . . . Let the Bulgarian people know that I am innocent!"[5]

The trial began on 7 December and sentences were handed down on the 14 December. Kostov was shot two days later. His codefendants received prison sentences ranging from life to fifteen years, but their lives were spared. Chervenkov later told the central committee that this was because they had shown how to behave during a trial.

"LITTLE STALIN"

Less than a month after Kostov's execution, Vasil Kolarov died. Thus, within six months, Dimitrov, Kostov, and Kolarov, the triumvirate that had dominated Bulgarian communism and led it to power, had all passed from the scene. There was something particularly ironic in Kolarov's brief period of leadership, for he had once been Blagoev's heir apparent, only to be surpassed on both the Bulgarian and world stage by Dimitrov. According to some sources, Kolarov always resented the fortuitous success of Dimitrov, and there is no doubt that he was enraged at being overshadowed by the younger Kostov, whom he helped to bring down.[6] Even in death Kolarov remained a subordinate, for his body was placed in a minor tomb as an appendage to Dimitrov's mausoleum.

Vŭlko Chervenkov, the successor Stalin selected, was born in 1900. He was the son of a soldier and, like Dimitrov, came from a Protestant family. He joined the party in 1919 and, after playing a small role in the organization of the cathedral bombing in 1925, emigrated to the Soviet Union, where he spent the next twenty years. In exile Chervenkov studied at the OGPU Academy in Moscow and later graduated from the Lenin International School, where he became a lecturer. He held various positions in the Comintern, and his rise in the Bulgarian party was facilitated by his marriage to Dimitrov's sister and by his own considerable intelligence. In 1936 or 1937 the NKVD sought his arrest, apparently in connection with a purge of the International School, but he was saved by his brother-in-law's intervention. According to party lore, Chervenkov also paid for his freedom by becoming a Soviet police agent reporting on Bulgarian party affairs.[7] Although there is no proof of this, it is certainly not impossible given the Soviet atmosphere in the 1930s and the tactics of Stalin's agents. Whether a police informer or not, Chervenkov was certainly molded in the Stalin bureaucracy, well connected with Soviet officials, and an obvious choice to cast the Bulgarian party in the Stalinist mode.

Chervenkov was named prime minister in February 1950, chairman of the national council of the Fatherland Front in March, and general secretary of the party in November. His consolidation of power was marked by the demotion or purge of the major figures who had led the party at home during the war and by the corresponding rise of men who had spent many years in Soviet exile. Interior Minister Anton Yugov was relieved of his post owing to "lack of vigilance" in connection with the Kostov affair. Dobri Terpeshev was accused of having supported Kostov's economic policies. He began a long slide that was ultimately to lead to expulsion from the party and internal exile. Tsola Dragoicheva was relegated to a series of minor posts. Petko Kunin, who headed the Ministry of Industry, was charged with sympathy for Tito and imprisoned. Partisan commander Slavcho Trŭnski was another victim who spent several years in prison.

As the number of arrests increased, so did apprehension throughout the party, for there were few who had never had any links with Kostov or had never worked in an agency under his direction. In the politburo, Vladimir Poptomov and Micho Neichev sought to bring the police under control and succeeded in establishing a special commission to investigate the evidence and the means used to obtain it. Chervenkov, however, led a politburo delegation to the Soviet Union, where Stalin told the Bulgarians that they stood at a crossroads, one path leading to Titoism, the other the path of loyalty to the USSR. After this meeting the terror resumed and continued until Stalin's death.[8]

The prewar political culture of Bulgaria lacked a strong democratic tradition, but it was egalitarian. The absence of a native nobility since the Turkish conquest in the fourteenth century, one of the most equal distributions of land in Europe, and social mobility fostered by a relatively well-developed system of compulsory public education had produced a society unaccustomed to hierarchies. Indeed, Bulgaria's first major political party coalesced around opposition to the elaborate forms of deference demanded by the German court that was imposed on the country by international politics. As Georgi Markov wrote:

> One of the characteristsics of our people that I most admire is its critical, cynical attitude toward idols. Looking at our entire history, we can say that the idolization of people and events is absolutely not a Bulgarian weakness. In this respect the Bulgarian people have shown more wisdom, intelligence, and realism than many other peoples, particularly the Russians, who it seems have idolatry in their very blood.[9]

Chervenkov, however, and many of the men who rose with him, had been raised in Stalin's court. The cult of Stalin's personality was transplanted in toto and Chervenkov bathed in its reflected light. Prolonged, rhythmic applause and chants of "Cher-ven-kov" greeted his public appearances. His pronouncements were treated as holy writ, and his portraits were on view everywhere. A Soviet-style rigid hierarchy replaced the more informal administrative relationships that had prevailed in the past.[10]

During the period of Chervenkov's dominance, Bulgaria became closed off from the outside world and even, in some senses, from itself. National heroes and cultural figures from the past were written off as relics of the country's bourgeois heritage, and all things Soviet or Russian were exalted. Literature and the arts were forced into the straitjacket of socialist realism as defined by Stalin and Zhdanov, and many of the prewar leaders of cultural life fell silent. Khristo Radevski's poem, "Guide Me, Oh Party," became a symbol of the entire sterile era and later was the target of sarcasm and satire.

During this period Bulgaria also withdrew from international life. The border with Yugoslavia was sealed when the conflict between Tito and Stalin came into the open. Macedonian-born Vladimir Poptomov, the fiercest enemy of the policy of cooperation with Yugoslavia in Pirin Macedonia, was named foreign minister. Bulgaria had no diplomatic relations with Greece, which was regarded as a hostile country after the collapse of the communist effort in the civil war. The Turkish border, too, was closed as a result of Bulgaria's effort to force resettlement on its citizens of Turkish descent. In February 1953 Greece, Yugoslavia, and Turkey signed a new Balkan Pact that further isolated Bulgaria.

Of all its neighbors, Bulgaria remained on nominally good terms only with Romania, but even here Stalinist policy permitted few direct contacts between satellites. Communication between Sofia and Bucharest had to go through Moscow. The United States broke off relations with Bulgaria in February 1950, when the Bulgarian regime refused to disavow charges made at the Kostov trial that the American ambassador was engaged in espionage.[11] Bulgaria denounced the West in general as the seat of all evil, filled with militarists, exploiters, and spies. According to Chervenkov, the Soviet Union was the only friend and ally that Bulgaria would ever need.

FOUNDATIONS OF THE SOCIALIST ECONOMY

The transformation of the Bulgarian economy began almost immediately after 9 September. Legislation provided for the confiscation of property acquired by wartime speculators and the property of individuals who had been convicted by the people's courts. As a result, nearly a quarter of Bulgaria's industrial production was in the hands of the state by the end of 1945.[12] More extensive nationalization was delayed until the conclusion of the peace treaties, perhaps because the Soviet Union had claims on Bulgarian industries that had been linked to the German war effort. With the consolidation of the communist regime, the USSR renounced most of these claims, although Bulgaria did have to pay the costs of Soviet military occupation. In a similar fraternal gesture, Yugoslavia remitted the $25 million in reparations promised in the peace treaty. Bulgaria owed another $45 million to Greece, but refused to pay.

Some instruments of state economic planning and control had already been created during the war. In May 1945 the Directorate of Civilian Mobilization was superceded by a Supreme Economic Council that began to coordinate the work of the various economic commissions of the party, the Fatherland Front, and the planning sections of the various economic ministries.[13] In May 1947 the government instituted a two-year plan aimed at recovery from the war through large-scale projects of industrial development and electrification. The plan envisioned an increase in industrial production of 67 percent over the 1939 level and an increase in agriculture of 34 percent.[14]

After the conclusion of the peace treaty and the defeat of the domestic opposition, the regime began to press more rapidly for the final elimination of the capitalist sector of the economy. At the end of 1947, in connection with the adoption of the Dimitrov Constitution, all large-scale industry, banks, and insurance companies were nationalized, and government monopolies were established over the major items of retail trade. By the end of 1948 approximately 85 percent of industrial production was in the hands of the state, with another 7 percent carried on by cooperative organizations.[15]

Permission for the formation of collective farms, called in Bulgaria "labor-cooperative farms" (*Trudovo-kooperativno zemedelsko stopanstvo*, or TKZS), was granted on 15 April 1945. Although differing in some respects, most significantly in its guarantee that members would receive a base percentage of the farm's income, the Bulgarian TKZS closely resembled the Soviet *kolkhoz*. Membership was supposed to be entirely voluntary, although the principle of land consolidation or "commassation" meant that a peasant's land could be expropriated for the TKZS if he was compensated with land outside the TKZS boundaries. In practice, considerable pressure was placed on the peasantry to join, and there was little concern for fair compensation to those whose land was taken. So much opposition appeared in the countryside, including opposition from rural party members, that the politburo reviewed the situation in May 1946. The party leadership again stressed that the TKZS was a voluntary institution and promised the peasantry that collectivization would not be forced upon it. Less than 7 percent of the country's farms, occupying 6 percent of Bulgaria's arable land, was collectivized by the end of 1948.[16]

The first five-year plan, covering the years 1949–1953, was approved by the fifth party congress at the end of 1948 and clearly reflected Soviet development strategy.[17] The output of heavy industry was scheduled to increase by 220 percent and the output of light industry by 75 percent. Priority was given to metallurgy and machine building, chemical production, electrification, and transportation. Such ambitious targets required enormous investments—over a quarter of the country's national income—with the result that living standards were held down. The situation was aggravated by the fact that light industry and agriculture had the lowest priorities and fell farthest short in receiving their planned share of resources.

Collectivization, held in abeyance since 1946, resumed with a vengeance in 1950. The signal was given by Chervenkov, who stressed that collectivization was required to transform the consciousness of the peasantry and to root out capitalism in the countryside as it had been destroyed in the cities. In May the government issued a Model Statute of the Collective Farm, and a new drive got under way. Local people's councils were directed to "lead" the peasantry into the TKZS, and at the same time a decree prohibited peasants from slaughtering livestock before joining the farms, an indication that the Bulgarian peasant was reacting to collectivization in the same way that his Russian counterpart had two decades earlier. As a result of this stepped-up pressure, the proportion of the land belonging to TKZSs increased from 11.3 percent at the end of 1949 to 44.2 percent by the end of 1950. There was obviously much hardship and discontent, and during the following year a number of local officials and representatives of the Ministry of Agriculture received token punishments for their overzealousness and arbitrary methods. The pace of collectivization briefly slowed but resumed again in 1952. After another hiatus, caused presumably by the uncertainties that followed Stalin's death, collectivization was substantially completed by 1958.[18]

During the period of the first five-year plan, the Soviet Union contributed to Bulgaria's economic development by providing expertise and material aid. But it is also true that the USSR purchased Bulgarian products at costs below world prices. Moreover, Soviet experts and officials who were sent to supervise the Bulgarian economy lived like the masters of a colonial regime, provided with special schools, privileges, and salaries four times those of their Bulgarian counterparts. Their arrogance and condescension provoked a considerable degree of resentment.[19]

It is difficult to evaluate with any degree of precision the results of Bulgaria's first five-year plan. The Bulgarian regime itself was confused: the plan was suddenly declared completed a year early, and the published statistics were both incomplete and confusing. Nonetheless, it is clear that the impact of the Stalinist pattern of industrialization was more beneficial in Bulgaria than it was in most of Eastern Europe. Although the Stalinist pattern caused extreme dislocations and retrenchment in the more developed countries, the primitive Bulgarian economy more closely resembled the Soviet prototype. During the first five-year plan, albeit at great human and material cost, Bulgaria began the process of constructing the foundation of a modern industrial economy, the achievement of which was to become the Communists' proudest achievement and their enduring claim to legitimacy.

STALIN'S DEATH AND THE NEW COURSE

Despite his emulation of Stalin's methods, Chervenkov had not succeeded in establishing a total monopoly of power by the time of the Soviet dictator's death. Indeed, Soviet authorities themselves probably did not allow this, since the continued existence of internal rivals worked to maximize their own power in the country. Influential "home Communists," such as Yugov and Terpeshev, were downgraded, but not entirely eliminated. Yugov, especially, remained both a minister and a member of the politburo. When several hundred tobacco workers in the Plovdiv region went on strike against the introduction of more onerous work regulations in May 1953, Yugov, who had himself once labored in the tobacco fields of the region, was sent to restore order. This he did by recognizing the legitimacy of the workers' grievances and promising significant changes.[20]

Among the population at large, Stalin's death brought feelings of relief and guarded hope. Georgi Markov, then a young engineer, recorded the following thoughts in his description of the day Stalin died.

> I remembered my parents' stories about the mass shootings around Pernik where they threw the dead and half-dead bodies down the ventilator shafts of the abandoned mines, and about the state security jeeps that prowled the country by night like modern vampires, inspiring dread in everyone. I thought of my friends who had been beaten in the left wing of Central Prison, of the endless trials in the four halls of the top floor of the Palace of Justice, where they handed out death sentences, of my fellow students and colleagues from the university in icy solitary confinement on Belene. I thought of how those loathsome invaders and a handful of our own traitors had launched their murderous, barbaric, sordid, vile assault on our entire people. Stalin was the one who turned our Bulgaria into a well-organized Soviet prison. Stalin was the one who banished forever the optimism, cheer, and individuality of my generation, who poisoned our future, and made us slaves of a most primitive and brutal feudalism.[21]

The immediate impact of Stalin's death on Bulgaria was not dramatic, but it affected the country's life in a number of ways. There was some amelioration of police terror, and an amnesty on the occasion of the eighth anniversary of 9 September saw the release of a substantial number of political prisoners. Several concessions were made to the peasantry, including a sizable reduction in compulsory deliveries from the TKZSs and cancellation of some back debts and taxes. The Agrarian Union, which had seemed destined for extinction, was revived as the BCP's "little brother," and a number of Agrarians emerged from retirement or prison. These included Stambolski's son and several associates of Nikola Petkov, who were persuaded to tour the countryside defending the regime's agrarian policies. During the following year, those organizers of the overthrow of the Agrarian government in 1923 who were still alive were placed on public trial as a further demonstration of the regime's solicitude for peasant interests.[22]

At the BCP's sixth congress (25 February–3 March 1954) Chervenkov followed the example of "collective leadership" set by the Soviet Union and gave up his post as party general secretary. Why did he relinquish party rather than state leadership? A number of answers are possible. He may have been influenced by the example of Malenkov, who seemed at the time the likely winner in the Soviet power struggle. Or he may have believed that he could continue to dominate the party apparatus through his successor, the little-known Todor Zhivkov. Or he may simply have been victimized by lack of historians' hindsight. In any case, his immediate control over the party was not substantially diminished, for he continued to be "responsible for the work of the politburo," and as such he led the Bulgarian delegation to the twentieth congress of the CPSU while Zhivkov stayed home.[23]

The sixth congress also saw the comeback of a number of figures who had been eclipsed in the Kostovite purges. The partisan leaders Terpeshev and Slavcho Trŭnski were restored to the central committee, the latter as a candidate, as were Boian Bŭlgaranov and Kiril Dramaliev. Dimitŭr Ganev, who had been in semiexile as ambassador to Prague, became a party secretary. Yugov remained on the politburo and soon became first deputy premier. The politburo elected by the sixth congress had nine full members—Vŭlko Chervenkov, Georgi Chankov, Georgi Damianov, Raiko Damianov, Ivan Mikhailov, Encho Staikov, Georgi Tsankov, Anton Yugov, and Todor Zhivkov—and two deputy members—Petŭr Panchevski and Todor Prahov. This gave a division of four "Muscovites" (Chervenkov, the two Damianovs, and Ivan Mikhailov), and five "home Communists." The latter group was not homogeneous, however, since Yugov and Staikov belonged to the prewar generation of leaders, whereas Zhivkov, Chankov, and Tsankov had more recently come to the forefront.

The death of Stalin and the emergence of the "New Course" in the USSR had a significant impact on Bulgaria's economic priorities. Toward the end of 1953 the regime reduced the prices of a large number of basic goods, particularly foodstuffs, and the goals set for the second five-year plan revealed a slowing of the pace of industrialization and a greater concern for consumer industry and agriculture. Concern for the standard of living was also shown by a provision that nearly quadrupled the level of investment in housing, a sorely needed measure in view of the urban expansion brought on by rapid industrial development.[24]

As in the Soviet Union, limited signs of a "thaw" in Bulgarian cultural life preceded Stalin's death. The key moment was the debate that followed the publication in 1951 of Dimitŭr Dimov's *Tiutiun* (Tobacco). Having as its theme the revolutionary movement among the tobacco workers before and during the Second World War, the book was denounced by party critics because its characters showed signs of multidimensionality, that is, the party organizers were not sufficiently positive and the workers were portrayed as having lives, ideas, and emotions independent of their involvement in the revolutionary struggle. The wave of condemnation had hardly passed when Chervenkov himself weighed in on the side of the novel and against its "unfortunate critics," who were attacked for their "dogmatism." Was he sincere or simply passing on signals from Moscow? The answer is not clear, but Bulgarian cultural life immediately responded. Liudmil Stoianov, who held the honorific post of president of the Writers' Union, called for a new antidogmatic approach to literature, and a younger group of critics and poets began an extended discussion of "craftsmanship" in poetry that ignored the standard of *partinost*. Stalin's death accelerated this process. In December 1953 Chervenkov wrote an open letter to the poetess Elizaveta Bagriana on the occasion of her sixtieth birthday that, in effect, called for a redefinition of socialist realism. Another sign of the shift in the regime's attitude was the "re-evaluation" of bourgeois writers, many of whom were restored to their places in Bulgarian cultural history. The classics of Bulgarian literature again appeared in the bookstores.[25]

THE APRIL PLENUM

The BCP still claims to be guided by the "April line" established at its central committee plenum of 2–6 April 1956. In party history this plenum marks the beginning of a new era, the overcoming of past "mistakes," and the acceptance of a greater measure of legality, internal democracy, and cultural liberalization.[26] In fact, the immediate effects of the April plenum were more limited and were soon undermined by the impact of events in Poland and Hungary. Some time was required before the ideals set forth at the plenum made a serious impression on Bulgarian reality.

Two factors, both associated with Khrushchev's rise to pre-eminence in the USSR, led to Bulgaria's April plenum. The first was Khrushchev's decision to pursue rapprochement with Tito. After the Soviet leader's visit to Yugoslavia in the summer of 1955, many Bulgarians believed that the complete downfall of Chervenkov, who was held in particularly low regard by Tito, was only a matter of time. Still, Chervenkov seemed in charge when the twentieth party congress of the CPSU convened in February 1956, and he led the Bulgarian delegation to Moscow while First Secretary Zhivkov remained at home. Khrushchev's sudden, direct attack on Stalin and the "cult of personality" brought the issue of party reform to the forefront and made a Bulgarian response inevitable.

Although he had not attended the CPSU's twentieth congress, Zhivkov delivered the main report on its significance and proved to be its main beneficiary. The resolution adopted by the plenum after "stormy discussions" stressed the importance of Soviet experience as a guide for combating the cult of personality and the "violations of Leninist norms" that had occurred under Stalin's rule. Vŭlko Chervenkov was explicitly criticized for having fostered his own personality cult and for undermining party legality and the principle of collective leadership. The persecution of Traicho Kostov was not directly mentioned, but "corrections" of past violations of legality were promised. This was further indicated by the expansion of the party secretariat from three to five. Zhivkov, Ganev, and Taskov were joined by Boris Bŭlgaranov, a partisan leader who had suffered in the Kostovite purges, and Encho Staikov, the wartime editor of *Rabotnicheski vestnik* and a specialist in propaganda and education.[27]

The plenum's focus on socialist legality required a short delay so that the proper forms could be observed, but on 17 April the National Assembly convened to accept Chervenkov's resignation as prime minister. A Yugoslav delegation headed by Mosa Pijade, invited especially for the occasion, looked on. Anton Yugov became the new prime minister, but Chervenkov was not entirely out. Demoted rather than purged, he became a deputy prime minister and retained his membership in the politburo, although he lost his leading role there to Zhivkov.[28] Chervenkov's survival near the top of the leadership was probably intended to reassure the apparatus that a wholesale purge of Stalinists was not contemplated, a message reinforced by the appointment of Yugov, who as postwar minister of the interior had a number of "violations of legality" on his own conscience. In fact, changes in personnel were very limited, and events soon demonstrated that even Chervenkov and his faction still had an important role to play.

The April plenum and subsequent demotion of Chervenkov gave rise among many Bulgarians to the expectation of further genuine liberalization. Vladimir Topencharov—the editor-in-chief of the Fatherland Front newspaper *Otechestven front*, president of the Union of Journalists, brother-in-law of Traicho Kostov, and a major spokesman for liberalization after Stalin's death—published a series of editorials accusing the party leadership of having divorced itself from the lives and interests of the people and calling for the fullest discussion of all aspects of the personality cult. But Topencharov's demands obviously went far beyond the bounds the Zhivkov-Yugov regime had set for reform. The party newspaper *Rabotnichesko delo* sharply criticized him, after which he was forced from his positions and sent as a correspondent to Cairo.[29]

Despite this setback, many younger writers and some of the older generation sought greater freedom of expression. Novelist Emil Manov published *An Unauthentic Case*, which contrasted idealistic communism with some of the realities of the Stalinist past. Todor Genov made the same point with his play *Fear*. A new literary journal, *Plamŭk* (The Flame), appeared in January 1957 and pledged to support "new forms, . . . new styles, new currents," and to feature the work of talented young writers. One of these, the poet Georgi Dzhagarov, published in it his influential poem, *"Predprolet"* (The Pre-spring), in which, with fairly obvious symbolism, he called for the young birds to find their voices and hasten the approach of a true spring. Many other works were written or emerged from *samizdat* circulation calling for greater literary freedom, and voices were raised against the conservative leadership of the Writers' Union.

This ferment, however, could not long survive in the atmosphere that prevailed after the Hungarian revolution, which shook the confidence of the Bulgarian leadership. Thousands of Bulgarians, some only recently freed by political amnesty, were placed under preventive detention by state security.[30] Because the regime was convinced that dissident intellectuals had been responsible for the events in Hungary, it determined to crack down on the intelligentsia. For this purpose, Chervenkov was appointed minister of education and culture, giving him broad control over the country's intellectual life, and the dogmatist philosopher Todor Pavlov, who had headed the Academy of Sciences since 1949, was given increased authority and was named to the party central committee. These moves may have had a double purpose, for they also involved the reassignment of Chervenkovites out of more powerful positions in the party, military, and economic bureaucracies. The fields of culture and education were regarded as a sort of dumping ground for the defeated faction. In any case, a purge of the intellectual community quickly followed. During the July 1957 meeting of the Bulgarian Writers' Union, Emil Manov, Todor Genov, and others were severely criticized. By the end of the year most of these men were removed from responsible positions, and the staffs of *Plamŭk*, the academic journal *Filosofska misŭl* (Philosophical Thought), and the newspaper *Otechestven front*, where liberal voices had been loudest, were dismissed. In April 1958 almost the entire leadership of the Writers' Union was replaced, not to encourage reform but to impose a firmer hand. Georgi Karaslavov, a rigid advocate of socialist realism and a member of the party's central committee, was placed in charge, and his conservative coterie monopolized the key positions in literary institutions and editorial staffs until the next wave of reform in the early 1960s.

In the wake of the Hungarian revolution, the party leadership was also purged to create a greater degree of uniformity. The inspiration, or perhaps signal, for this was the Soviet purge of the so-called antiparty group (Malenkov, Molotov, Kaganovich, and Shepilov) in July 1957. Only days later, a plenum of the BCP's central committee announced the dismissals of Dobri Terpeshev, Yanko Panov, and Georgi Chankov. The charges against the three were vaguely formulated, but it was believed that Terpeshev and Panov, a partisan general during World War II and more recently a deputy minister of defense, did not think that the April plenum had gone far enough to encourage party reform. Georgi Chankov was accused of "unhealthy ambition," a charge that may well have had some foundation, since he was a natural rival to Zhivkov. All three were removed from the central committee, and Chankov lost his place on the politburo and his post as deputy prime minister as well.[31]

Although the hopes that the April plenum would rapidly be followed by extensive liberalizing reforms were disappointed, the plenum was not without effect. Some of the worst abuses of the earlier period were curbed, cultural life became a little freer, and real progress was made in improving the living standard of industrial workers and collective farmers. Moreover, the April plenum set out ideals that could be appealed to against the immediate conservative reaction and that later re-emerged after that reaction had had its day. It provided the framework within which it became possible, at least in limited ways, to criticize existing practices from the standpoint of "ideal communism." Moreover, the April plenum was followed by a stronger assertion of Bulgarian national feeling, although this was probably due at least as much to the deterioration of relations between the Soviet Union and Yugoslavia after the suppression of the Hungarian revolution.

The old line still prevailed, however, in December 1956 when a census found that there were 187,789 Macedonians in Bulgaria and that they constituted the majority of the population of the Blagoevgrad Province (Pirin Macedonia).[32] In March 1958, in a speech commemorating the eightieth anniversary of the liberation of 1878, Encho Staikov referred to the Treaty of San Stefano as having unified all Bulgarians in a single state and he made no mention of a Macedonian nationality. Later in the year, in a speech delivered on the occasion of the fiftieth anniversary of the September Uprising, Dimitŭr Ganev explicitly denied the existence of a separate Macedonian nationality and accused Yugoslavia of suppressing Bulgarian national consciousness among the population of its portion of Macedonia. The Bulgarian position was stated vigorously in the central committee's historical journal at the end of the year:

> There is no foundation for the recognition of the population of the [Pirin] region as a separate nationality. Such a distinction would be artificial . . . There are no differences in language, culture, or economy between the population of the Pirin region and the Bulgarians, nor are there legal or political differences. It would be an act of oppression to force on the inhabitants of the Pirin region the half-Serbian literary language that has been invented in Skoplje.

With only small modifications this has remained the Bulgarian position since that time.[33]

THE GREAT LEAP FORWARD

In June 1958 the BCP's seventh congress approved the third five-year plan for the development of the economy. The plan set relatively moderate goals and increased the share of investment devoted to consumer industry. Over the course of the plan, industrial production was scheduled to increase by 62 percent, agriculture by 35 percent.[34] Suddenly, during October, the press discovered a "nationwide demand" to achieve the goals of the plan in a shorter time. The party responded in plenums of October and November 1958 and January 1959, the last of which approved the "Zhivkov Theses," which substantially increased the pace of development. According to the revised goals, industrial production by the end of 1962 would be double that of 1957 and by 1965 it would be three to four times greater than 1957 production. More dramatic still, agricultural production for 1959 was to double the 1958 level and to triple that level in 1960. To achieve these goals "Chinese methods" were used—the slogan "Great Leap Forward" was borrowed by the Bulgarian press—and all the party's resources and experience in agitation and propaganda were employed to mobilize the population to a frenzy of effort.

What caused this burst of activity? Several factors seem to have been at work. Economic development was being speeded up throughout the Soviet bloc. Bulgaria had recently assumed increased obligations toward its

CMEA partners, particularly in supplying agricultural products; and there was a stubborn problem of unemployment caused by the displacement of labor from agriculture by collectivization and by the suppression of artisanry and private trade.[35] Still, it is unlikely that the Chinese character of the new program was due primarily to economic causes. Internal party conflicts were almost certainly a key factor. During the course of the great leap forward, especially as problems developed, Zhivkov and others began to denounce critics within the party, who were accused of expressing doubt that the new goals could be achieved. One of these critics was apparently Boris Taskov, who was purged from the politburo and from his post as minister of trade during the spring of 1959. His dismissal was given considerable publicity as a warning to others who might "waver" or "whisper against the party line." [36] Later, when Yugov was purged, he too was accused of having opposed the accelerated economic development.

If the main architect of the great leap was Zhivkov, he did not suffer from its failure. Indeed, failure was never recognized, for by the end of 1960 the party announced that the goals had been met. The actual results, however, fell far short of what the Zhivkov Theses had set out. In most areas the economy also failed to meet the targets of the original five-year plan. Moreover, the frenetic pace of development had magnified the importance of Bulgaria's lack of skilled labor and technical expertise, as the proportion of resources tied up in unfinished projects more than tripled from 1958 to 1960.[37] There was much wasted effort that provoked a cynical response from the population. Peasants complained that the hens laid no better after the Zhivkov Theses were read to them, and Georgi Markov recorded the following memory of the "Sofia Sea":

> For many years at the Pavlovo stop on the Kniazhevski tramline there stood a huge sign with the inscription: "Site of the future Pavlovo harbor." Under the inscription was a map of the "Pancharevo-Pavlovo Shipping Canal" with its would-be ports of call. I know that some of my readers will already have recalled the anecdote about the crocodiles one could expect to see in the Sofia waters, the jokes about how we would turn shovels into oars, and the question whether we would have water with which occasionally to sprinkle the flowers once we had built the sea and canal. But most of all they will think of that long stream of Sundays when all we simple mortal inhabitants of Sofia had to turn out to work for free to dig the Sofia Sea.[38]

The great leap forward was the last major undertaking of the Zhivkov-Yugov-Chervenkov triumvirate. The economic upheaval it caused was over by the end of 1960. But the political upheaval was not finished for two more years.

ZHIVKOV'S CONSOLIDATION OF POWER

The appointment of Todor Zhivkov as first secretary at the BCP's sixth congress in 1954 came as a surprise to almost everyone. At 42, he was the youngest man ever to become head of a ruling communist party, and he was neither well known nor highly respected. Chervenkov had once called him an "empty person." [39] In the 1955 edition of Bulgaria's standard history text, Zhivkov received only 2 minor references, as opposed to 149 for Dimitrov and 42 for Chervenkov. [40] But if he was little known, he was not without talent or acumen. By swimming with the tides set in motion in the Soviet bloc by Stalin's death and Khrushchev's reforms, Zhivkov emerged as Bulgaria's undisputed leader at the BCP's eighth congress in 1962.

Todor Khristov Zhivkov was born on 7 September 1911 in Pravets, a small, poor village in what is now the Botevgrad District north of Sofia. [41] Like many men of the village, Zhivkov's father left to seek work elsewhere, eventually becoming a fur-dresser in a factory in Gabrovo and later a hauler of construction materials in Sofia. His mother worked the family land and sent her son to the village's elementary and intermediate schools. According to Zhivkov's official biography, it was while he was in the latter, at the age of thirteen, that he was first introduced to Marxist ideas. His "teacher in communism" was the secondary-school student Marin Raichinov, who had returned to his native village to form a "temperance society," the sort of organization that frequently served as a front for communist groups after 1923. [42] In 1926 Zhivkov received a "certificate of poverty" enabling him to enroll without tuition in the secondary school in Orkhanie (Botevgrad), the major town of the region. There he was again active in the school "temperance society" and was introduced to communist groups that operated further underground. He also supposedly occupied himself with study of the classics of Marxism-Leninism, but this is probably an exaggeration; Zhivkov's ideological commitments, like Khrushchev's, arose from emotion and personal experience rather than academic study.

In 1929, one year before graduation, Zhivkov was compelled to leave the Orkhanie school. This followed, but was not necessarily caused by, his involvement in a student strike the preceding year. Moving to the capital, he entered the Secondary School of Book Printing and Graphic Arts attached to the State Printing Office, where he received training as a printer and joined the clandestine Communist Youth League. After graduating in 1932, Zhivkov was taken on by the State Printing Office as a type founder. In the same year he was admitted into the BCP in the "Kofardzhiev recruitment" that followed the murder of Nikola Kofardzhiev. He quickly became the secretary of the underground party organization at the printing office.

Zhivkov's involvement in an effort to establish a cooperative canteen for the workers cost him his job, although he remained head of the party organization in the printing office. In 1934 he was made secretary of the third party region in Sofia and became a member of the party committee for the entire Sofia district. At this time Zhivkov apparently shared the outlook of the "left sectarians" who dominated the party at home, for after the coup d'état against the People's Bloc government he was placed in charge of organizing street demonstrations in the capital. In recollections published in the literary magazine *Septemvri* (September) in 1972, he departed from the traditional condemnation of the "left sectarians" and found much to praise about the comrades of his youth.

> Occasionally, those of us who participated in the struggle and lived through the times will smile condescendingly at our recollections. But I should duly stress that our struggle of that period is not and should not be judged with any measure of contemptuous irony, for despite all weaknesses, errors of the leadership, unrealistic assessments and inflicted harm, that was a heroic time. The overwhelming majority of leftist sectarians were honest, true, and devoted Party members. Their misfortune was that almost all of them belonged to the young Party generation, lacking revolutionary experience and theoretical background . . . Yet one cannot help paying tribute to the heroism of the communists of that time; they faced the police head on, and the street paving was often smeared with their blood.[43]

Failure to carry out an operation planned by the central committee led to a quarrel with the leadership and Zhivkov's expulsion from the Sofia district committee, so that he was at odds with the left-sectarian leadership at the time that the tide was turning in favor of Dimitrov and the so-called Old Guard. Moreover, while Dimitrov and Kolarov were organizing the purge of the left, Zhivkov was called to perform his compulsory military service, so that he spent these critical years in comparative safety.[44]

Discharged in 1937, Zhivkov returned to Sofia to find the party in the hands of a new leadership. His expulsion from the district committee was annulled, and he was given new duties in the Komsomol and as secretary of the Koniovitsa region, a proletarian section of the capital. During this time he met and married Mara Maleeva, a medical student with leftist sympathies. After she became a doctor in 1938, Zhivkov divided his time between Sofia and the towns and villages to which she was assigned as a medical officer. He was then involved primarily in legal work, organizing libraries, reading rooms, and theatrical presentations. The local press recognized him as a talented director and actor, and there is some indication that he aspired to a career in the theater in these years before the war.[45]

During the first stage of the war, Zhivkov remained in Sofia, where he again became the secretary of the third party district and organized communist participation in the campaign to protect the Jews.[46] After Stalingrad, when the Bulgarian partisan effort was reorganized, he was appointed to the political staff of the first VOZ (Sofia Province) under Georgi Chankov, whom he later purged. Zhivkov also became liaison with the Chavdar Partisan Brigade that was active in his native Botevgrad region. Zhivkov reorganized the brigade, recommending Dobri Dzhurov, ever after a close ally, as its military commander, and he participated in several of its operations. During the 9 September coup Zhivkov led the partisan detachments into Sofia, and immediately thereafter he was placed in charge of reorganizing the civilian police force.

During the consolidation of the communist regime, Zhivkov held a number of posts in the Sofia party organization. He became its organizational secretary in November 1944. Three months later, at the party's eighth plenum, he was made a candidate member of the central committee. At the fifth party congress in January 1948 he became a full member and was placed on the party's organizational bureau. According to one source, Zhivkov was put in charge of the Household Department, which furnished the apartments of party leaders with property taken from the various residences of the royal family, a job that allowed him to make contacts and earn good will among the party elite. At the same time he also became first secretary of the Sofia city and provincial party organizations and played a prominent part in the campaign against Traicho Kostov.[47] His further rise was extremely rapid. He became a secretary of the central committee in January 1950, a candidate member of the politburo in November of the same year, and a full member in June 1951. Little is known of his activities from that time until his appointment as BCP first secretary, except that his main concern was agriculture.

Two factors were primarily responsible for Zhivkov's success in defeating his rivals in the Chervenkov-Yugov-Zhivkov triumvirate that emerged after the BCP's April plenum. The first was the power of patronage that he could command as first secretary, which allowed him to create and advance his own followers. At the seventh party congress in June 1958, he added Mitko Grigorov and Pencho Kubadinski to the secretariat. They joined Stanko Todorov, who had become a member in 1957 and was one of Zhivkov's wartime colleagues, thus guaranteeing the first secretary a solid majority.[48] During the following year, Todorov moved up to a candidate membership on the politburo and became chairman of the State Planning Commission, where he could make inroads into Yugov's domain of state administration. At the same time Boris Velchev and Tano Tsolov, men of Zhivkov's generation who also proved to be long-term supporters, were added to the secretariat.[49] At lower levels, Zhivkov's experience in organizational work and his power of appointment steadily eroded the bases of support for the Chervenkov and Yugov factions.

The second factor operating in Zhivkov's favor was Khrushchev's ascendancy in the Soviet Union and the beginning of a new wave of reform at the twenty-second CPSU congress. Little real information exists about the personal relationship between Khrushchev and Zhivkov, but it is not hard to imagine a degree of rapport between these two men, whose backgrounds contained so many similarities. It was widely rumored in party circles that there was a deep antipathy between Khrushchev and Chervenkov, whereas Zhivkov consistently echoed in Bulgaria whatever the Soviet leader said on the larger stage.

The twenty-second CPSU congress marked a renewal of the destalinization process and the condemnation of the Chinese Communists for their defense of dogmatism. The Bulgarian response came at a plenum of the central committee on 28–29 November, one month after the Soviet congress concluded. Here, Chervenkov was expelled from the politburo, the central committee, and his current government post as deputy premier, and he was subjected to extensive criticism. According to Zhivkov's report, Chervenkov was guilty of a host of errors and abuses of power. He forced down the incomes of farm workers, slowed the pace of industrialization, overcentralized state and party administration, put himself above the politburo and central committee, and failed to accept the criticism of his colleagues. Zhivkov himself noted that there were many party members who shared Chervenkov's outlook, did not understand the need fully to discredit the personality cult, and opposed the policies of the CPSU congress. Chervenkov declined to make any act of contrition and, though defeated, stepped down without humiliating himself.[50] Zhivkov's position was further strengthened by the addition of Stanko Todorov and Mitko Grigorov to the politburo.

That there was substantial opposition in the Bulgarian party to further measures of destalinization and the purge of the Chervenkovites was demonstrated by the visit of Khrushchev and a high-ranking Soviet delegation in May 1962. Khrushchev stumped the country exhuberantly praising Zhivkov and the "normalization" in Bulgarian party life that had taken place under his leadership. It was obvious that Zhivkov had become Khrushchev's chosen instrument to rule Bulgaria, for the Soviet leader praised him far more than Yugov, and on several occasions he stressed their "warm personal relationship."[51]

The first substantial sign that Yugov was in trouble came in March 1962, when Georgi Tsankov, who had held the Interior Ministry since 1951, was "promoted" to an honorific position as a deputy prime minister, and control of the police apparatus was given to General Diko Dikov, who purged or transferred a number of prominent ministry officials. Still, the fate of Yugov and his faction was probably not decided until the eve of the party's eighth congress. On 31 October the party central committee held a plenum to prepare for the opening of the congress five days later. Presumably Yugov tried to rally support, for Zhivkov interrupted the plenum to fly to Moscow for consultation with Khrushchev, after which he returned to deliver the knockout punch.

In his opening address to the congress, Zhivkov announced the expulsion of Yugov and Tsankov from their offices and from the central committee. Vŭlko Chervenkov was expelled from the party altogether. Several other officials, most connected with the Interior Ministry, were also criticized and punished. Raikov Damianov, a member of the Yugov faction, left the politburo quietly and was not publicly criticized. Zhivkov himself assumed the post of prime minister, thus combining party and effective state leadership as Khrushchev and János Kádar in Hungary had already done. Two of his close associates, Boris Velchev and Zhivko Zhivkov (no relation), were added to the politburo, giving the first secretary a clear majority. Twenty-eight full members and fourteen candidates were dropped from the central committee, including a number of prominent figures from both the Yugov and Chervenkov factions. In replacing these men and expanding the central committee, Zhivkov harvested his first crop of younger party apparatchiks, who were to shape Bulgarian policy under his control.

7
The Zhivkov Era

Inside the domed monument built at the site of the BCP's founding, scenes from the party's past have melded with traditional iconography, so that mosaics depict the martyrdom of early party heroes and the slaying of the dragon of "fascism-capitalism" by a partisan St. George. One end of the interior hall is dominated by the trinity of Marx-Engels-Lenin; the other, by its Bulgarian reflection, Blagoev-Dimitrov-Zhivkov. Of the three, Todor Zhivkov, who has held power longer than any other Soviet-bloc leader, has done the most to shape the face of contemporary Bulgaria.

THE POLITICS OF THE ZHIVKOV ERA

Despite his victory over Chervenkov and Yugov, Zhivkov still faced formidable problems. If he had driven his enemies from the commanding heights of Bulgarian politics, opposition remained in the foothills and valleys. The sudden fall of Khrushchev in 1964 both removed his most influential patron and demonstrated that even an entrenched, powerful leader was vulnerable to a well-coordinated palace revolution. According to Stefan Svirdlev, a colonel in the state security who defected in 1971, between 1965 and 1971 there were no less than six coup attempts aimed at the forcible overthrow of the first secretary. Of these, only one was ever made known to the public.[1] This was the "April conspiracy," whose leader was General Ivan Todorov-Gorunia. Todorov-Gorunia, who killed himself to avoid arrest, had been the political commissar of the Gavril Genov Partisan Detachment that operated around Vratsa during the war, was secretary of the Vratsa Province party committee until 1961 when he was made a deputy minister for agriculture, and became a full member of the central committee after the eighth party congress. He was joined in the conspiracy by Tsolo Krŭstev and Major General Tsviatko Anev, who had been the commander and deputy commander, respectively, of the Genov detachment. Among the others who were brought to trial were two active-duty major generals and other military figures. According to the official version of the case, the conspirators sympathized with Maoism and wished to impose a Chinese line in Bulgaria. Unofficial rumors suggested that they had opposed Zhivkov's excessive subservience toward the Soviet Union or that they simply resented his favoritism of other partisan veterans, particularly those of his own Chavdar brigade. The ten men who were brought to trial received remarkably light sentences— these ranged from three to fifteen years imprisonment—considering the nature of their crimes. Others rumored to have been involved were not immediately punished, although during the next two years several high-ranking military figures were transferred from their positions to posts in foreign embassies, and an unusually large number of district party secretaries were replaced. Zhivkov waited three years before suddenly purging the Vratsa party organization amid charges that it harbored sympathy for Todorov-Gorunia's Chinese line. This purge expelled 359 people in the Vratsa organization from the party.[2]

There is little doubt that, despite his own lack of formal education, Zhivkov came to believe that Bulgaria's future lay with younger, better-trained, and more professional cadres. He once complained in front of Georgi Markov that: "We have some members on the politburo who have no reason for being there. They can't finish any kind of work. They just sit there. Members of the politburo!"[3] But the Old Guard was deeply entrenched in the party apparatus and was frequently well connected with Soviet officialdom. Zhivkov showed great circumspection when dealing with the generation of "tested revolutionaries," as indicated by the light sentences given to the April conspirators and the long delay in cleaning out their Vratsa nest. One means Zhivkov used to win over the Old Guard was direct material support, in the form of large monthly stipends to the wartime "Active Fighters Against Fascism and Capitalism."[4] Another has been to ensure their representation at the highest levels. At the party's ninth congress in 1966, the two oldest members of the politburo, Boris Bŭlgaranov (70) and Ivan Mikhailov (69), who had been expected to retire, kept their positions and were joined by Tsola Dragoicheva (68) and Todor Pavlov (76). Bŭlgaranov remained in the politburo until his death in 1972; Pavlov retired at the eleventh party congress in 1976 and died the following year; Mikhailov stayed on until the twelfth congress in 1981 and died within a year of his retirement; and Dragoicheva was re-elected at the twelfth congress, finally retiring in January 1984.

While making sure the older generation continued to be represented in the highest party circles, Zhivkov also brought along a group of younger men—and one woman, his daughter Liudmila—that he entrusted with serious responsibilities. These included Stanko Todorov and Alexander Lilov in administration and ideology, Ognian Doinov and Todor Bozhinov in economic policy, and Ivan Bashev and Petŭr Mladenov in foreign policy. Zhivkov's daughter Liudmila came to dominate the field of cultural policy, and after her death Georgi Yordanov was brought up from the Sofia party organization to take her place.[5] At the same time Zhivkov did not allow any of his younger supporters to become serious rivals for power. Mitko Grigorov dropped unexpectedly from the politburo and party secretariat at the party's ninth congress in 1966. Boris Velchev was purged suddenly in 1974. Stanko Todorov was downgraded from the post of prime minister to the less prestigious presidency of the National Assembly in 1982. And Alexander Lilov was dropped from the politburo and secretariat in 1983. Zhivkov also moved to break up regional loyalties; for example, in 1981 he thoroughly purged the Varna party organization whose leader, Todor Stoichev, had controlled the region since 1959.

Despite his steadily firmer grasp on power, Zhivkov did not introduce a personality cult like those of Stalin, Chervenkov, or his northern neighbor, Nicolae Ceauşescu. On the contrary, "Bai Tosho," as he came to be widely called, cultivated a common touch that, whether natural or feigned, was in keeping with the country's egalitarian tradition. When a Soviet film director proposed a Bulgarian segment of a film on wartime resistance that portrayed Zhivkov as a major figure both in the party and among the partisans, Zhivkov protested and published his 1944 party *kharakteristika* with its statement of modest though real accomplishments.[6] It became his habit when addressing a public body such as the Fatherland Front or the General Congress of Trade Unions to ask permission to speak "as one of the delegates." Permission was never denied, but the impression of equality among comrades remained.

Zhivkov also developed a reputation for accessibility. "I am not in power because of my attractive eyes," he told the *New York Times*. "I go around visiting the towns and villages, and I know what the people think." Georgi Markov considered him unique among the top people in the party because he seemed genuinely willing to listen to what outsiders told him.[7] The importance of personal relationships is magnified in a small country such as Bulgaria with a relatively narrow elite. Zhivkov apparently cultivated friendships with individuals outside party ranks—with the writer

Georgi Dzhagarov, for example—who established "Zhivkov factions" in many areas of public life.

The ordinary Bulgarian's sense of justice may also have been satisfied by the knowledge that under Zhivkov the venal crimes of party figures were not always beyond the reach of punishment. At the tenth party congress in 1971, Lŭchezar Avramov, who had been minister of foreign trade, head of the Komsomol, and a candidate member of the politburo, was purged and disgraced amid accusations of corruption. After the death of Liudmila Zhivkova, a number of high officials from the Committee on Culture and the Foreign Ministry were prosecuted for misappropriating funds allocated for the purchase of art from abroad. During 1982 Yancho Takov and Atanas Taskov were sent to prison for smuggling and currency violations. The former was the son of Peko Takov, who was simultaneously dropped from the politburo, and the latter was the son of Boris Taskov, a retired minister and politburo member.[8]

Zhivkov had boasted that his children were not like those of many other high party figures, who became "princes and princesses" with a well-developed taste for a sybaritic existence. His Liudmila, he told Georgi Markov, took her studies seriously. And others associated with her confirmed that she developed as a genuine scholar and intellectual. Born in 1942, Liudmila Zhivkova specialized in historical studies at Sofia University in the late 1960s, and in 1970 she spent a year at St. Antony's College, Oxford. In 1971 she completed her dissertation on Anglo-Turkish relations between 1933 and 1939 and joined the Institute for Balkan Studies under the Academy of Sciences. At the same time, following the death of her mother, she became more active in politics, assuming the role of "first lady" and gaining appointment to a few government commissions. In March 1972 she became deputy chairman of the Committee of Art and Culture: she was in fact the committee's actual head. This committee was eventually reorganized under her chairmanship as the Committee on Culture, with power over education, publishing, and international cultural relations, as well as the traditional cultural fields. Her position gave her cabinet rank, and at the eleventh BCP congress in 1976 Zhivkova became a full member of the central committee. In 1979 she became a full member of the politburo and took charge of a newly formed politburo commission on science, culture, and education. She remained the regime's dominant figure in the field of cultural policy until her death in 1981.[9]

Zhivkov's son, Vladimir, born in 1952, had no public role before Liudmila's death, but since that time he has been rapidly pushed forward. During 1982 he was appointed secretary general of the Banner of Peace Center, which Liudmila had created to organize the International Children's Assembly, and he was elected to the bureau of the Komsomol's central committee. During the following year he was sent to the National Assembly after a by-election in Mikhailovgrad. Liudmila's rise was accepted because of her obvious talent and energy. Vladimir Zhivkov has yet to demonstrate these qualities, although he may possess them. But his youth is against him, for his father may not have time to bring him into the highest levels of leadership.

During Zhivkov's years in power, the structure of the Bulgarian government has undergone several changes, beginning with the territorial-administrative reform of 1959. The system that the regime had partly inherited and partly thrown together after World War II was cumbersome and overbureaucratized, and its faults became increasingly obvious as the problems of industrial development became more complex. Beneath the ministries of the central government stood three levels of regional administration: the thirteen provinces (*okrŭzi*), 117 districts (*okolii*), and 1,930 village and municipal communities (*obshtini*). The new system, which probably owed its inspiration to the reforms in Soviet regional administration in 1957, attempted to integrate the needs of political and economic administration and to bring about a greater degree of decentralization. The old provinces were replaced by 30 new ones (also called *okrŭzi*), the districts were abolished altogether, and the village and municipal communities were consolidated and reduced in number to 897. The elimination of one entire level of bureaucracy and the consolidation of local governments tended to facilitate the planning of regional industrial projects. In agriculture, collective and state farms were at the same time amalgamated into large-scale agroindustrial complexes whose territorial extent largely coincided with the boundaries of the old *okolii*, thus preserving much of the old system of rural administration.[10]

In 1971 the tenth party congress, the National Assembly, and a national referendum approved a new constitution to replace the Dimitrov Constitution that had been adopted in 1947. In contrast to its forerunner, the new constitution explicitly recognized the Communist Party as the "governing force" in society. The Council of Ministers, which had been the chief executive authority, was made subordinate to a State Council, whose chairman became the official head of state. When the constitution went into effect, Todor Zhivkov resigned as prime minister to assume this post.[11]

The new constitution also explicitly recognized the "fraternal cooperation" of the BANU in governing the country, a reflection of the regime's decision to preserve the Agrarian Union as a transmission belt for the conveyance of party policy to the countryside. Membership in the BANU has been reported as 120,000, a figure that remained unchanged for a decade. Agrarians usually occupy a quarter of the National Assembly's 400 seats and about a fifth of the positions on local councils, and they head the ministries of justice, public health, communications, and forestry. The post of first deputy chairman of the State Council, whose occupant is the formal successor to the head of state, has also been held by an Agrarian, permitting Zhivkov to avoid designating an official heir apparent from the BCP. Until his death in 1974 the BANU was led by Georgi Traikov, who developed a close relationship with Zhivkov and became one of the most publicized men in the country. He was succeeded by Petŭr Tanchev, who continues to depict the BANU as the loyal "little brother" of the BCP. The regime uses the Agrarian Union both to implement agricultural policies in the country-side and to establish or maintain contacts with noncommunist agrarian parties around the world.[12]

The National Assembly had been the focal point of Bulgarian politics from the time of its establishment to the crushing of the opposition in 1947. The new constitution seemed to promise a revitalization of that institution by creating permanent assembly commissions to supervise the work of the ministries and by permitting a variety of groups—such as the trade unions, Komsomol, or Fatherland Front—to initiate legislation. This measure was probably intended to encourage political mobilization rather than to bring about any genuine democratization. Candidates for assembly seats are handpicked by the Fatherland Front and are representative in that they include a token proportion of industrial workers, Komsomol milkmaids, and so on, as well as the truly powerful.[13] When it meets, the assembly simply rubber-stamps the legislation and policies prepared elsewhere. Ordinary Bulgarians regard it as "the aquarium," where the country's big fish are on occasional public view.

The tenth party congress also updated the program of the BCP to adapt it to a newly defined stage of "mature socialism," which was described as "the highest and concluding development of socialism as a phase in the building of communism." The new program recognized the importance of the April plenum for guiding the party's conduct but focused primarily on the party's role in construction, emphasizing the necessity of mastering science and technology for the improvement of production.[14]

Certain trends in party membership developed during the Zhivkov era. As shown in Table 11, the party grew by nearly 300,000 (or about 56 percent) between 1962 and 1981. This substantially outpaced population growth over the same period, so that whereas one in fifteen citizens was a party member in 1962, in 1981 it was one in eleven. With regard to the party's composition, the proportion of workers has grown very slightly and that of the peasantry has declined sharply. This reflects both the changing social composition of the country as a whole and the deliberate policy of the leadership to keep blue-collar membership, "the backbone of the party" as Zhivkov called it, at a high level.[15] The biggest growth has been in white-

TABLE 11   SOCIAL COMPOSITION OF PARTY MEMBERSHIP, 1948–1981

Year	BCP Membership	Workers	Peasants	White-Collar	Others
1948	463,682	122,896	207,490	75,401	57,895
%		26.5	44.7	16.3	12.5
1954	455,251	155,081	180,998	81,664	37,508
%		34.1	39.8	17.9	8.2
1958	484,255	174,805	165,420	105,164	38,866
%		36.1	34.2	21.7	8.0
1962	528,674	196,449	169,601	124,587	38,037
%		37.2	32.1	23.6	7.2
1966	611,179	234,752	178,500	159,789	38,138
%		38.4	29.2	26.1	6.2
1971	697,641	279,751	181,779	196,657	39,454
%		40.1	26.1	28.2	5.6
1976	788,211	326,573	181,302	238,059	42,277
%		41.4	23.0	30.2	5.4
1981[a]	825,876	352,649	—	473,227	—
%		42.7	—	57.3	—

SOURCE: Atanas Atanasov et al., *Organizatsionen stroezh na BKP* (Sofia, 1978); and Todor Zhivkov, *Otchet na Tsentralniiat komitet na BKP pred XII kongres* (Sofia, 1981), pp. 112–13.
[a] Zhivkov's report to the twelfth party congress gave figures only for total membership and proletarian membership. The white-collar figures for 1981 thus represent all nonproletarian party members.

collar membership, of which the largest component is the state and party bureaucracy. The party has also grown older (see Table 12), but this is in keeping with the aging of the general population in a country that for some time has had one of the world's lowest birthrates. The proportion of women in party membership has also grown substantially, reflecting their higher educational levels and importance in the labor force. Women are not, however, well represented at higher levels in the party. Only 11 of the 197 members of the central committee elected at the twelfth party congress in 1981 were women, and Tsola Dragoicheva and Liudmila Zhivkova are the only women to have been accorded politburo status since the end of World War II.

There is little information available about the membership of national minorities in the party, although it is generally believed that ethnic Turks, Gypsies, and Pomaks are not represented in accordance with their numbers in the general population. In the 1981 central committee there were three Jews, one Turk, one Pomak, and no Gypsies.[16]

TABLE 12   PARTY MEMBERSHIP BY AGE, 1948–1981
(PERCENTAGES)

Age	1948	1958	1971	1976	1981[a]
under 21	1.0	0.3	0.5	0.3	11.4
21 to 30	25.0	21.0	15.6	14.7	
31 to 40	39.0	35.5	27.8	25.4	
41 to 50	25.0	25.0	28.5	26.8	88.6
51 to 60	8.0	13.2	15.5	17.9	
over 60	2.0	5.0	12.1	14.9	

SOURCE: Atanas Atanasov et al., *Organizatsionen stroezh na BKP* (Sofia, 1978); and Todor Zhivkov, *Otchet na Tsentralniiat komitet na BKP pred XII kongres* (Sofia, 1981), p. 113.
[a] Zhivkov's report for 1981 gave percentages only for members over and under 30.

TABLE 13   PROPORTION OF WOMEN IN BCP MEMBERSHIP,
1948–1981

1948	1954	1958	1962	1966	1971	1976	1981
13.4%	19.3%	20.4%	21.3%	22.8%	25.2%	27.6%	29.7%

SOURCES: Atanas Atanasov et al., *Organizatsionen stroezh na BKP* (Sofia, 1978); and Todor Zhivkov, *Otchet na Tsentralniiat komitet na BKP pred XII kongres* (Sofia, 1981), p. 242.

ECONOMIC DEVELOPMENT SINCE 1960

The BCP's most frequently made claim to legitimacy is that it has transformed a backward, peasant nation into a modern, industrial state; Bai Ganiu, the irrepressible and semicivilized symbol of post-Ottoman Bulgaria, has become "Engineer Ganev," an enthusiastic participant in an ongoing "scientific-technological revolution" fostered by party leadership.[17] Certainly, Bulgaria has enjoyed an unusually long period of continuous growth. In his study of the Bulgarian economy, American economist George Feiwel estimated that Bulgaria's growth in national income between 1951 and 1967 averaged 9.6 percent annually, and between 1967 and 1974 it was about 7.5 percent. This was accompanied by substantial structural change; the share of industry in national income rose from 37 percent in 1950 to 51 percent in 1972. By 1979 it had reached 58 percent.[18] The late 1970s saw worldwide economic retrenchment, but the Bulgarian economy continued to grow, although at a slower rate of between 4 and 5 percent. Thus, Bulgaria's long-term record of economic growth is the best of any CMEA nation. This has had significant political consequences, for Bulgarians tend to judge their achievements not against the standards of the West but against those of their closer neighbors. In the late 1960s and early 1970s an awareness of relative Yugoslav prosperity and the passage through the country of Turkish "guest workers" in Western cars laden with Western goods provoked feelings of resentment, which declined when Bulgaria's situation improved while economic conditions in neighboring states worsened.

After a period of retrenchment following the disruptions of the great leap forward, the priorities of the 1950s reappeared in the twenty-year plan for development adopted by the party's eighth congress in 1962. Extensive material and technological assistance from the USSR supported industrial growth, although it was aimed at coordinating Bulgarian development with Soviet needs. The contribution of the Soviet Union was particularly marked in such large-scale projects as the Maritsa-iztok energy-industrial complex near Stara Zagora, the Kremikovtsi metallurgical combine near Sofia, the Burgas petrochemical complex, and others. It is a matter of debate whether these examples of Soviet "giantism" were appropriate to Bulgaria's needs and resource base.[19]

Economic growth became more difficult in the 1970s for a number of reasons. Industrial development had been supported first by the availability of surplus labor from the countryside and then by the massive entry of women into the labor force. By the beginning of the 1970s, these processes had been nearly completed, so that there were no longer untapped reservoirs of labor. Nor was Bulgaria any longer at the most primitive stage of industrialization; further progress required higher levels of knowledge and technology than could be found in the country or borrowed from the Soviet Union. And, although the USSR insulated Bulgaria from the worst impact of the oil shock, the country was nonetheless affected both because Soviet supplies could not be counted on indefinitely and because the worldwide recession restricted the international market for Bulgarian products.

The Bulgarian responses were to stress quality and efficiency (the theme of the seventh five-year plan), to expand economic ties to the West, and to renew the search for ideologically acceptable ways to provide incentives for improved quality and output. During 1979 the regime introduced the so-called New Economic Mechanism, or NEM, in agriculture. Its central idea, creating quasi-market relationships and profits in the economy, as well as its name, was borrowed from Hungarian experience, although Bulgarian planners have been far more cautious than their Hungarian counterparts. As described when introduced, agricultural enterprises when setting up their plans first had to arrange contracts for marketing all production above a compulsory minimum. For their part, procurement organizations were required to buy only products for which there was demand on the home or foreign market, and they were empowered to encourage output of high-demand products by offering bonuses for them. According to Todor Bozhinov, supposedly the architect of the reform, the agroindustrial complexes were no longer to be taxed by income but by land value, thus permitting the more productive ones to retain a greater surplus for their wage funds while the less efficient could see a sharp drop in income. Although on the surface Bulgaria's NEM seemed a straightforward case of market socialism, the reform was carefully hedged with measures allowing for intervention from central authority and permitting subsidies for enterprises that found themselves in difficulty. And in fact complaints did appear in the economic press that inefficient producers were being shielded and that the process of negotiating contracts between producers and procurement agencies was overcomplex and muddled. In the fall of 1980 the apathy of these organizations was blamed for endangering the harvest and requiring national mobilization of the trade unions and the Komsomol to bring in the harvest. Nevertheless, in 1981 the twelfth party congress highly praised the NEM and put it into effect for the entire economy at the beginning of the following year, even though its procedures were still clearly in flux.

The increasing difficulty of maintaining Bulgarian competitiveness was revealed in an unusually strong speech by Zhivkov in the spring of 1983. He condemned the poor quality of Bulgarian-made products and the lagging technical proficiency of the country's industries, blaming them for the loss of foreign markets that had been painfully won in the past. Even the borrowing of Western technology was not effective, Zhivkov confessed, since the output was "Bulgarized" by low standards of labor discipline and efficiency during the production process.[20] He announced that a national party conference would be convened to discuss methods of raising the quality of production, which seems likely to be the central economic theme of the 1980s.

Bulgarian agriculture, whose productivity grew more slowly than the regime had called for, has gradually improved its ability to supply the population with an adequate diet and to export quality food products to both its CMEA partners and Western Europe. Between 1965 and 1981 Bulgarians increased their annual per capita consumption of meat from 48 to 61 kilograms, of milk from 148 to 198 liters, and of eggs from 167 to 203. Queues, which were omnipresent for even basic food products in the 1960s, were largely wiped out during the following decade. A significant part of this improvement came from the peasantry's private plots, which the regime has tended to favor. According to a 1983 report, the state acquired 33

TABLE 14   BULGARIAN EXPORTS, 1960–1981
(IN MILLIONS OF TRADE LEVA)

Year	USSR	Other Socialist Countries	Developed Capitalist Countries	Developing Countries
1960	359.5	202.2	83.5	23.4
%	53.8	30.2	13.2	2.8
1965	717.9	374.7	217.9	65.2
%	52.2	27.2	15.9	4.7
1970	1,261.4	597.5	333.6	152.0
%	53.8	25.5	14.2	6.5
1975	2,480.7	1,151.9	420.6	488.2
%	54.6	25.4	9.3	10.7
1976	2,817.9	1,359.3	543.3	479.3
%	54.2	26.1	10.5	9.2
1977	3,249.8	1,568.4	576.5	627.3
%	53.9	26.1	9.6	10.4
1978	3,584.1	1,672.9	650.5	742.1
%	53.9	25.2	9.8	11.1
1979	4,019.6	1,679.3	1,104.7	863.2
%	52.4	21.9	14.4	11.3
1980	4,444.8	1,858.9	1,407.0	1,190.8
%	49.9	20.9	15.8	13.4
1981	4,767.8	2,043.3	1,326.1	1,723.1
%	48.4	20.7	13.4	17.5

SOURCE: *Statisticheski godishnik na narodna republika Bŭlgariia, 1982* (Sofia, 1982), pp. 382–383.

percent of its meat, 14 percent of its milk, and 27 percent of its eggs from private plots.[21]

Tables 14 and 15 indicate the principal developments in Bulgaria's foreign trade. During the 1970s, imports from the West rose sharply and then leveled off. But, exercising restraint, Bulgaria managed to avoid the sort of serious balance-of-payments problem with the West that led to major difficulties in Poland and Romania by the end of the decade. Bulgaria also worked successfully to expand its exports to Third World nations. But throughout the postwar era the Bulgarian economy has been dominated by its Soviet partner, which continues to account for half of Bulgaria's imports and exports. Bulgaria has signed comprehensive agreements covering economic coordination with the USSR into the 1990s. Although their full contents remain secret, they are known to call for the expansion of the huge atomic power complex at Kozlodui on the Danube, which will generate

TABLE 15   BULGARIAN IMPORTS, 1960–1981
(IN MILLIONS OF TRADE LEVA)

Year	USSR	Other Socialist Countries	Developed Capitalist Countries	Developing Countries
1960	388.8	232.2	101.6	17.5
%	52.5	31.4	13.7	2.4
1965	688.7	334.3	306.8	48.1
%	49.9	24.3	22.3	3.5
1970	1,117.6	514.4	409.4	100.9
%	54.9	21.3	19.1	4.7
1975	2,653.0	1,129.8	1,237.6	215.2
%	50.7	21.6	23.6	4.1
1976	2,957.8	1,234.2	1,002.4	241.6
%	54.4	22.7	18.5	4.4
1977	3,461.3	1,382.4	944.4	273.6
%	57.1	22.8	15.6	4.5
1978	4,046.9	1,493.7	1,022.4	237.9
%	58.1	22.0	15.0	3.5
1979	4,336.0	1,628.3	1,142.2	256.9
%	58.9	22.1	15.5	3.5
1980	4,743.2	1,789.4	1,426.2	324.1
%	57.3	21.6	17.2	3.9
1981	5,450.6	2,058.5	1,988.3	460.5
%	54.7	20.7	20.0	4.6

SOURCE: *Statisticheski godishnik na narodna republika Bŭlgariia, 1982* (Sofia, 1982), pp. 382, 384.

over 40 percent of the country's electricity by 1990, and the opening of another large metallurgical combine near Burgas.

Lenin observed that in 1917 the Russian army voted with its feet. In recent years, Bulgarian state and party officials have begun to recognize that their people have been balloting on the future with other parts of their anatomy. Since 1974 the number of births per 1,000 people has fallen steadily from 17.2 to 14.1 in 1981. This caused a corresponding drop in the rate of population increase from 7.4 per 1,000 in 1974 to 3.0 in 1981, and some regions—Viden, Lovech, and Mikhailovgrad provinces—have experienced sharply negative rates of growth. Moreover, although population statistics broken down by ethnic group have not been published for several years, it is probably true that ethnic Bulgarians have the lowest birthrate. The Turkish, Gypsy, and Muslim Pomak minorities probably have substantially higher ones, for population growth in these years was greatest in the provinces with the highest concentration of minorities. During 1982 both Pencho Kubadinski, chairman of the Fatherland Front, and Georgi Dzhagarov, a deputy chairman of the State Council, issued warnings about the long-term implications of this trend for Bulgaria's future. Various remedies were proposed, ranging from higher prices for abortions and taxes on single people and childless families to improved housing and subsidies for child care and education. A genuine reversal, however, will probably require changes beyond the economic sphere to improve the quality of life and raise the level of optimism about the future.[22]

CULTURAL POLICIES UNDER ZHIVKOV

Discontent, even on a significant scale, is likely to dissipate or prove self-destructive without the focus and direction provided by intellectuals. The role of dissident intellectuals in formulating challenges to political authority and official values has been evident in every major crisis in Eastern Europe since Stalin's death. Bulgarian intellectuals, unlike their counterparts elsewhere in the region, have never developed any formal organization. This is due primarily to the small size of the country and its intellectual communities. Secret clubs or an underground press are hardly necessary to facilitate and exchange ideas among people who see each other regularly at work, in Sofia's café society, or during vacations together on the Black Sea. Discussions among trusted personal friends or colleagues is the preferred Bulgarian arena for advancing critical ideas or policies.[23]

In the early 1960s Bulgarian writers, the largest and most influential of the country's intellectual communities, were sharply divided. On one side were the conservatives, led by Georgi Karaslavov, first secretary of the Writers' Union, who were sponsored by Chervenkov and Todor Pavlov. They controlled the Writers' Union and the editorial boards of most literary journals and publishing houses. Arrayed against them was a diverse group that included a number of prewar and wartime radicals who had suffered under the Stalinist system (Emil Manov was the outstanding figure among them). A younger generation, for whom Georgi Dzhagarov was the emerging spokesman, joined the search for greater diversity and freedom. Few in the conservative literary establishment were favorably disposed toward Zhivkov or regarded him as of more than temporary importance. Consequently, the first secretary had quietly cultivated some of the outsiders, a fact that encouraged their expectations that the dogmatists' control over literature might be overthrown. Then came the Soviet twenty-second party congress, at which Khrushchev sought to reinvigorate the process of reform. The twenty-second congress was followed in Bulgaria by the ousting of Yugov and the final purge of Chervenkov. The conservatives were thrown on the defensive as it again became possible openly to criticize the personality cult and its abuses of power and to call attention to at least some areas of life where such problems still remained. A barrage of criticism was launched at Karaslavov, who was forced to give up the post of first secretary of the Writers' Union in April 1962.

Another sign of the changes in cultural policy was a greater openness to developments in the West. More translations of Western writers appeared, and a number of Western films and plays reached Bulgarian movie houses and theaters. In this relatively brief period, even Soviet imports could be unsettling. Solzhenitsyn's *One Day in the Life of Ivan Denisovich* was published in Bulgarian translation, which perhaps facilitated the publication of Nikola Lankov's long poem, "Recollection." Lankov had been a radical poet during the 1930s and had gone to prison during Chervenkov's purges. Knowing that he was dying of cancer, he composed "Recollection" to describe his experience at the hands of state security. Although poetry is an unlikely medium for the description of life in a concentration camp, the publication of Lankov's work indicated that new doors had been opened for literary investigation.[24]

The outstanding example of the ferment that developed during 1962 was the Improvisational Theater of satirist Radoi Ralin. Probably the most popular writer in Bulgaria, Ralin brought his own satires and those of other critical writers to the Sofia stage. Marked by tremendous energy and constantly changing to evade censorship, these performances sought to push back the limits on cultural life, and they gained tremendous attention throughout the country.[25]

In April 1963 Zhivkov called a halt to the process of cultural liberalization. This was probably inevitable given the switch in Soviet cultural policies that had been signaled by the attack on modern art and formalism that Khrushchev had made the preceding month. In a speech delivered before a huge rally in front of the headquarters of the central committee, Zhivkov denounced the increasing signs of Western influence in the country and drew particular attention to the tendency of youth to idolize Western music and fashions. Attacking several writers by name, he charged that the proponents of cultural liberalization were guilty of formalism, pessimism, decadence, and infatuation with Western forms alien to Bulgarian national traditions. Defending the literary Old Guard, he demanded strict adherence to the canons of socialist realism and a strong infusion of *partinost* (party spirit) into cultural life.[26] Zhivkov did more than threaten. *Literaturni novini* (Literary News), which had published some of the most daring works, was closed down, and liberals were removed from the editorial staffs of other publications.

Despite the severity of its tone, Zhivkov's April speech did not mark a complete return to the rigidities of the past. If he had forbidden certain directions to the country's writers, he had not prescribed a single path, and many remained active by turning to nonpolitical themes. Moreover, Zhivkov showed no desire to alienate the creative intelligentsia permanently, and in the following years he went to considerable lengths to win it over. The technique that he used was to open the way to material success and even political power for those willing to support the regime's policies. Membership in the Writers' Union or the other unions of the cultural intelligentsia became much more than honorific. Immensely high salaries, sinecures, commissions, lecture tours, vacation resorts, good-will assignments abroad, and other incentives were provided to elevate the successful intellectual to a status only slightly below that of the party leadership. Under Zhivkov, the regime made sure that if members of the intellectual community were alienated it was not because of material want. Moreover, there was a high cost associated with the public expression of alienation. Or, as Georgi Markov expressed his discovery: "They don't pay us to write, they pay us not to write."[27] Another method of killing with kindness was to "encourage" an individual to shift fields.

> Over the past ten years or so [since 1963] this idea of shifting people from one area to another has developed into a refined mechanism for the manipulation of dissenters among the Bulgarian humanistic intelligentsia. In addition, it enables officials to avoid creating martyrs, which might happen in the case of the open suppression of ideas. The officials control the money and the press, and they are able to arrange things so that the slamming of a door in someone's face is always accompanied by the opening of another one through which the victim may discharge whatever creative energy he still has left. And, of course, once you have given up your distinctive creative identity, you become a passive "good conductor" for their manipulations, just another copper wire in the state machine.[28]

Zhivkov also lavished time and his personal attention to cultivate members of the creative intelligentsia. The most striking example was Georgi Dzhagarov, the rebellious poet of the late 1950s, whom Zhivkov treated with a kind of paternal solicitude. Although Dzhagarov was one of those criticized in Zhivkov's speech, the immediacy of his repentance suggested that it all had been a put-up job. Two years later his play, *The Prosecutor*, which dealt very critically with the abuses of power of the Stalin era, was produced in Sofia and attracted wide attention. It may have been intended, however, as a pre-emptive strike, since other writers who wished to pursue this theme were told to seek another since "Dzhagarov has already taken care of it." [29] Dzhagarov became Zhivkov's viceroy as head of the Writers' Union, and in 1971 he was elevated to a deputy chairmanship of the State

Council. His protégé, Liubomir Levchev, a poet of greater talent who also began his career as a rebel, also became an intimate of the Zhivkov family and, as head of the Writers' Union and deputy chairman of Liudmila Zhivkova's Committee on Culture, became one of the chief managers of Bulgarian culture. Undoubtedly in these relationships there is a question of who was using whom. Did Zhivkov use the lures of wealth and power to rein in the intelligentsia or did its members exploit their relationships with him gradually to expand their own freedom of action? Probably there was an element of both, but the primary beneficiary has been the state, which, by making the creative intelligentsia a privileged social stratum, has severed the elite's links with the people.

It should be added that the Bulgarian regime has employed more brutal tactics when its efforts to win support have failed. When Solzhenitsyn won the Nobel Prize, Dzhagarov forced the members of the Writers' Union to sign a letter denouncing him. Those who refused, including the prominent figures Valeri Petrov, Khristo Ganev, Gocho Gochev, and Blagoi Dimitrov, lost their privileges and were expelled from the party. The critic Lazar Tsvetkov was jailed for circulating the works of Russian dissidents in *samizdat*. Blaga Dimitrova, perhaps Bulgaria's greatest living writer, was subjected to a brutal campaign of denunciation in 1982 when her novel *Litso* (Face) offended the party leadership with its depiction of cynicism and hypocrisy among the elite. And Georgi Markov, who left the country in 1969, was murdered by the state security in 1978 for his Bulgarian-language broadcasts on the BBC.[30]

Every Bulgarian knows the words of the monk Paisi, who inaugurated the Bulgarian national awakening more than 200 years ago with his plea for Bulgarians to know and take pride in their language and their past. "Have not the Bulgarians had a kingdom and an empire of their own?" he asked. "Why should you, O Foolish One, be ashamed of your nation and speak in a foreign tongue?" Zhivkov echoed Paisi's call in 1967 in a series of theses on the problems of youth and education. The theses were presented to the politburo and received wide attention in the press. Bulgaria, Zhivkov maintained, was guilty of neglecting the patriotic education of its young people. "Behind our motherland Bulgaria there is a dramatic and heroic history . . . but there is hardly any other state that allows such an underestimation and even belittling of its historic past . . . We must be proud of our history, our past, and our glorious revolutionary traditions." [31]

What accounted for Zhivkov's new interest in patriotism? It was certainly true that since 1944 the regime had neglected the traditional sources of national sentiment. All things Soviet or Russian were exalted over Bulgaria's own past and culture. National heroes and cultural figures from the past, as well as the church, were dismissed as relics of the country's bourgeois heritage. Bulgaria had even bowed to Soviet diplomacy in recognizing the existence of a separate Macedonian nationality. In seeking to undo some of the damage to the national psyche, Zhivkov was undoubtedly seeking some common ground on which to stand with the creative intelligentsia and with the population in general. He may also have been motivated by the 1965 military conspiracy, or perhaps he was following his genuine instincts.

The process of appropriating the national past has involved the rehabilitation of individuals and institutions that the party once despised. Bourgeois cultural figures were the first to be restored to legitimacy. In the 1970s the Agrarian movement received recognition as a positive, progressive force. Later the entire prewar bourgeois political opposition was granted the same status. Castigated in the past as foreign agents and spies, its members came to be seen as components of a broadly democratic movement of which the BCP was only the most advanced element. Rehabilitation was also extended to the church, which came to be regarded as a valuable cultural artifact, the principal defender of Bulgarian nationality before the party took over to fulfill this obligation in the modern world. On national holidays it became common to see portraits of Saints Cyril and Methodius, Paisi, and Kliment Okhridski carried alongside those of Blagoev, Dimitrov, and Zhivkov—although, to be sure, the latter remained more numerous. At the banquet concluding the celebration of the 1300th anniversary of the Bulgarian state, Zhivkov and Patriarch Maksim smilingly toasted each other, separated only by the great suckling pig on the table between them. The whole scene was a perfect symbol of the reconciliation between throne and altar for the greater glory of Bulgarian culture.

Since the regime's decision to appeal to the depths of national feeling, it had devoted enormous resources to the celebration of the national past and culture. The central role in the process was played by Zhivkov's daughter, Liudmila, who before her untimely death in 1981 became the dominant force in shaping the regime's cultural policies. Liudmila Zhivkova's impact on Bulgarian culture was felt in several ways. She brought more resources, both material and political, to scholarly and intellectual enterprises than they had ever received before. She removed the lawyers to the Sofia suburbs and converted the Palace of Justice into a national historical museum, and her agents went on an around-the-world buying spree to find works of art for new Bulgarian cultural centers.[32] Vast sums were spent to finance international exhibitions devoted to aspects of Bulgarian culture or to bring foreign specialists to Bulgaria. And her creation, the International Children's Assembly, put Bulgaria on the circuit of international cultural events.

Zhivkova also sent cultural life in new directions. A devotee of Eastern religions and certain forms of mysticism, she paid little more than lip service to party dogmatism in the arts.[33] She strongly encouraged both the avant-garde and the exploration of traditional nationalist themes. Zhivkova also promoted a coterie of liberals, prominent among them Liubomir Levchev and Alexander Fol, who became her minister of education. Her death in 1981, however, brought the curtailment of many of these changes. In the colder atmosphere brought on by the deterioration in East-West relations, Bulgarian cultural policies became more conservative. Contacts and exchanges with the West were diminished, though not entirely eliminated, and "pessimistic" literature was discouraged. Several from Zhivkova's entourage were purged for abusing their authority for personal gain, and it was rumored that Alexander Lilov's expulsion from the politburo in 1983 was due to his close association with her policies. The nationalist element, however, has hardly diminished, and Liudmila Zhivkova received a place in the great mural, dedicated to the "awakeners" of the Bulgarians, in the Palace of Culture that bears her name.

FOREIGN POLICY UNDER ZHIVKOV

Bulgaria is unique among the Soviet-bloc nations of Eastern Europe in that it has never experienced a significant crisis in its relationship with the Soviet Union. On the contrary, Zhivkov and the various Soviet leaders with whom he has dealt consistently described their relationship as a model one for nations with similar social systems. Zhivkov outshone all other East European leaders in the search for expressions of loyalty and adoration for the USSR. He said that the Bulgarian watch runs on Moscow time and that the two countries "have a single circulatory system," and he repeated Dimitrov's metaphor that Soviet friendship is Bulgaria's "air and sun." [34] During Zhivkov's years in power, Bulgaria has been the most consistent echo of Soviet positions both on the international stage and within the communist world, where it has condemned all movements that have questioned the necessity of the USSR's leading role. Some Western observers have been so struck by Bulgaria's lack of independence that they have described the country as a sixteenth Soviet republic. [35]

Numerous explanations for Bulgaria's extreme subservience have been offered. Yugoslav literature, particularly the portion that originates in Skoplje, emphasizes the supposed national character of the Bulgarians: dull, passive, naturally accustomed to following orders or, perhaps, "culturally conditioned toward evil." [36] A second explanation, which the Bulgarian regime supports and is widely held by those in the West with some knowledge of the Balkans, stresses the historic links between the Bulgarian and Russian peoples. Both are Slavic and Orthodox, Russian pan-Slav societies supported the Bulgarian national revival, and Russian armies liberated the Bulgarians from the Ottoman yoke. Signs of Bulgarian gratitude to *Diado* Ivan abounded even before 9 September 1944. Consequently, it is often assumed that there is an unusual depth of sympathy between Bulgarian and Russian. But this overlooks the equally strong anti-Russian tradition that has also existed in Bulgaria. Even at the time of the country's liberation, the nationalist leader Liuben Karavelov qualified his gratitude toward Russia in his famous statement that "if Russia comes to liberate, she will be met with great sympathy; but if she comes to rule she will find many enemies." [37] Nor was Blagoev a supporter of either pan-Slavism or Russian expansion. And the supposed pro-Russian feelings of the Bulgarians did not prevent them from taking the opposing side in two world wars. At best, this argument should be stated negatively. That is, the reservoir of anti-Russian feeling is less deep in Bulgaria than in the rest of Eastern Europe, and so represents less of a problem to be overcome. [38]

The close links between Bulgaria and the Soviet Union are due less to the residue of romantic pan-Slavism than to a hard calculation of interest on both sides. From the Soviet point of view, Bulgaria has considerable strategic significance. The Balkan peninsula is occupied by two NATO states, Greece and Turkey: two nonaligned communist states, Yugoslavia and Albania; and one ally of doubtful dependability, Romania. Bulgaria alone makes it possible for the USSR to assert a firm presence in the region, a fact underlined by the opening in 1978 of the Varna-Illichevsk ferry, which permits the movement of Soviet military forces to Bulgarian soil without relying on the land route through Romania. From the Bulgarian perspective, loyalty to the Soviet Union brings economic support, inflated prestige in the communist world, and the security of Soviet military protection, a factor that should not be discounted for a nation that has lost three wars in the twentieth century and whose territorial integrity is not recognized by its largest neighbor. As a small state surrounded by traditionally unfriendly neighbors, Bulgaria's diplomatic freedom of action has always been narrowly circumscribed, and, since the achievement of independence, the main task of Bulgarian foreign policy has been to find a patron among the great powers. The country's one attempt to achieve its national goals by itself ended in the catastrophe of the second Balkan war. Consequently, if there is no realistic alternative to the Soviet embrace, Zhivkov's policy of trying to make the best of it, although less than heroic, may well be Bulgaria's most reasonable course of action. And if Zhivkov was disturbed, as he sometimes must have been, by his obsequious behavior toward the USSR and visiting Soviet officials, he could console himself with the belief that he at least spared his people the ordeals suffered by Hungary or Czechoslovakia. [39]

Newton discovered that when an apple falls toward the earth, the earth also falls toward the apple, although the difference in mass makes this imperceptible to normal observation. The Soviet Union exercises a preponderant force on Bulgaria's foreign policy, but there is also a reciprocal action that, though rarely measurable, is nonetheless real. Zhivkov privately boasted that the marked improvement in Bulgaria's relations with Greece in the early 1960s was taken at his own initiative, carried through against Khrushchev's objections.[40] According to Soviet dissident Anton Antonov-Ovseyenko, at the twenty-third CPSU congress in 1966 Zhivkov spoke very forcefully behind the scenes against plans for a comprehensive rehabilitation of Stalin.[41] During the development of the Polish crisis over Solidarity, Bulgaria took a moderate position, stating consistently that the Poles were able to work out their own problems. Bulgarian officials have also quietly objected to Soviet foreign radio broadcasts in the "Macedonian language", and they have managed to delay indefinitely the publication of a Soviet linguistic atlas, again over the question of the existence or extent of Macedonian speech. Such disagreements, however, are rarely if ever made explicit in public in order to preserve the image of complete harmony.

Zhivkov's years in power were marked by a considerable improvement in Bulgaria's relations with her Balkan neighbors. Relations with Greece had been particularly bad after that country joined NATO and accepted American bases. Bulgaria had refused to pay its reparations bill and allowed its territory to be used as a refuge by leftist opponents of the Greek regime. Furthermore, Bulgaria had resurrected an old claim to compensation for the repatriation of Bulgarians from Greek territory after World War I. Quiet discussions between the two countries began in 1960 and reached a sudden conclusion in July 1964, when the Bulgarian foreign minister visited Athens to sign a whole series of agreements. The reparations issue was resolved by Bulgaria's payment of about $7 million in goods against a claim of over $65 million. Other agreements called for improved trade, communications, tourism, and cultural cooperation.[42] This breakthrough was followed by a more thorough normalization of relations and even a growing cordiality that was only slightly modified by the 1967 military coup in Athens. Since the fall of the military regime, the two countries have become even closer. Bulgaria particularly welcomed the victory of Andreas Papandreou's Panhellenic Socialist Movement (PASOK) in 1981, for an agreement on friendship and cooperation between PASOK and Bulgaria's Fatherland Front had been in existence since 1979.

The principal obstacle to rapprochement with Turkey was the issue of Bulgaria's Turkish minority. In 1969 the two countries concluded an agreement that permitted Turkish emigration from Bulgaria for a ten-year period, during which between eighty and ninety thousand ethnic Turks, about 10 percent of Bulgaria's Turkish minority, left the country. Although various Turkish governments were concerned by Sofia's alleged trafficking in guns and drugs with the Turkish political and criminal undergrounds, relations have generally been cooperative.

Relations with Romania worsened in the wake of the Soviet invasion of Czechoslovakia in 1968, which Bulgaria supported but Romania did not. Nevertheless, they soon recovered in spite of Romania's maverick foreign policy. During the late 1970s Zhivkov and Ceauşescu began the tradition of an annual exchange of visits, and they also agreed to undertake several large-scale, joint projects of industrial development and power generation along the Danube.

Yugoslavia continued to be the missing link in Bulgaria's policy of Balkan détente, and, as always, the key issue was Macedonia. Some improvement in relations between the two regimes did take place in the early 1960s, marked by Zhivkov's visit to Belgrade in 1962 and Tito's to Sofia in 1965. On neither occasion was Macedonia specifically mentioned, and polemics on this issue were held in check on both sides.[43] A change in Bulgarian policy became evident by the end of 1967 and was marked by Zhivkov's emphasis on patriotism. This was followed by a series of polemics asserting the historically Bulgarian character of Macedonia and denying the existence of a separate Macedonian nationality. In November 1968, the Historical Institute of the Academy of Sciences issued a pamphlet setting out in detail Bulgaria's position, the contents of which were broadcast over Radio Sofia and widely disseminated. Since that time the controversy between the two countries has gradually but steadily escalated, reaching a high point on the Bulgarian side with the publication of Tsola Dragoicheva's memoirs in 1979, which asserted that the Macedonians were "flesh of the flesh, blood of the blood" with the Bulgarian people. Soon after that, Todor Zhivkov delivered a state-of-the-nation report to the National Assembly that dealt primarily with the state of relations with Yugoslavia. He stated that Bulgaria had no claim on Yugoslav territory and that he would meet with Tito at any time or place to sign a treaty guaranteeing the inviolability of the borders established after World War II.[44]

The Yugoslavs made no response to Zhivkov's offer, which was repeated after Tito's death, stating that it was without significance, since Bulgaria still did not admit the existence of the distinct Macedonian nationality. For their part, the Bulgarians argued that recognition of a Macedonian nationality would have no foundation in linguistics, culture, or history, and that it would serve to legitimize Yugoslav claims to the Pirin region. In August 1983, the Bulgarian press suggested that only in the Pirin do Macedonians enjoy genuine freedom, whereas the other nine-tenths of Macedonia remains under "foreign rule." A conference devoted to the seventieth anniversary of the Balkan wars reached the conclusion that they were not the product of "bourgeois imperialism" but were wars of national liberation for the Macedonians.[45] Although such polemics keep scholars and journalists on both sides at fever pitch, there is little likelihood of this becoming anything more than a war of words, for the controversy serves mainly domestic purposes on both sides. For the Yugoslavs, the image of a hostile and irredentist Bulgaria serves as a perpetual reminder of the Soviet threat and the need to moderate hostilities between its own nationalities. For the Bulgarians, emphasis on the Macedonian question promotes patriotism and diverts national feeling away from resentment of the regime's subservience to the USSR.

During the 1970s Bulgaria sought expanded contacts and improved relations with the West. In part this was a continuation of the decision made in the early 1960s to open the country to Western tourism. Supposedly, it was Khrushchev himself who convinced Zhivkov of the potential gain in hard currency to be made from developing resort complexes on the Black Sea coast. But conservatives in the party were distrustful, and, although the resorts were built, the regime sought to segregate Western visitors from the public as much as possible.[46] During the following decade, however, a number of factors coincided to give impetus to the development of a new Western policy. These included the need for Western technology, the more open cultural policies associated with Liudmila Zhivkova, and, above all, the emergence of détente in the relations between the two superpowers, which allowed Sofia to pursue its goals without calling into question its close relationship with the Soviet Union. Bulgarian diplomacy undertook numerous good-will missions, expanded cultural and scholarly contacts, and sought to attract Western investments. Bulgaria's legislation covering foreign investment was described as the most liberal in Eastern Europe.[47]

By the end of the decade, however, Bulgaria's policy of improving relations with the West was undergoing retrenchment. The principal cause was the breakdown of détente in the wake of the USSR's long military buildup and the invasion of Afghanistan. As tension between the Soviet Union and the West increased, Bulgaria responded to pressure to close ranks behind its Soviet patron. Bulgaria's relations with the West were also hurt by the accusation that Bulgarian agents had organized the attempted assassination of Pope John Paul II in May 1981. These charges, which first surfaced in a *Reader's Digest* article and were repeated in an NBC television documentary, led Italian authorities to reopen their investigation. Mehmet Ali Agca, the Turkish would-be assassin, reportedly described a network of Bulgarian intelligence agents and Turkish underworld figures, who were deeply involved in international trafficking in drugs and arms and who hired him to kill the Pope at the behest of the Soviet KGB. In November

1982 Italian authorities arrested Sergei Ivanov Antonov, head of Bulgaria's Balkan Airlines office in Rome and allegedly a state security agent, and they sought the arrest of two Bulgarian embassy officials who had previously returned to Bulgaria. Antonov remained in custody for more than a year while the investigation continued. Although some of the information that Agca supplied, and which had been leaked to the press, was demonstrably false, Italian magistrates continued to insist that a substantial case against Antonov remained.[48] Regardless of whether the charges are ever proved, they represented a substantial setback to Bulgaria's efforts to improve its image in the West. During 1984 the United States Senate adopted a resolution branding Bulgaria a "terrorist nation," even though Antonov had still not been brought to trial, and other American officials charged that Bulgaria played a major role in international narcotics traffic and supplying arms to terrorists.[49]

CONCLUSION

During the Zhivkov era, Bulgaria moved slowly and haltingly along the path traveled more rapidly by Kádár's Hungary. This is probably the most progress that could reasonably be expected, given the constraints imposed by history and geography. In some ways Bulgaria's current circumstances recall the period of national awakening during the last century of Ottoman rule. The country's national revival was not revolutionary, at least not until Ottoman deterioration and a changing international constellation made it so. The majority of the creators of modern Bulgarian nationalism looked with optimism toward a future of cultural and economic progress within the borders of a Turkish empire that was itself gaining in enlightenment and toleration. This vision is probably close to Zhivkov's hopes for contemporary Bulgaria within the Soviet bloc.

The easing of great-power tensions in the 1970s provided an international environment congenial to this vision, and Zhivkov's frequent speeches pleading for a return to détente undoubtedly reflected his genuine conviction that it served Bulgarian interests well. But if conditions characteristic of cold war return, Bulgaria will shape its policies, both internal and international, to conform with Soviet desires. Indeed, it is difficult to visualize any alternative policy available to Zhivkov or the men who will succeed him. Bulgaria has always had to pay a price for being a small state in a critical and volatile region. Bulgarians may take some comfort in the knowledge that their culture and sense of national identity survived for centuries despite submersion in the empires of Byzantium and the Ottoman Turks. For the Bulgarians, endurance has always been the primary national virtue.

Appendixes

A. BCP POLITBURO AND SECRETARIAT, 1944–1981

First Postwar Politburo and Secretariat (Members co-opted
September–October 1944)

Politburo Members
Georgi Chankov
Raiko Damianov
Georgi Dimitrov
Tsola Dragoicheva
Dimitŭr Ganev
Vasil Kolarov
Traicho Kostov
Petko Kunin

Candidate Members
Vŭlko Chervenkov
Georgi Damianov
Ivan Vinarov

First Secretary
Traicho Kostov

Secretaries
Georgi Chankov
Vŭlko Chervenkov

B. Eighth Enlarged Plenum (27 February–1 March 1945)

Central Committee Chairman
Georgi Dimitrov

Politburo Members
Georgi Chankov
Vŭlko Chervenkov
Georgi Damianov
Raiko Damianov
Georgi Dimitrov
Tsola Dragoicheva
Dimitŭr Ganev
Vasil Kolarov
Traicho Kostov
Petko Kunin
Vladimir Poptomov
Dobri Terpeshev
Anton Yugov

Candidate Members
Titko Chernokolev
Dimitŭr Dimov
Gocho Grozev

First Secretary
Traicho Kostov

Secretaries
Georgi Chankov
Vŭlko Chervenkov

Nikola Pavlov was added to the secretariat in 1946.

C. Fifth Party Congress (18–25 December 1948)

Politburo Members	*Candidate Members*
Georgi Chankov	Titko Chernokolev[6]
Vŭlko Chervenkov	Raiko Damianov
Georgi Damianov	Mincho Neichev[7]
Georgi Dimitrov[1]	
Vasil Kolarov[2]	*General Secretary*
Traicho Kostov[3]	Georgi Dimitrov[1]
Vladimir Poptomov[4]	
Dobri Terpeshev[5]	*Secretaries*
Anton Yugov	Georgi Chankov
	Vŭlko Chervenkov

[1]Died 2 July 1949.
[2]Died 23 January 1950.
[3]Purged in March 1949; executed in December.
[4]Died 1 May 1952.
[5]Purged in 1950.
[6]Made a full member of the politburo in 1949; purged in 1951.
[7]Made a full member of the politburo in 1949.

Although Vasil Kolarov became de facto head of the party after the death of Dimitrov, he was never formally elected general secretary. Vŭlko Chervenkov was named to this office following Kolarov's death in January 1950.

Mincho Neichev and Titko Chernokolev were made full members of the politburo in 1949; Dimitŭr Dimov and Dimitŭr Ganev became candidate members. Todor Zhivkov became a candidate member in 1950 and a full member in 1951. Georgi Tsankov was added to the politburo in 1951.

Dimitŭr Dimov was made a secretary in 1949. Ruben Avramov, Georgi Tsankov, and Todor Zhivkov were added to the secretariat in 1950. Avramov left that body in 1952. Ivan Raikov and Encho Staikov were added to the secretariat in 1952.

D. Sixth Party Congress (25 February–3 March 1954)

Politburo Members	*Candidate Members*
Georgi Chankov[1]	Petŭr Panchevski
Vŭlko Chervenkov	Todor Prakhov
Georgi Damianov	
Raiko Damianov	*First Secretary*
Ivan Mikhailov	Todor Zhivkov
Encho Staikov	*Secretaries*
Georgi Tsankov	Dimitŭr Ganev
Anton Yugov	Boris Taskov[2]
Todor Zhivkov	

[1]Purged in July 1957.
[2]Released in September 1959 following appointment to politburo.

In September 1957 Dimitŭr Ganev, Boris Taskov, and Boian Bŭlgaranov were made full members of the politburo; Dimitŭr Dimov and Mladen Stoianov were made candidate members.

The plenum of April 1956 added Boian Bŭlgaranov and Encho Staikov to the secretariat. Staikov was released from this body in September 1957, at which time Dancho Dimitrov and Stanko Todorov were added.

E. Seventh Party Congress (2–7 June 1958)

Politburo Members	*Candidate Members*
Boian Bŭlgaranov	Dimitŭr Dimov
Vŭlko Chervenkov[1]	Todor Prakhov
Georgi Damianov[2]	Mladen Stoianov
Raiko Damianov	
Dimitŭr Ganev	*First Secretary*
Ivan Mikhailov	Todor Zhivkov
Encho Staikov	
Boris Taskov[3]	*Secretaries*
Georgi Tsankov	Boian Bŭlgaranov
Anton Yugov	Dimitŭr Ganev
Todor Zhivkov	Mitko Grigorov
	Pencho Kubadinski
	Stanko Todorov

[1]Purged in November 1961.
[2]Died 28 November 1958.
[3]Purged in April 1959.

F. Eighth Party Congress (5–14 November 1962)

Politburo Members
Boian Bŭlgaranov
Dimitŭr Ganev[1]
Mitko Grigorov
Ivan Mikhailov
Encho Staikov
Stanko Todorov
Boris Velchev
Todor Zhivkov
Zhivko Zhivkov

Candidate Members
Dimitŭr Dimov
Pencho Kubadinski
Tano Tsolov

First Secretary
Todor Zhivkov

Secretaries
Lŭchezar Avramov
Boian Bŭlgaranov
Mitko Grigorov
Nacho Papazov
Boris Velchev

[1]Died 21 April 1964.

G. Ninth Party Congress (14–19 November 1966)

Politburo Members
Boian Bŭlgaranov
Tsola Dragoicheva
Pencho Kubadinski
Ivan Mikhailov
Todor Pavlov
Ivan Popov
Stanko Todorov
Tano Tsolov
Boris Velchev
Todor Zhivkov
Zhivko Zhivkov

Candidate Members
Ivan Abadzhiev
Lŭchezar Avramov
Dimitŭr Dimov
Kostadin Giaurov
Peko Takov
Krŭstiu Trichkov
Angel Tsanev

First Secretary
Todor Zhivkov

Secretaries
Boian Bŭlgaranov
Venelin Kotsev
Ivan Prumov
Stanko Todorov
Boris Velchev

Members of the Secretariat
Georgi Bokov
Stoian Giaurov[1]
Stefan Vasilev[1]

[1]Released in connection with appointments to other positions during 1967. They were replaced by Roza Koritarova and Vladimir Bonev. The position "member of the secretariat" was created at the sixth congress. It seems to have been abolished at the twelfth congress in 1981.

H. Tenth Party Congress (20–25 April 1971)

Politburo Members
Boian Bŭlgaranov[1]
Tsola Dragoicheva
Pencho Kubadinski
Ivan Mikhailov
Todor Pavlov
Ivan Popov
Stanko Todorov
Tano Tsolov
Boris Velchev
Todor Zhivkov
Zhivko Zhivkov

Candidate Members
Ivan Abadzhiev[2]
Kostadin Giaurov[2]
Venelin Kotsev[2]
Peko Takov
Krŭstiu Trichkov
Angel Tsanev[3]

First Secretary
Todor Zhivkov

Secretaries
Ivan Abadzhiev[2]
Peniu Kiratsev
Venelin Kotsev[4]
Ivan Prumov
Stanko Todorov
Boris Velchev

Members of the Secretariat
Georgi Bokov
Vladimir Bonev

[1]Died 26 December 1971.
[2]Purged in July 1974.
[3]Purged in July 1973.
[4]Removed from this position in July 1972.

In July 1974 Grisha Filipov and Alexander Lilov were added to the politburo. At the same time Dobri Dzhurov, Petŭr Mladenov, Drazha Vŭlcheva, and Todor Stoichev were made candidate members.

Additions to the ranks of central committee secretaries came in July 1971 (Grisha Filipov); February 1972 (Konstantin Tellalov); July 1972 (Alexander Lilov); and January 1973 (Sava Dŭlbokov).

I. ELEVENTH PARTY CONGRESS (29 MARCH–2 APRIL 1976)

Politburo Members
Tsola Dragoicheva
Grisha Filipov
Pencho Kubadinski
Alexander Lilov
Ivan Mikhailov
Stanko Todorov
Tano Tsolov
Boris Velchev[1]
Todor Zhivkov

Candidate Members
Dobri Dzhurov[2]
Petŭr Mladenov[2]
Todor Stoichev
Peko Takov[3]
Krŭstiu Trichkov
Drazha Vŭlcheva

First Secretary
Todor Zhivkov

Secretaries
Ognian Doinov[4]
Grisha Filipov
Alexander Lilov
Ivan Prumov[5]
Boris Velchev[1]

Members of the Secretariat
Vladimir Bonev
Sava Dŭlbokov
Misho Mishev
Georgi Yordanov

[1]Purged in May 1977.
[2]Raised to full member status in July 1977.
[3]Raised to full member status in July 1978.
[4]Released in July 1979 in connection with appointment to politburo.
[5]Purged in July 1978.

Dobri Dzhurov, Petŭr Mladenov, and Ognian Doinov were added to the politburo in December 1977. In July 1979 a party plenum made Todor Bozhinov, Peko Takov, and Liudmila Zhivkova full members of the politburo and made Georgi Yordanov and Andrei Lukanov candidate members.

Dimitŭr Stanishev, Petŭr Diulgerov, and Georgi Atanasov were made central committee secretaries in December 1977. In July 1978 the same plenum that removed Ivan Prumov made Todor Bozhinov and Stoian Mikhailov secretaries and made Nacho Papazov a member of the secretariat. Milko Balev and Misho Mishev were made central committee secretaries in July 1979.

J. Twelfth Party Congress (31 March–4 April 1981)

Politburo Members
Todor Bozhinov
Ognian Doinov
Tsola Dragoicheva[1]
Dobri Dzhurov
Grisha Filipov
Pencho Kubadinski
Alexander Lilov[2]
Petŭr Mladenov
Peko Takov[3]
Stanko Todorov
Todor Zhivkov
Liudmila Zhivkova[4]

Candidate Members
Petŭr Diulgerov
Andrei Lukanov
Georgi Yordanov

General Secretary
Todor Zhivkov

Secretaries
Chudomir Alexandrov[5]
Georgi Atanasov
Milko Balev
Ognian Doinov
Grisha Filipov[6]
Alexander Lilov[2]
Stoian Mikhailov
Misho Mishev[7]
Dimitŭr Stanishev
Vasil Tsanov

[1]Retired in January 1984.
[2]Purged from politburo and secretariat in September 1983.
[3]Resigned in March 1982.
[4]Died 21 July 1981.
[5]Released from secretariat in January 1984 in connection with election to the politburo.
[6]Released from secretariat in March 1982 in connection with appointment as prime minister.
[7]Died 3 February 1984.

Milko Balev was added to the politburo in March 1982, at the time of Takov's resignation. In January 1984, following the purge of Lilov and the retirement of Dragoicheva, Chudomir Alexandrov and Yordan Yotov were elected to the politburo. At the same time, four new candidate members were named: Georgi Atanasov, Stanish Bonev, Dimitŭr Stoianov, and Grigor Stoichov.

The secretariat has had two additions: Kiril Zarev in March 1982 and Emil Khristov in January 1984.

Notes

CHAPTER 1

1. V.D. Konobeev, *Bŭlgarskoto natsionalno osvoboditelno dvizhenie: Ideologiia, programa, razvitie* (Sofia, 1972), pp. 366–67, 428–37.

2. On the impact of the liberation on Bulgaria's peasant society, see N. G. Levintov, "Agrarnye otnosheniia v Bolgarii nakanune osvobozhdeniia i agrarny perevorot 1877–1879 godov," in *Osvobozhdenie Bolgarii ot turetskogo iga: sbornik statei* (Moscow, 1953), pp. 186–99; and G. D. Todorov, "Deinostta na vremennoto rusko upravlenie v Bŭlgariia po urezhdane na agrarniia i bezhanskiia vŭpros prez 1877–1879 gg.," *Istoricheski pregled* 6 (1955): 27–59. An excellent recent survey in English of Bulgaria's history between the liberation and World War I is Richard Crampton, *Bulgaria, 1878–1918: A History* (Boulder, Colo., 1983).

3. Nikolai Todorov et al., *Stopanska istoriia na Bŭlgariia, 681–1981* (Sofia, 1981), pp. 215–62. On the development of the Bulgarian economy in this period, see also S. Sh. Grinberg, "Iz istorii razvitiia bolgarskoi promyshlennosti v kontse XIX v.: Perekhod k politike proteksionizma i pooshchreniia krupnoi promyshlennosti, *Uchenye zapiski Instituta slavianovedeniia* 30 (1956): 136–52; and Ivan N. Chastukhin, "Razvitie kapitalizma v Bolgarii v kontse XIX veka, "*Vestnik Moskovskogo universiteta: Seriia obshchestvennykh nauk* 7 (1953): 55–70.

4. Alexander Gerschenkron, *Economic Backwardness in Historical Perspective* (New York, 1962), p. 221.

5. *Spisanie na Bŭlgarskoto ikonomichesko druzhestvo* 1 (1895): 1–2; and John R. Lampe and Marvin Jackson, *Balkan Economic History, 1550–1950* (Bloomington, Ind., 1982), pp. 237–77.

6. Kiril Popoff, *La Bulgarie économique, 1878–1911* (Sofia, 1920), p. 11.

7. Ilcho Dimitrov's *Burzhoaznata opozitsiia v Bŭlgariia, 1939–1944* (Sofia, 1969) inspired considerable controversy when it first appeared, and has since come to be seen as a landmark in the development of modern Bulgarian historiography. See also Stoicho Grŭncharov, "Bŭlgarskata burzhoazna demokratsiia, 1879–1918 g.," in Vasil Giuzelev, ed., *Bŭlgarskata dŭrzhava prez vekovete* (Sofia, 1982), 1: 455–63.

8. The political events of the first years of Bulgarian independence are described in Cyril E. Black, *The Establishment of Constitutional Government in Bulgaria* (Princeton, N.J., 1943). See also Joel N. Searles, "The Emergence of the Leadership Element in Bulgaria: A Social and Political Investigation, 1877–1881" (Ph.D. diss., University of Washington, 1976).

9. Dimo Kazasov, *Ulitsi, khora, sŭbitiia* (Sofia, 1959), p. 200.

10. There are biographies in English of the two men who dominated Bulgaria in these years; see A. H. Beamon, *Stambuloff* (London, 1895); and Stephen Constant, *Foxy Ferdinand: Tsar of Bulgaria* (New York, 1980).

11. R. W. Seton-Watson, *Europe in the Melting Pot* (London, 1919), p. 358. See also Radoslav Popov, "Monarkhicheskiiat institut, burzhoaznite partii i problemata za konstitutsionnoto upravlenie v Bŭlgariia v nachaloto na XX vek," in Vasil Giuzelev, ed., *Bŭlgarskata dŭrzhava prez vekovete*, 1: 464–76.

12. *Mezhdunarodnye otnosheniia v epokhe imperializma* (Moscow, 1963), 8: 117. Leon Trotsky wrote several colorful and insightful observations of Bulgarian politics and society while in the country as a correspondent during the Balkan wars. They are reprinted in Lev Trotsky and Khristo Kabakchiev, *Ocherki politicheskoi Bolgarii* (Moscow, 1923).

13. A survey of Blagoev's career and the early history of Bulgarian socialism should begin with Blagoev's own *Prinos kŭm istoriiata na sotsializma v Bŭlgariia*, first published in 1906 (reprint, Sofia, 1976). See also Iordan Iotov et al., *Dimitŭr Blagoev: Biografiia* (Sofia, 1979); "Diskusiia po niakoi sporni vŭprosi ot istoriiata na BKP: Kharakterŭt na BRSDP prez 1894–1903 g.," *Izvestiia na Instituta po istoriiata na BKP* 20 (1969): 315–439; and Kosta Andreev, "Prinosŭt na Dimitŭr Blagoev za razvitieto na marksistkata teoriia," in Kostadin Baichinski et al., eds., *Simpozium: Teoretichniiat prinos na BKP do 1944 g. i v sotsialisticheskoto stroitelstvo* (Sofia, 1982), pp. 4–30. In English this period is covered in the first two chapters of Joseph Rothschild, *The Communist Party of Bulgaria: Origins and Development, 1883–1936* (New York, 1959); and in Marin Pundeff, "Marxism in Bulgaria Before 1891," *Slavic Review* 30 (1971): 523–50.

14. Angel Vekov, "D. Blagoev and G. V. Plekhanov," *Izvestiia na Instituta po istoriia na BKP* 36 (1977): 83–118.

15. Lenin, *Collected Works*, 4th ed., (London, 1960), 20: 247.

16. Blagoev, *Prinos*, p. 133.

17. R. K. Karakolov, "Kharakterni momenti ot borbata na Bŭlgarskata rabotnicheska partiia—komunisti," *Istoricheski pregled* 2 (1948): 130.

18. There has been some controversy over the membership of the first central committee. In addition to Blagoev and Sakŭzov, the members were apparently Georgi Bakalov, Gavril Georgiev, and Georgi Bogoev. See Ivan Tanchev, "Sŭstavŭt na Ts. K. na BRSDP prez 1894–1897 godina," *Vekove* 1 (1979): 38–42.

19. Blagoev, *Prinos*, p. 241.

20. Quoted in Blagoev, *Prinos*, pp. 260–61.

21. Ibid., p. 262.

22. On the efforts of the Social Democrats to influence the early organized Agrarian movement, see John D. Bell, *Peasants in Power: Alexander Stamboliski and the Bulgarian Agrarian National Union, 1899–1923* (Princeton, N.J., 1977), pp. 33–37; and Vladislav Topalov, "Osnovavane na Bŭlgarskiia zemedelski sŭiuz," *Izvestiia na Instituta za istoriia* 8 (1960): 153–204.

23. Quoted in Rothschild, *Communist Party of Bulgaria*, p. 25.

24. Blagoev, *Prinos*, pp. 503–12. On the early history of trade unionism in Bulgaria, see the two volumes of Kiril Lambrev, *Nachenki na rabotnicheskoto i profsŭiuznoto dvizhenie v Bŭlgariia, 1878–1891* (Sofia, 1960), and *Rabotnicheskoto i profesionalnoto dvizhenie v Bŭlgariia, 1891–1903* (Sofia, 1966).

25. A diligent search found Bulgarian translations of only nine items, none of them major, from Lenin's pre-1917 writings. Before 1917, Lenin or his works were mentioned twelve times in the Bulgarian press; this includes critical comments and Blagoev's mistaken attribution of *What Is to Be Done?* to Plekhanov. See P. Edreva, *Lenin na Bŭlgarski: Bibliografiia* (Sofia, 1970), pp. 1–2, 37–38.

26. Iotov et al., *Blagoev*, pp. 200–201; and Stavri Georgiev, "Raztseplenieto na BRSDP prez 1903 g. i negovite istoricheski posleditsi," *Istoricheski pregled* 4 (1983): 34–42.

27. A collection of Kolarov's memoirs, *Spomeni*, was published in Sofia in 1968; see also Todor Borov and Elena Savova, eds., *Vasil Kolarov: Bio-bibliografiia* (Sofia, 1947). There is an immense literature on Georgi Dimitrov. Two of the standard works on his life are Stela Blagoeva, *Georgi Dimitrov: Biografichen ocherk* (Sofia, 1953); and Elena Savova, ed., *Georgi Dimitrov: Letopis na zhivota i revoliutsionnata mu deinost* (Sofia, 1952). A less flattering picture is presented in Peter Semerjeev, *Dimitrov and the Comintern: Myth and Reality*, Soviet and East European Research Centre, Hebrew University of Jerusalem, Paper no. 7, 1976.

28. Blagoev, *Prinos*, pp. 494–502.

29. Blagoev's version of the schism may be found in *Prinos*, pp. 494–502. See also Rothschild, *Communist Party of Bulgaria*, pp. 29–35.

30. Trotsky's comments on the Bulgarian scene may be found in George Weissman and Duncan Williams, eds., *The War Correspondence of Leon Trotsky: The Balkan Wars, 1912–13* (New York, 1980), pp. 29–54.

31. Iotov et al., *Blagoev*, pp. 264–66.

32. Bell, *Peasants in Power*, p. 82.

33. Rothschild, *Communist Party of Bulgaria*, p. 42.

34. For a discussion of Stamboliski, Agrarian ideology, and the growth of the Agrarian Union, and for additional bibliography on these subjects, see Bell, *Peasants in Power*, pp. 55–84.

35. *Istoriia na BKP* (Sofia, 1981), pp. 98–102.

36. Iotov et al., *Blagoev*, pp. 267–68.

37. According to the Tŭrnovo Constitution, a Grand National Assembly was required to elect the monarch and to approve any alteration of the country's borders or modification of the constitution. It differed from an ordinary National Assembly in that it was twice as large and met at Tŭrnovo. Previous Grand National assemblies had been held in 1879 to elect Alexander Battenberg to the throne, in 1881 to suspend the constitution, in 1887 to elect Ferdinand, and in 1893 to correct some minor inconsistencies in the wording of some constitutional provisions and to formulate religious requirements for the heir to the throne.

38. *Statisticheski godishnik na Bŭlgarskata tsarstvo, godina chetvŭrta* (Sofia, 1912), pp. 388–89.

39. Ibid., p. 391.

40. *Bŭlgarskata komunisticheska partiia v rezoliutsii i resheniia* (Sofia, 1957), 1: 289.

41. Iotov et al., *Blagoev*, pp. 297–99.

42. Ibid., pp. 302–3.

43. Rothschild, *Communist Party of Bulgaria*, pp. 59–60.

44. *Statisticheski godishnik na bŭlgarskoto tsarstvo, godini X–XIV, 1913–1922* (Sofia, 1924), sec. 30, p. 58.

45. Iotov et al., *Blagoev*, pp. 317–18, 325.

46. Ibid., pp. 321–24.

47. Rothschild, *Communist Party of Bulgaria*, pp. 64–67.

48. Iotov et al, *Blagoev*, p. 316.

CHAPTER 2

1. For a survey of the general impact of the war on Bulgaria, see A. Ts. Tsankov, "Bŭlgariia prez voinata i sled neia," *Spisanie na Bŭlgarskoto ikonomichesko druzhestvo* 1–2–3 (1921): 36–55; and G. T. Danaillow, *Les Effets de la guerre en Bulgarie* (Fontenay-aux-Roses, 1932).

2. S. S. Arabadzhiev, "Selski zhenski buntove vŭv velikotŭrnovsko prez 1918 g.," *Istoricheski pregled* 5 (1966): 73–80.

3. *Istoriia na BKP* (Sofia, 1981), pp. 175–87.

4. Iordan Iotov et al., *Dimitŭr Blagoev: Biografiia* (Sofia, 1979), p. 385; and P. Edreva, *Lenin na Bŭlgarski: Bibliografiia* (Sofia, 1970), p. 40.

5. Lev Trotsky and Khristo Kabakchiev, *Ocherki politicheskoi Bolgarii* (Moscow, 1923), p. 148; and A. M. Koren' kov, "Internatsionalistskaia pozitsiia Bolgar-

skikh Tesnykh Sotsialistov v period pervoi mirovoi voiny, 1914–1918 gg.,"
Uchenye zapiski Instituta slavianovedeniia 10 (1954): 385–86.

6. Iotov et al., *Blagoev*, pp. 375–79.

7. There is a large literature on the Radomir Rebellion. Two of the basic works
are Mikhail A. Birman, *Revoliutsionnaia situatsiia v Bolgarii v 1918–1919 gg.*
(Moscow, 1957); and, especially, Khristo Khristov, *Revoliutsionnata kriza v
Bŭlgariia prez 1918–1919* (Sofia, 1957). For further bibliography see John D.
Bell, *Peasants in Power: Alexander Stamboliski and the Bulgarian Agrarian National
Union, 1899–1923* (Princeton, N.J., 1977), pp. 130–40.

8. Iotov et al., *Blagoev*, pp. 379–80; *Istoriia na BKP* (Sofia, 1981), pp. 183–84.

9. Tatiana Koleva, "Bŭlgarskata komunisticheska partiia i leninizmŭt," in Tatiana
Koleva, ed., *Sotsialni i revoliutsionni dvizheniia v Bŭlgariia* (Sofia, 1982), p. 21. See
also the discussion of this issue in Petko Boev, "Kŭm vŭprosa za nachaloto na
leninizatsiiata na BKP," *Izvestiia na Instituta po istoriia na BKP* 32 (1975): 345–71.

10. Petko Boev, *Kongres istoricheski* (Sofia, 1980), pp. 130–40.

11. The proceedings of the congress are described in Boev, *Kongres istoricheski*, pp.
26–150. Two other significant essays dealing with this period are Khristo
Kristov, "Velikata oktomvriska sotsialisticheska revoliutsiia i razvitieto na revoliutsionnoto dvizhenie v Bŭlgariia," in Khristo Khristov et al., eds., *Oktomvriskata
revoliutsiia i bŭlgaro-sŭvetskata druzhba* (Sofia, 1967), pp. 9–40; and Tatiana Koleva, "Oktomvriskata revoliutsiia i bolshevizatsiiata na Bŭlgarskata komunisticheska partiia, 1917–1923," in ibid., pp. 41–65.

12. Veselin Khadzhinikolov, "Niakoi problemi na koalitsionnoto pravitelstvo na
Aleksandŭr Stamboliski," in Khristo Khristov et al., eds., *Aleksandŭr Stamboliski: Zhivot, delo, zaveti* (Sofia, 1980), p. 256.

13. Marko Turlakov, *Istoriia, printsipi i taktika na Bŭlgarski zemedelski naroden sŭiuz*
(Stara Zagora, 1929), p. 136; and Dimo Kazasov, *Burni godini* (Sofia, 1949), p.
36. The details of these negotiations were also described by Dimo Kazasov,
then a Socialist, and Alexander Obbov, an Agrarian minister, in conversations
with the author in June and July 1973.

14. Joseph Rothschild, *The Communist Party of Bulgaria: Origins and Development,
1883–1936* (New York, 1959), pp. 100–101.

15. The Treaty of Neuilly obliged Bulgaria to cede a strip of territory along her
western frontier to the newly formed Serb-Croat-Slovene Kingdom; confirmed
Romania's possession of the Dobruja; and assigned Western Thrace, Bulgaria's
outlet to the Aegean, to Britain, France, and Italy for later award to Greece.
The treaty also disarmed Bulgaria, prohibited conscription, and imposed a
heavy reparations burden.

16. Birman, *Revoliutsionnaia situatsiia*, p. 348.

17. Khristov, *Revoliutsionnata kriza*, pp. 526–33.

18. Khristo Mashkov, "Uchastieto na pernishkite (dimitrovskite) rudnichari v transportnata stachka prez 1919/1920 g.," *Istoricheski pregled* 2 (1956), 65–71.

19. Bell, *Peasants in Power*, pp. 154–207.

20. Todor Zhivkov, "Do uchastnitsite v mezhdunarodnata nauchna konferentsiia, posvetena na 100-godishninata ot rozhdenieto na Aleksandŭr Stamboliski," in Khristov et al., *Aleksandŭr Stamboliski,* pp. 9–11. See also Khristo Khristov, "Aleksandŭr Stamboliski v novata i nai-novata istoriia na Bŭlgariia," in ibid., pp. 21–61; and Alexander Manko, "Politika splocheniia levykh sil v strategii i taktike bolgarskoi kommunisticheskoi partii, 1918–1923 gg.," in Tatiana Koleva, ed., *Sotsialni i revoliutsionni dvizheniia v Bŭlgariia,* pp. 120–28.

21. B., "Kommunisticheskoe dvizhenie v Bolgarii," *Kommunisticheski internatsional* 11 (1920): 1820.

22. "Godishen otchet na Ts. K. na BKP(t.s.) za 1921–1922 partina godina, iznesen na IV kongres na BKP(t.s.)," *Izvestiia na Instituta po istoriia na BKP* 30 (1974): 357–405.

23. Iotov et al., *Blagoev,* p. 430; Veselin Khadzhinikolov, "Pomoshtta na bŭlgarskiia narod za postradalite ot glada v Povolzhieto prez 1921 g.," *Istoricheski pregled* 3 (1952): 283–84.

24. Bell, *Peasants in Power,* pp. 195–97.

25. *Bŭlgarskata komunisticheska partiia v rezoliutsii i resheniia na kongresite, konferentsite i plenumite na Ts. K., 1919–1923* (Sofia, 1951), p. 159.

26. Iaroslav Iotsov, "Upravlenieto na Zemedelskiia sŭiuz, 1919–1923 g." *Istoricheski pregled* 3 (1951): 266–67.

27. *BKP v rezoliutsii i resheniia,* p. 245.

28. For further details on the 9 June coup, see Bell, *Peasants in Power,* pp. 208–41.

29. M. Shishiniova, Z. Litsova, and E. Stoianov, *Vrŭzki i edinodeistvie na BKP i BZNS v Pazardzhiski okrŭg v perioda 1894–1925 g.* (Pazardzhik, 1973), pp. 103–4.

30. Khristo Kabakchiev, "Posle perevorota," *Kommunisticheski internatsional* 28–29 (1923): 7695–96. See also the comments of Georgi Dimitrov reported in *Rabotnicheski vestnik,* 28 June 1923.

31. Gregori Zinoviev, "Uroki bolgarskogo perevorota," *Kommunistichski internatsional* 26–27 (1923): 7343.

32. Vasil Kolarov, "Taktika Bolgarskoi kommunisticheskoi partii v svete sobyti," *Kommunisticheski internatsional* 1 (1924): 625.

33. Karl Radek, "Perevorot v Bolgarii i kommunisticheskaia partiia," *Kommunisticheski internatsional* 26–27 (1923): 7327–42.

34. *BKP v rezoliutsii i resheniia,* pp. 270–72.

35. Kabakchiev's defense appears as "Posle perevorota" and "Kriticheskie zametki," *Kommunisticheski internatsional* 28–29 (1923): 7680–740, 7741–64.

36. *BKP v rezoliutsii i resheniia,* pp. 275–76, 358.

37. Doncho Daskalov, "Za podgotovkata na septemvriskoto vŭstanie v Sofiia prez 1923 g.," *Istoricheski pregled* 4 (1983): 3–15. There is an immense literature on the September Uprising. The classic work on the subject is still Dimitŭr Kosev's *Septemvriskoto vŭstanie 1923 g.* (Sofia, 1954).

38. *Istoriia na BKP,* pp. 258–62.

39. A recent Bulgarian study seems to confirm the belief that the peasantry provided the backbone of the uprising. Donko Dochev, "Sotsiologicheski nabliudeniia vŭrkhu uchastnitsite v septemvriskoto vŭstanie prez 1923 g. v plovdivska oblast," *Istoricheski pregled* 4 (1983): 45–46.

CHAPTER 3

1. Boian Grigorov, *Po pŭtia na reformizma: Sotsial-demokratsiiata i borbite na trudeshtite se v Bŭlgariia 9 iuni–19 mai 1934* (Sofia, 1981), pp. 122–32.

2. Stela Dimitrova, "Uchastieto na BKP v parlamentarnite izbori–noemvri 1923 g.," *Izvestiia na Instituta po istoriia na BKP* 1–2 (1957): 166–201.

3. *Istoriia na BKP* (Sofia, 1981), pp. 271–73; and L. Panaiotov, "Rezoliutsii na Vitoshkata partina konferentsiia, 1924 g.," *Izvestiia na Instituta po istoriia na BKP* 1–2 (1957): 457–75.

4. The Agrarian version of these negotiations is given in Kosta Todorov, *Balkan Firebrand* (New York, 1943), pp. 200–224. For the communist side, see Iono Mitev, "Kŭm vŭprosa za teoriiata i praktikata na BKP pri izgrazhdaneto na edinen antifashistki front sled porazhenieto na Septemvriskoto vŭstanie, 1923–1924 g.," *Izvestiia na Instituta po istoriia na BKP* 11 (1964): 110–23; and Zdravka Micheva, "Georgi Dimitrov i emigratsiiata na BZNS, 1923–1934," in Khristo Khristov et al., eds., *Georgi Dimitrov, rabotnichesko-selskiiat sŭiuz i BZNS* (Sofia, 1982), pp. 85–96.

5. Voin Bozhinov and L. Panaiotov, eds., *Macedonia: Documents and Material* (Sofia, 1978), pp. 749–51; Joseph Rothschild, *The Communist Party of Bulgaria: Origins and Development, 1883–1936* (New York, 1959), pp. 181–204; and Todorov, *Balkan Firebrand*, pp. 212–13.

6. *Istoriia na BKP*, pp. 276–79.

7. Tsola Dragoicheva, *Povelia na dŭlga* (Sofia, 1980), 1: 431–85.

8. A vivid account of the bombing and its aftermath may be found in Petŭr Peshev, *Istoricheskite sŭbitiia i deiateli* (Sofia, 1929), pp. 811–28.

9. Georgi Dimitrov, *Politicheski otchet na Ts. K. na BRP(k) pred V Kongres na BRP(k)* (Sofia, 1948), p. 28.

10. Peter Semerjeev, *Dimitrov and the Comintern: Myth and Reality*, pp. 26–29.

11. Dragoicheva, *Povelia na dŭlga*, 1: 489–596.

12. Nissan Oren, *Bulgarian Communism: The Road to Power, 1934–1944* (New York, 1971), pp. 35–49. Oren's study is particularly valuable for its material on the Bulgarian emigration in the USSR.

13. Iaroslav Iotsov, "Upravlenieto na ' Demokraticheski sgovor,' " *Istoricheski pregled* 3–4 (1948–49): 468.

14. Dimitrina Petrova, *BZNS prez perioda na ikonomicheskata kriza, 1929–1934* (Sofia, 1979), pp. 74–77, 107–17.

15. Dimitrina Petrova, "Obshtinski izbori v Sofiia—25 septemvri 1932 g.," *Vekove* 2 (1978): 58–64.

16. Nikolai Todorov et al., *Stopanska istoriia na Bŭlgariia, 681–1981* (Sofia, 1981), pp. 353–67.

17. Dimo Kazasov's *Zveno bez grim* (Sofia, 1936) states the movement's principles. Kazasov's memoirs, *Burni godini, 1918–1944*, are also important, although it is dangerous to rely on them because their content changed markedly in later editions. They are as slippery as the man himself was. Further material on *Zveno* may be found in "Kharakter na 19-tomaiskiia prevrat prez 1934 g.: Diskusiia," *Izvestiia na Instituta po istoriia na BKP* 21 (1969): 219–72; and Ganka Slavcheva, "Evoliutsiia na politicheskiia krŭg 'Zveno' kŭm antifashistko sŭtrudnichestvo s BKP v navecherieto na Vtorata svetovna voina," *Izvestiia na Instituta po istoriia na BKP* 25 (1971): 75–112.

18. S. S. Arabadzhiev, "Borbata na BKP protiv dogmatizma i sektantstvoto na 'levite' komunisti prez perioda 1919–1922 g.," *Izvestiia na Instituta po istoriia na BKP* 14 (1964): 90–99.

19. As with many medieval heresies, the ideas of left sectarianism must be found in the works of those who fought it. See Vasil Kolarov, *Protiv liavoto sektantstvo i Trotskizma v Bulgariia* (Sofia, 1949): and Zhak Natan, "Borbata na BKP protiv 'liavoto' sektantstvo," *Izvestiia na Instituta po istoriia na BKP* 11 (1964): 124–44.

20. *Istoriia na BKP*, pp. 300–302; and *BKP v rezoliutsii i resheniia* (Sofia, 1953), 3: 148.

21. Oren, *Bulgarian Communism*, pp. 56–60.

22. *Istoriia na BKP*, p. 313.

23. Aneta Stoilkova, "Tretiiat plenum na Ts. K. na BKP i niakoi vŭprosi ot borbata sreshtu 'liavoto' sektantstvo," *Izvestiia na Instituta po istoriia na BKP* 32 (1975): 372–98.

24. Dragoicheva, *Povelia na dŭlga*, 2: 119–23.

25. Petra Radenkova, "Novi danni za zhivota i revoliutsionnata deinost na Georgi Dimitrov, ianuari 1929–mart 1933 g.," *Izvestiia na Instituta po istoriia na BKP* 16 (1967): 213–29.

26. The ninth volume of Georgi Dimitrov's 14-volume *Sŭchineniia* (Sofia, 1951–1955) covers the Leipzig trial. The controversies that still surround such questions as who actually started the Reichstag fire and whether Dimitrov knew in advance he would be acquitted are beyond the scope of this work. Both Rothschild and Oren discuss these issues.

27. *Pravda*, 28 February 1934.

28. E. H. Carr, *Twilight of the Comintern, 1930–35* (New York, 1982), pp. 124–28, 423–24.

29. Semerjeev, *Dimitrov and the Comintern*, pp. 8–9.

30. Ibid., p. 12; Todorov, *Balkan Firebrand*, pp, 245–46; and Kolarov, *Protiv liavoto sektantstvo*, p. 127.

31. *Istoriia na BKP*, pp. 343–44.

32. Ibid., pp. 344–46; and Oren, *Bulgarian Communism*, pp. 72–75.

33. Carr, *Twilight of the Comintern*, p. 132; and *Istoriia na BKP*, pp. 353–55.

34. Oren, *Bulgarian Communism*, pp. 83–93; and Semerjeev, *Dimitrov and the Comintern*, pp. 51–55.

35. Blagoi Popov, *Za da ne se povtori nikoga veche* (Paris, 1981), p. 45. Following the publication of Popov's memoirs in the West, the principal Bulgarian historical journal published a biographical article about him, admitting that he been sent into exile in the 1930s. The article excused his conduct during the Leipzig trial because of his poor command of German and his lack of deep revolutionary experience. It also stressed the fact that Popov remained a loyal Communist after his return to Bulgaria. Boian Grigorov. "Blagoi Popov—Edin ot podsŭdimite po laiptsigskiia protses prez 1933 g.," *Istoricheski pregled* 4 (1983): 74–84.

36. Milovan Djilas, *Conversations with Stalin* (New York, 1962), p. 34.

37. Georgi Dimitrov, *Politicheski otchet*, p. 30; and Popov, *Za da ne se povtori nikoga veche*, pp. 21–22, 101, 118.

38. Trendafila Angelova, "Za reorganiziraneto na komunisticheskata i rabotnicheskata partiia, 1934–1940 g.," *Izvestiia na Instituta po istoriia na BKP* 20 (1969): 455–502.

39. Dimitrina Petrova, "Vŭznikvane na BZNS 'Aleksandŭr Stamboliski' ('Pladne')," *Vekove* 6 (1976): 38–52.

40. Veselin Khadzhinikolov, "Georgi Dimitrov, narodniiat front i rabotnichesko-selskiiat sŭiuz, 1934-1941 g.," in Khristov et al., eds., *Georgi Dimitrov*, pp. 165–92.

41. Oren, *Bulgarian Communism*, pp. 133–38.

CHAPTER 4

1. Todor Pavlov, *Protiv obŭrkvaneto na poniatiata* (Sofia, 1939).

2. *Istoriia na BKP* (Sofia, 1981), p. 374; *Rabotnichesko delo: Izbrani statii i materiali, 1927–1944* (Sofia, 1954), p. 346–47; and Marshall Lee Miller, *Bulgaria During the Second World War* (Stanford, 1975), pp. 17–18.

3. Tsola Dragoicheva, *Povelia na dŭlga*, 2: 262–63, 278–81.

4. Ibid., pp. 298–303; and Miller, *Bulgaria During the Second World War*, pp. 33–35.

5. Nissan Oren, *Bulgarian Communism: The Road to Power, 1934–1944* (New York, 1971), pp. 158–59.

6. *Istoriia na BKP*, p. 376.

7. Stoian Rachev, *Angliia i sŭprotivitelnoto dvizhenie na Balkanite, 1940–1945* (Sofia, 1978), pp. 21–25; and Charles Moser, *Dimitrov of Bulgaria* (Ottawa, Ill., 1979), pp. 143–53.

8. Dragoicheva, *Povelia na dŭlga*, 2: 335–42.

9. *BKP v rezoliutsii i resheniia* (Sofia, 1953), 3: 447–50.

10. Dragoicheva, *Povelia na dŭlga*, 2: 357.

11. Orlin Vasilev, *Vŭoruzhenata sŭprotiva sreshtu fashizma v Bŭlgariia* (Sofia, 1946), p. 126.

12. Dragoicheva, *Povelia na dŭlga*, 2: 361.

13. Ibid., 2: 402–6; Traicho Kostov, *Politicheskoto polozhenie i zadachite na partiiata* (Sofia, 1945), pp. 5–8; Oren, *Bulgarian Communism*, pp. 171–72; and Peniu Stavrev, "Nachalo na sŭprotivata na bŭlgarskiia narod protiv khitleristkoto khozainichene," *Istoricheski pregled* 2–3 (1969): 30–42.

14. This expedition is described in Kiril Vidinski, *Podvodnicharite* (Sofia, 1963). See also Mariia Ereliska, "Geroichniiat podvig na bŭlgarskite politemigranti prez 1941 g.," *Izvestiia na Instituta po istoriia na BKP* 10 (1963): 325–54.

15. Dragoicheva, *Povelia na dŭlga*, 3: 7; 2: 573–78.

16. Peter Semerjeev, *Sudebny protsess Traicho Kostova v Bolgarii, 7–12 dekabria 1949*, Soviet and East European Research Center Paper, The Hebrew University of Jerusalem, 1980, p. 13.

17. Dragoicheva, *Povelia na dŭlga*, 2: 578–90; and Mariia Ereliska, "Protsesŭt sreshtu chlenove i sŭtrudnitsi na Ts. K. na Bŭlgarskata rabotnicheska partiia prez 1942 g.," *Izvestiia na Instituta po istoriia na BKP* 10 (1963): 313–24.

18. Semerjeev, *Sudebny protsess Traicho Kostova*, pp. 13–14; and Oren, *Bulgarian Communism*, pp. 183–84.

19. Miller, *Bulgaria During the Second World War*, p. 79; and Ereliska, "Protsesŭt," pp. 313–24.

20. Dragoicheva, *Povelia na dŭlga*, 3: 41–60.

21. The work of the terrorist groups is described in ibid., pp. 167–79; and in Boris Stoinov, *Boinite grupi, 1941–1944* (Sofia, 1969), pp. 92–101.

22. *Istoriia na BKP*, pp. 396–97; and Dragoicheva, *Povelia na dŭlga*, 3: 197–200.

23. Oren, *Bulgarian Communism*, pp. 203–4. A useful bibliography of partisan accounts is given in two articles by I. Dolapchieva: "Nashata memoarna literatura za partizanskoto dvizhenie: Anotirana bibliografiia na knigi, izdadeni prez 1944–1961 g.," *Izvestiia na Instituta po istoriia na BKP* 9 (1962): 442–75; and "Nashata memoarna literatura za partizanskoto dvizhenie: Anotirana bibliografiia na knigi, izdadeni prez 1962–avgust 1965 g.," in ibid. 15 (1965): 422–31.

24. Dragoicheva, *Povelia na dŭlga*, 3: 207–22; and Donko Dochev, "Ofanzivata na monarkho-fashistkata vlast sreshtu antifashistkite sili (okt.–dek. 1943 g.)," *Izvestiia na Instituta po istoriia na BKP* 39 (1978): 351–79.

25. Rachev, *Angliia i sŭprotivitelnoto dvizhenie*, pp. 190–206; and Dragoicheva, *Povelia na dŭlga*, 3: 538–39.

26. See the discussion of the size of the partisan movement in Oren, *Bulgarian Communism*, pp. 214–20.

27. Donko Dochev, "Sotsialno-klasova kharakteristika na pŭrva rodopska brigada 'Georgi Dimitrov,' " *Istoricheski pregled* 2–3 (1969): 43–60; and Dimitŭr Tishev,

"BZNS i vŭoruzhenata borba na bŭlgarskiia narod protiv monarkho-fashistkata diktatura, 1941–1944 g.," *Istoricheski pregled* 3 (1966): 3–32.

28. Yugoslav sources state that Shatorov immediately went to Sofia to "hand over" the Macedonian party organization to the Bulgarian Communists. In her memoirs, Tsola Dragoicheva calls this a fabrication. According to her account, when the war broke off contacts between the CPY and the Macedonian Regional Committee, Shatorov sent emissaries to Sofia to seek guidance. "We could not refuse, we did not have the right to refuse them our help" (Dragoicheva, *Povelia na dŭlga*, 3: 353).

29. The text is given in ibid., p. 354.

30. Ibid., 3: 357–60. Dragoicheva's memoirs provide by far the most comprehensive statement of the Bulgarian side. The Yugoslav position is presented in Lazo Mojsov, *Bulgarskata rabotnichka partiia (komunisti) i mukedonskoto natsionalno prashanie* (Skoplje, 1948). See also Oren, *Bulgarian Communism*, pp. 187–99.

31. Dragoicheva, *Povelia na dŭlga*, 3: 362–64; see also Dobrin Michev, "Iugoslavskata istoriografiia za bŭlgaro-iugoslavskite otnosheniia, 1941–44," *Vekove* 5 (1980): 57–66.

32. Dragoicheva, *Povelia na dŭlga*, 3: 366–68.

33. Ibid., pp. 328–29, 386–87; and Milovan Djilas, *Wartime* (New York, 1977), pp. 357, 398–99.

34. *Govori radiostantsiia "Khristo Botev"* (Sofia, 1950), 1: 347–48.

35. Dimitrina Petrova, *BZNS v kraia na burzhoaznoto gospodstvo v Bŭlgariia, 1939–1944 g.* (Sofia, 1970), p. 68.

36. *Govori radiostantsiia "Khristo Botev,"* 3: 12–14.

37. Dragoicheva, *Povelia na dŭlga*, 3: 16–21.

38. Ibid., pp. 93–94, 100–107.

39. Ibid., pp. 131–35; and Petrova, *BZNS v kraia na burzhoaznoto gospodstvo*, pp. 80–81.

40. Dragoicheva, *Povelia na dŭlga*, 3: 108–10, 113–14, 118, 140–41.

41. Ibid., pp. 120–32, 136–38; and Petrova, *BZNS v kraia na burzhoaznoto gospodstvo*, pp. 72–80.

42. Dragoicheva, *Povelia na dŭlga*, 3: 225.

43. Todor Zhivkov, then secretary of the party's third Sofia district, which contained most of the capital's Jewish population, was in charge of the Communists' preparations (ibid., p. 212; and *Todor Zhivkov: A Biographical Sketch* [Sofia, 1980] pp. 63–65).

44. The resistance to the Jewish deportations has been the subject of numerous studies. See Frederick B. Chary, *The Bulgarian Jews and the Final Solution, 1940–1944* (Pittsburgh, Pa., 1972), pp. 129–99, and its bibliographical essay; and David Koen, "Provalŭt na natsistkite planove za unichtozhavane na bŭlgarskite evrei," *Istoricheski pregled* 2–3 (1969): 61–81.

45. Dragoicheva, *Povelia na dŭlga*, 3: 239–40.

46. The popular belief that Boris was murdered by the Nazis will probably never be extinguished even though it has been rejected by scholarship. See Ilcho Dimitrov, "Smŭrtta na tsar Boris III," *Istoricheski pregled* 2 (1968): 40–59; and Miller, *Bulgaria During the Second World War*, pp. 135–48.

47. Dimitrov, *Burzhoaznata opozitsiia*, pp. 124–25.

48. Dimo Kazasov, *Burni godini, 1918–1944* (Sofia, 1949), p. 730.

49. Dragoicheva, *Povelia na dŭlga*, 3: 245.

50. Ibid., pp. 294–98, 309; and Petrova, *BZNS v kraiata na burzhoaznoto gospodstvo*, p. 147.

51. Dragoicheva, *Povelia na dŭlga*, 3: 546–48.

52. Kazasov, *Burni godini*, pp. 748–49.

53. Dragoicheva, *Povelia na dŭlga*, 3: 549–68. Division in the party leadership over dealing with Bagrianov had been hinted at earlier by Traicho Kostov (Kostov, *Politicheskoto polozhenie*, pp. 11–12). Dragoicheva's confirmation makes comprehensible what had seemed a very puzzling episode. See Oren, *Bulgarian Communism*, pp. 237–39.

54. Dragoicheva, *Povelia na dŭlga*, 3: 570–71; and Kazasov, *Burni godini*, pp. 751–52.

55. Petrova, *BZNS v kraiat na burzhoaznoto gospodstvo*, p. 157; and Dimitrov, *Burzhoaznata opozitsiia*, pp. 174–77.

56. Miller, *Bulgaria During the Second World War*, pp. 186–87.

57. Kazasov, *Burni godini*, pp. 756–58, 780; and Dragoicheva, *Povelia na dŭlga*, 3: 594–95.

58. Dragoicheva, *Povelia na dŭlga*, 3: 585–93.

59. Semerjeev suggests that Dimitrov-Marek's death was not an accident—that he was killed because he was the last living, authoritative witness to Dimitrov's and Kolarov's responsibility for the disasters of 1923 (Semerjeev, *Sudebny protses Traicho Kostova*, p. 28).

60. Vojtech Mastny, *Russia's Road to the Cold War* (New York, 1979), pp. 200–201.

61. The most interesting account of the Muraviev government is in Ilcho Dimitrov's *Burzhoaznata opozitsiia*, pp. 167–236, which inspired a spirited debate among Bulgarian historians published as "Diskusiia po vŭprosa za burzhoaznata opozitsiia i kharaktera na pravitelstvoto na Muraviev," *Izvestiia na Instituta po istoriia na BKP* 30 (1974): 165–354.

62. Miller, *Bulgaria During the Second World War*, p. 210; and Ivan Marinov, "Pet dni v pravitelstvo na K. Muraviev," *Istoricheski pregled* 3 (1968): 81–102.

63. Dragoicheva, *Povelia na dŭlga*, 3: 600–20; and Boris Mateev, "Za glavniia udar na devetoseptemvriskoto vŭoruzheno vŭstanie," *Istoricheski pregled* 2–3 (1969): 82–105.

64. Dragoicheva, *Povelia na dŭlga*, 3: 644.

65. Ibid., pp. 646–57.

Chapter 5

1. Milovan Djilas, *Conversations with Stalin* (New York, 1962), p. 114.

2. A valuable recent study of the diplomacy of World War II with particular regard to developments in Eastern Europe is Vojtech Mastny's *Russia's Road to the Cold War* (New York, 1979). Albert Resis ("The Churchill-Stalin Secret 'Percentages' Agreement on the Balkans, Moscow, October 1944," *American Historical Review* 83 [1978]: 368–87) casts new light on British, and indirectly American, policy during this crucial period. Soviet diplomacy with regard to Bulgaria is surveyed in Angel Nakov, *Bŭlgaro-sŭvetski otnosheniia, 1944–48* (Sofia, 1978).

3. Sergei S. Biriuzov, *Surovye gody* (Moscow, 1966), p. 157. Biriuzov's memoirs were first published as *Sovetski soldat na Balkanakh* (Moscow, 1963). In a slightly reworked form they appeared again as *Surovye gody*. The main differences between the two redactions lie in the deletion in the later volume of nearly all references to Khrushchev and most of the unfavorable commentary on Stalin. Neither provides much detailed information on the working of the Allied Control Commission or on Soviet involvement in Bulgarian affairs, although they indicate Biriuzov's outlook fairly well. Biriuzov later became a deputy minister of defense, commander of the air defense forces, and finally commander of the strategic rocket forces. He was killed in an airplane crash en route to the celebration of the twentieth anniversary of the liberation of Yugoslavia.

4. Mito Isusov, "Sŭzdavane na legalnite rŭkovodni organi na BRP(k)," *Vekove* 1–2 (1982): 43–44.

5. Ibid., p. 46

6. "Nepublikovani radiogrami na Georgi Dimitrov do Ts. K. na BRP(k), avgust–dekemvri, 1944 g.," *Izvestiia na Instituta po istoriia na BKP* 27 (1972): 22–23.

7. Mito Isusov, *Politicheskite partii v Bŭlgariia 1944–1948* (Sofia, 1978), p. 36.

8. The reorganization of the party after 9 September is described in Isusov, *Politicheskite partii*, pp. 32–58; Petŭr Avramov, "Organizatsionno izgrazhdane na BKP sled izlizaneto i ot nelegalnost, 9 septemvri 1944 g.–fevruari 1945 g.," *Istoricheski pregled* 2 (1965): 3–31; I. V. Ganevich, *Deiatel'nost' Bolgarskoi kommunisticheskoi partii po ukrepleniiu diktatury proletariata, sentiabr' 1944–1948 gg.* (Kiev, 1974); and Petŭr Ostoich, *BKP i izgrazhdaneto na narodno-demokraticheskata dŭrzhava, 9 septemvri 1944–dekemvri 1947* (Sofia, 1967).

9. Ilcho Dimitrov and Nikolai Genchev, *Izgrazhdane na edinen mladezhski sŭiuz v Bŭlgariia* (Sofia, 1964), p. 11.

10. Nikolai Genchev, "Razgromŭt na burzhoaznata opozitsiia v Bŭlgariia prez 1947–1948 godina," *Godishnik na Sofiskiia universitet (ideologichni katedri)* 56 (1962): 235.

11. Mito Isusov, "Revoliutsionniiat protses i politicheskata sistema na narodnata demokratsiia v Bŭlgariia, 1944–48 g.," *Istoricheski pregled* 4–5 (1979): 85.

12. Nissan Oren accepts the extreme claims made by some historians and political figures in his *Revolution Administered: Agrarianism and Communism in Bulgaria* (Baltimore, 1973), p. 80.

13. The issue is discussed extensively in Ostoich, *Izgrazhdaneto*, pp. 39–65. See also Isusov, *Politicheskite partii*, pp. 22–30; and Anatoly Kopylov, "K voprosu o funktsiiakh komitetov otechestvennogo fronta neposredstvenno posle 9 sentiabria 1944 goda," in Tsvetana Todorova and Mito Isusov, eds., *Bŭlgarska dŭrzhava prez vekovete* (Sofia, 1982), 2: 383–88.

14. Ivan Peikov, *Razgrom na svalenata ot vlast monarkho-fashistka burzhoaziia v Bŭlgariia 9.IX.1944–IX.1945* (Sofia, 1982), p. 22. See also Vladimir Migev, "Politicheskite aspekti v izgrazhdaneto i razvitieto na dŭrzhavnite organi prez prekhodniia period v Bŭlgariia, 1944–1958," in Todorova and Isusov, eds., *Bŭlgarskata dŭrzhava prez vekovete* 2: 359–60.

15. Ostoich, *Izgrazhdaneto*, p. 70.

16. Ibid., p. 91.

17. Biriuzov, *Surovye gody*, p. 501.

18. This account is based largely on Ivan Peikov, "Podgotovka, provezhdane i znachenie na narodniia sŭd prez 1944–1945 g.," *Istoricheski pregled* 2–3 (1964): 151–70.

19. Georgi Batalski, "Otechestvenata voina na Bŭlgariia 1944–1945 godina," in Todorova and Isusov, eds., *Bŭlgarskata dŭrzhava prez vekovete*, 2: 439–43. According to one Bulgarian historian, the Yugoslav Communists showed no gratitude for Bulgarian help and urged the Soviet command to keep the Bulgarian army out of Macedonia (Dimitŭr Dimitrov, "Pŭrva armiia i iugoslavskite narodoosvoboditelni voiski na Kiustendilsko-Skopskoto i Skopska-Prishtinskoto napravlenie prez Otechestvenata voina, 1944–1945 g.," *Istoricheski pregled* 1 [1983]: 64-76).

20. On the purge of the army, see Filiu Khristov, "Deveti septemvri i bŭlgarskata narodna armiia," *Istoricheski pregled* 2–3 (1969): 172–93; and Ostoich, *Izgrazhdaneto*, pp. 85–90.

21. According to Peter Semerjeev, Dimitrov's original text, sent to the USSR for comment, did not contain this formulation. It was added by the document's Soviet editors (*Myth of Georgi Dimitrov*, p. 120). A recent Bulgarian article states that it was Stalin himself who edited Dimitrov's speech (Petŭr Avramov, "Razvitie na vŭzgleda za Devetoseptemvriskoto vŭstanie i narodno-demokraticheskata vlast, 1944–1948 g.," *Istoricheski pregled* 3 [1982]: p. 92).

22. Isusov, "Sŭzdavane," p. 49.

23. The best Bulgarian work on the noncommunist parties after 9 September is Isusov's *Politicheskite partii*. The works of Peikov, Ostoich, and Ganevich previously cited are also important.

24. Iordan Zarchev, "Bŭlgarskiiat zemedelski naroden sŭiuz, 9 septemvri 1944–1948 g.," *Izvestiia na Instituta po istoriia na BKP* 32 (1975): 120–21.

25. Charles Moser's *Dimitrov of Bulgaria* (Ottawa, Ill., 1979) is a biography of the

Agrarian, not the Communist, Dimitrov. See also Stratiia Skerlev, *D-r G. M. Dimitrov: Lichnost, delo i idei* (Paris, 1977).

26. "Nepublikovani radiogrami na Georgi Dimitrov i Ts. K. na BRP(k), avgust–dekemvri 1944," *Izvestiia na Instituta po istoriia na BKP* 32 (1975): 61.

27. Peikov, *Razgrom*, p. 153.

28. Petŭr Avramov (Petkov), "Borbata na BKP protiv gemetovshtinata i restavrator-skata opozitsiia, za krepŭk rabotnichesko-selski sŭiuz, 1944–1947 g.," *Izvestie na vissha partina shkola "Stanke Dimitrov" pri ts. k. na BKP: Otdel istoriia* 4 (1959): 111.

29. Oren, *Revolution Administered*, p. 96; and Moser, *Dimitrov*, p. 213.

30. Isusov, *Politicheskite partii*, p. 92.

31. The role of the American diplomatic mission in Bulgaria during this period is described in Cyril E. Black, "The View from Bulgaria," in Thomas Hammond, ed., *Witnesses to the Origins of the Cold War* (Seattle, Wash., 1982), pp. 60–97.

32. The text of Petkov's letter may be found in *Foreign Relations of the United States, Conference of Berlin (Potsdam), 1945* (Washington, D.C., 1960), 2: 724–25.

33. *Foreign Relations of the United States, 1945,* (Washington, D.C., 1968), 4: 308–9, 311–12.

34. Their freedom was short-lived. By 1948 most had been rearrested, and the majority died in prison or labor camps.

35. Isusov, *Politicheskite partii*, p. 174.

36. James F. Byrnes, *Speaking Frankly* (New York, 1947), p. 107. The Ethridge mission is described by Cyril E. Black, who accompanied Ethridge, in "The View from Bulgaria," pp. 81–85.

37. Memorandum by Mark Ethridge, 7 December 1945, with attached covering letters, Box 172, President's Secretary File, Papers of Harry S. Truman. See also Mark Ethridge and Cyril Black, "Negotiating in the Balkans, 1945–1947," in Raymond Dennett and Joseph Johnson, eds., *Negotiating with the Russians* (Boston, 1951), 171–206.

38. Isusov, *Politicheski partii*, p. 230.

39. Byrnes, *Speaking Frankly*, pp. 115–21, 237.

40. The account of the negotiations with the opposition is from Isusov, *Politicheskite partii*, pp. 243–65.

41. Ibid., pp. 288–89.

42. Ibid., pp. 297–309; and Ganevich, *Deiatel'nost' bolgarskoi kommunisticheskoi partii*, p. 174.

43. Genchev, "Razgromŭt na burzhoaznata opozitsiia," pp. 201–10.

44. Ibid., pp. 214–22; Isusov, *Politicheskite partii*, pp. 330–37; and Zarchev, "BZNS," pp. 144–52.

45. *Foreign Relations of the United States, 1945*, 4: 140, 179–82.

46. Maynard Barnes, who had returned to Washington before Petkov's arrest, asked

the State Department's permission to return to Bulgaria to work for his defense. The secretary of state's staff meeting, chaired by Dean Acheson, denied this request on 9 June (*Foreign Relations of the United States, 1947*, 4: 163). As a result Barnes resigned from the Foreign Service.

47. *The Trial of Nikola D. Petkov* (Sofia, 1947) contains the official record of Petkov's trial. See also Michael Padev, *Dimitrov Wastes No Bullets* (London, 1948); and Dr. Georgi M. Dimitrov, "The Bravest Democrat of All," *Saturday Evening Post* (6 December 1947): 28–29, 208–10.

48. Zbigniew K. Brzezinski, *The Soviet Bloc* (New York, 1967), pp. 61–63.

49. Isusov, *Politicheskite partii*, pp. 429–30.

50. Zarchev, "Razgromŭt," pp. 55–66; and Isusov, *Politicheskite partii*, pp. 387–90, 454–66.

51. Isusov, *Politicheskite partii*, p. 390.

52. Peikov, *Razgrom*, pp. 209–39; and Petko Petkov, "Obshtoto i spetsifichnoto v likvidiraneto na kapitalisticheskata sobstvennost v promishlenostta v Bŭlgariia," *Izvestiia na Instituta po istoriia na BKP* 20 (1969): 10–28.

53. Velichko Georgiev, "Sŭzdavane i ukrepvane na obshtiia rabotnicheski profesionalen sŭiuz prez perioda ot 9 septemvri 1944 do dekemvri 1947 g.," *Profsŭiuzni letopisi* 2 (1963): 8–56.

54. Robert Tobias, *Communist-Christian Encounter in Eastern Europe* (Indianapolis, Ind., 1956), pp. 352–79; Marin Pundeff, "Church-State Relations in Bulgaria Under Communism," in Bohdan R. Bociurkiw and John W. Strong, eds., *Religion and Atheism in the U.S.S.R. and Eastern Europe* (Toronto, 1975), pp. 328–36; D. Lazov, *Ekzarkh Stefan I: Zhivot, apostolstvo i tvorchestvo* (Sofia, 1947), pp. 257–59.

55. Pundeff, "Church-State Relations," pp. 337–40. The government's statement of this case may be found in *The Trial of Fifteen Protestant Pastors-Spies* (Sofia, 1949); and *Subversive Activities of the Evangelical Pastors in Bulgaria: Documents* (Sofia, 1949).

56. Oren, *Revolution Administered*, pp. 122–25; and Semerjeev, *Sudebny protsess Traicho Kostova*, p. 88.

57. Robert L. Wolff, *The Balkans in Our Time* (New York, 1967), pp. 476–80.

58. Dragoicheva, *Povelia na dŭlga*, 3: 387–88; and Adam Ulam, *Titoism and the Cominform* (Cambridge, Mass., 1955), pp. 92–93.

59. Dragoicheva, *Povelia na dŭlga*, 3: 393. Information from the Yugoslav side may be found primarily in Djilas, *Conversations with Stalin;* Vladimir Dedijer, *Tito Speaks* (London, 1953); and in the memoirs of Svetozar Vukmanovic-Tempo published in *Politika*, 16 May—9 June 1980. The Bulgarian position is most fully presented by Dragoicheva in her memoirs and in interviews dealing with Yugoslav criticism published in the newspaper *Otechestven front*, 9 February and 5 April 1979. See also Georgi V. Dimitrov, "Za taka narechenata 'kulturna avtonomiia' v blagoevgradski okrŭg, 1946–1948 g.," *Istoricheski pregled* 6 (1979): 70–82.

60. Djilas, *Conversations with Stalin*, pp. 172–84.

61. Georgi V. Dimitrov, "Za taka narechenata 'kulturna avtonomiia,' " pp. 74–81.

Chapter 6

1. Even after Kostov's rehabilitation, the party made no effort to present the facts of the case or to place responsibility for his persecution. The introduction to a recent edition of a collection of Kostov's speeches and writings, *Izbrani sŭchineniia* (Sofia, 1978), made no reference to his downfall or execution. In 1979 the obituaries of Petko Kunin, who was imprisoned as a Kostovite in 1949 and was rehabilitated and restored to the central committee after 1956, failed even to mention this period of persecution. Information on Kostov's career and purge comes primarily from Semerjeev, *Sudebny protsess Traicho Kostova v Bolgarii* (Jerusalem, 1980) and the official *The Trial of Traicho Kostov and His Group* (Sofia, 1949).

2. Rumors exist to the effect that Dimitrov did not die a natural death, but these were almost inevitable given the environment of Stalinism. There is nothing to substantiate the rumors.

3. Georgi Dimitrov, *Sŭchineniia* (Sofia, 1955), 14: 373.

4. The distinction between "home" and "Moscow" Communists was less clear in the BCP than in the other East European parties, since there were few Bulgarian party leaders from the older generation who had not spent time in the Soviet Union. Still, the men who advanced at this time were usually those with long service in the USSR—men who had been integrated into Soviet or Comintern institutions.

5. Kostov's complete statement could not be heard, owing to the shouts and disturbance created by agents planted in the courtroom.

6. Semerjeev, *Sudebny protsess Traicho Kostova*, pp. 39–40.

7. Ibid., p. 106. See also Vŭlko Chervenkov, *Bio-bibliografiia, 1900–1950* (Sofia, 1950).

8. Semerjeev, *Sudebny protsess Traicho Kostova*, pp. 110–14.

9. Georgi Markov, *Zadochni reportazhi za Bŭlgariia* (Zurich, 1981), 1: 45.

10. For a description of the trappings of Chervenkov's personality cult, see ibid., pp. 45–51.

11. *Foreign Relations of the United States, 1950*, 4: 518–25.

12. Peikov, *Razgrom na svalenata ot vlast monarkho-fashistka burzhoaziia* (Sofia, 1982), pp. 230–31.

13. Nikolai Todorov et al., *Stopanska istoriia na Bŭlgariia, 681–1981* (Sofia, 1981), pp. 440–41.

14. Zlatko Zlatev, "Sotsialno-ikonomicheski preobrazovaniia v Bŭlgariia, 1944–1948 g.," *Istoricheski pregled* 1 (1981): 13.

15. L. A. D. Dellin, ed., *Bulgaria* (New York, 1957), p. 269.

16. Mito Isusov, *Politicheskite partii v Bŭlgariia, 1944–1948* (Sofia, 1978), pp. 273–74; Dellin, *Bulgaria*, p. 300; and Vladimir Migev, "Za etapite na kooperiraneto na selskoto stopanstvo v Bŭlgariia, 1944–1959 g.," *Vekove* 1 (1984): 52–57.

17. Todorov et al., *Stopanska istoriia na Bŭlgariia*, pp. 454–62.

18. Ibid., pp. 462–70; Robert L. Wolff, *The Balkans in Our Time* (New York, 1967), pp. 524–32; and Migev, "Za etapite," pp. 47-59.

19. Angel Nakov, "Bŭlgaro-sŭvetskite otnosheniia v razvitieto na sotsialisticheska Bŭlgariia," *Istoricheski pregled* 4–5 (1979): 56–57; and Markov, *Zadochni reportazhi*, 2: 154.

20. J. F. Brown, *Bulgaria Under Communist Rule* (London, 1970), pp. 25–26.

21. Markov, *Zadochni reportazhi*, 1: 106.

22. Brown, *Bulgaria Under Communist Rule*, pp. 27–29; and Iordan Zarchev, "Bŭlgarskiiat zemedelski naroden sŭiuz i sotsializmŭt, 1944–1971," *Istoricheski pregled* 4–5 (1979): 65–72.

23. *Istoriia na BKP* (Sofia, 1981) p. 490.

24. Todorov et al., *Stopanska istoriia na Bŭlgariia*, p. 451; and Brown, *Bulgaria Under Communist Rule*, pp. 39–52.

25. The most detailed work on the Bulgarian thaw is Atanas Slavov's *The "Thaw" in Bulgarian Literature* (New York, 1981). Further information can be found throughout the two volumes of Markov's *Zadochni reportazhi*. See also Brown, *Bulgaria Under Communist Rule*, pp. 240–44.

26. Liubomir Ognianov, "Istoricheskite zavoevaniia na sotsialisticheska Bŭlgariia sled aprilskiia plenum na TsK na BKP, 1956 g.," *Istoricheski pregled* 2 (1981): 20.

27. Brown, *Bulgaria Under Communist Rule*, p. 67.

28. *Istoriia na BKP*, p. 505.

29. See expecially *Otechestven front*, 18 April, 5 May, and 20 May 1956.

30. Markov, *Zadochni reportazhi*, 1: 253.

31. Brown, *Bulgaria Under Communist Rule*, pp. 78–80. Chankov eventually became Bulgarian ambassador to Brazil.

32. Robert R. King, *Minorities Under Communism: Nationalities as a Source of Tension Among Balkan Communist States* (Cambridge, Mass., 1973), p. 189. This census has remained a permanent source of embarrassment to Sofia.

33. P. Georgiev, "Natsionalisticheska kritika," *Izvestiia na Instituta po istoriia na BKP* 3–4 (1958): 509. The chapter on Macedonia in King's *Minorities Under Communism* presents both the Bulgarian and the Yugoslav positions in some detail.

34. *Istoriia na BKP*, p. 517: and Brown, *Bulgaria Under Communist Rule*, p. 85.

35. George Feiwel, *Growth and Reforms in Centrally Planned Economies: The Lessons of the Bulgarian Experience* (New York, 1977), p. 46.

36. Brown, *Bulgaria Under Communist Rule*, p. 91.

37. Feiwel, *Growth and Reforms in Centrally Planned Economies*, p. 46.

38. Markov, *Zadochni reportazhi*, 1: 174.
39. Semerjeev, *Sudebny protsess Traicho Kostova*, p. 107.
40. Dimitŭr Kosev et al., *Istoriia na Bŭlgariia* (Sofia, 1955), vol. 2.
41. Information on Zhivkov's early life and career comes from *Todor Zhivkov: A Biographical Sketch* (Sofia, 1981); Robert Maxwell, ed., *Todor Zhivkov: Statesman and Builder of New Bulgaria* (London, 1982), which contains excerpts from a number of Zhivkov's speeches and writings; and the biographical entry in *Kratka bŭlgarska entsiklopediia* (Sofia, 1964), vol. 2.
42. Zhivkov used the phrase "teacher in communism" in a letter to Raichinov's widow. It is quoted in Maxwell, ed., *Todor Zhivkov*, p. 40.
43. Quoted in ibid., pp. 59–60.
44. This is the version given in Zhivkov's official biography. His party "kharakteristika" written in 1944 states that he was called to compulsory labor service.
45. Vera Maleeva et al., *Tia obichashe khorata: Spomeni za d-r Mara Maleeva-Zhivkova* (Sofia, 1982), pp. 115, 119.
46. See my discussion above.
47. Slavov, *The "Thaw" in Bulgarian Literature*, p. 143.
48. Brown, *Bulgaria Under Communist Rule*, pp. 97–98.
49. Zhivkov has never hesitated to purge or downgrade supporters who grew too powerful themselves. Grigorov was demoted in 1966, Todorov in 1981, and Velchev was purged in 1977. Tano Tsolov remained a powerful figure until incapacitated in 1980, and Kubadinski remains prominent at the time of writing.
50. Chervenkov was quietly readmitted to the party in 1969 but remained in obscurity until his death in 1980.
51. On Khrushchev's visit and the purge of Yugov, see Brown, *Bulgaria Under Communist Rule*, pp. 126–42, which deals with these events in some detail.

CHAPTER 7

1. *Newsweek*, 3 January 1983, p. 29. In a private conversation that included Georgi Markov, Zhivkov discussed an attempt by "a tank commander" to seize the capital in 1968. Markov was unable to confirm this story or to learn the name of the commander (Georgi Markov, *Zadachni reportazhi za Bŭlgariia* (Zurich, 1980), 2: 372–73).
2. Only limited information about this conspiracy ever appeared in the Bulgarian press. The best account is still that given in J. F. Brown, *Bulgaria Under Communist Rule* (London, 1970), pp. 173–87.
3. Markov, *Zadochni reportazhi*, 2: 333.
4. In 1962 this amounted to 300 leva a month over and above salary; the average monthly wage was then about 90 leva (Slavov, *The "Thaw"*, p. 15).
5. Ivan Bashev was killed in a hiking accident in 1971.

6. Maxwell, ed., *Todor Zhivkov*, pp. 21–23.

7. *New York Times*, 1 September 1982; and Markov, *Zadochni reportazhi*, 2: 319.

8. After serving in minor diplomatic posts, Avramov was quietly readmitted to the central committee at the party's twelfth congress in 1981.

9. Her impact on cultural policies is discussed below. Zhivkova's death at age 38 gave rise to speculation that she had been killed on Soviet orders because of her strongly nationalistic policies. There is no evidence to support this belief, and her death probably was the consequence of a near-fatal automobile accident five years earlier in which she had suffered severe head injuries.

10. Thomas M. Poulson, "Administrative and Economic Regionalization of Bulgaria: The Territorial Reform of 1959," in Thomas Butler, ed., *Bulgaria Past and Present* (Columbus, Ohio, 1976), pp. 187–201; Kostadin Petrov, *Bŭlgariia po pŭtia na razvitiia sotsializŭm* (Sofia, 1981), pp. 35–37; and Vladimir Migev, "Izgrazhdane na razvitiia sotsializŭm v Bŭlgariia," *Istoricheski pregled* 3–4 (1981): 7. Migev gives slightly different figures from other sources. By 1978 the number of village and municipal councils had grown to over 1,400. During 1978–1979 they were consolidated into 291 "inhabited systems."

11. Boris Spasov, "Bŭlgarskite konstitutsii," in Vasil Giuzelev, ed., *Bŭlgarskata dŭrzhava prez vekovete* (Sofia, 1982), 1: 486–90.

12. G. A. Cherneiko, *BZNS—Veren sŭiuznik na bŭlgarskite komunisti* (Sofia, 1980), pp. 145–74.

13. Joint Publications Research Service, "East Europe Report No. 1906: Elections for National Assembly Deputies in Bulgaria," (Washington, D.C., 5 August 1981), pp. 1–38.

14. *Istoriia na BKP*, pp. 600–604; and *Besedi po ustava na BKP* (Sofia, 1982), pp. 3–8.

15. Todor Zhivkov, *Otchet na Tsentralniia komitet na Bŭlgarskata komunisticheska partiia pred Dvanadesetiia kongres i predstoiashtite zadachi na partiiata* (Sofia, 1981), p. 113.

16. "The BCP Politburo, Secretariat, and CC after the 12th Congress," *Radio Free Europe Research*, Background Report no. 134, 12 May 1981.

17. Bai Ganiu, a sort of Uncle Sam or John Bull figure for Bulgaria, was the creation of the writer Aleko Konstantinov in the 1890s. His transformation into Engineer Ganev was portrayed in the humor magazine *Stŭrshel*.

18. *Rabotnichesko delo*, 28 April 1979; and Feiwel, *Growth and Reforms*, pp. 270, 276.

19. Nikolai Todorov et al., eds., *Stopanska istoriia na Bŭlgariia*, pp. 494–503; and George W. Hoffman, *Regional Development Strategy in Southeast Europe: A Comparative Analysis of Albania, Bulgaria, Greece, Romania, and Yugoslavia* (New York, 1972), pp. 97–99. The journalist Paul Lendvai recorded some remarks critical of the Soviet pattern of industrialization from Bulgarian economic officials in the late 1960s (*Eagles in Cobwebs: Nationalism and Communism in the Balkans* [New York, 1969], pp. 252–55).

20. A translation of Zhivkov's speech appeared in the Foreign Broadcast Information Service's (FBIS) press survey of Eastern Europe, 2 June 1983.

21. *Bŭlgarska telegrafna agentsiia*, 8 September 1983, quoted in FBIS, 9 September 1983, and 28 January 1983, quoted in FBIS, 31 January 1983.

22. Robert Wesson, ed., *Yearbook on International Communist Affairs, 1983* (Stanford, 1983), pp. 254–55. See also Georgi Markov's perceptive and moving essay, "Nai-goliamata tragediia," in *Zadochni reportazhi*, 2: 18–33.

23. This fact of Bulgarian intellectual life makes it very difficult for the outsider to catch more than dim outlines of what is going on beneath the surface. This is why such insider accounts as those of Georgi Markov and Atanas Slavov are extremely valuable.

24. Slavov, *The "Thaw,"* p. 76. Lankov died in 1965.

25. Ibid., pp. 101–2.

26. *Rabotnichesko delo*, 24 April 1963.

27. Markov became acutely embarrassed at giving readings to workers' groups, for each of which he was paid far more than a worker's monthly wage. His description of the material incentives made available to cooperative writers may be found in *Zadochni reportazhi*, 1: 308–56.

28. Slavov, *The "Thaw,"* p. 124.

29. Markov, *Zadochni reportazhi*, 2: 221.

30. Markov's work abroad and the "umbrella murder" are described in *Encounter*, November 1978.

31. *Rabotnichesko delo*, 1 December 1967.

32. To be sure, after her death several of them were sent to prison for misappropriating the funds placed at their disposal. For a further discussion of the revival of Bulgarian nationalism under Zhivkov, see Marin Pundeff, "Nationalism and Communism in Bulgaria," *Südost-Forschungen* 29 (1970): 161–70.

33. Liudmila Zhivkova's exotic ideas as well as the attempt to force them into Marxist categories may be examined in the collection of her most important speeches, *Za usŭvŭrshenstvuvane na choveka i obshtestvoto* (Sofia, 1980).

34. For a recent statement of Zhivkov's views on the identity of Soviet and Bulgarian interests, see his interview in Robert Maxwell, ed., *Todor Zhivkov*, pp. 374–76.

35. Nissan Oren, *Revolution Administered: Agrarianism and Communism in Bulgaria* (Baltimore, 1973), pp. 171–83; L. A. D. Dellin, "The Communist Party of Bulgaria," in Stephen Fischer-Galati, ed., *The Communist Parties of Eastern Europe* (New York, 1979), pp. 71–82.

36. See, for example, the article by the anti-Bulgarian specialist Mihajlo Apostolski in *NIN*, 4 March 1979.

37. Cited in Cyril E. Black, *The Establishment of Constitutional Government in Bulgaria* (Princeton, N.J., 1943), p. 41.

38. For an interesting discussion of the historic ties between Russia and Bulgaria, see Markov, *Zadochni reportazhi*, 2: 142–57.

39. According to Georgi Markov, Zhivkov did complain in private of the excessive

importance given to Soviet experience as a guide to solving Bulgarian problems (ibid., 2: 333).

40. Ibid., 2: 331–32.

41. Anton Antonov-Ovseyenko, *In Stalin's Time* (New York, 1981), p. 321. Antonov-Ovseyenko's source was allegedly Anastas Mikoyan.

42. Brown, *Bulgaria Under Communist Rule*, pp. 273–75.

43. Ibid., pp. 281–83.

44. *Rabotnichesko delo*, 28 April 1979.

45. *Narodna armiia*, 26 March 1983; the Bulgarian position was also set out in a recent handbook *Balkanite: Politiko-ikonomicheski spravochnik* (Sofia, 1982).

46. Markov, *Zadochni reportazhi*, 1: 442; and Petŭr Popov et al., eds., *Borbata sreshtu otritsatelnite iavleniia v sotsialisticheskoto obshtestvo* (Sofia, 1980), pp. 231–34.

47. *Financial Times* (London), 8 September 1979.

48. The case for KGB and Bulgarian guilt was made in Paul Henze, *The Plot To Kill the Pope* (New York, 1983). Luigi Barzini raised numerous doubts about the evidence in his review of Henze's book in *Washington Post Book World*, 11 December 1983. The Bulgarians themselves charged that the case against Antonov was fabricated by Western intelligence agencies. See *A Subversion of the Neo-Crusaders* (Sofia, 1983); *Free Antonov!* (Sofia, 1983); and Iona Andronov, *On the Wolf's Track* (Sofia, 1983). At the end of 1983 Claire Sterling, whose article in the *Reader's Digest* originally drew attention to the "Bulgarian connection," published *The Time of the Assassins*, making her case in greater detail.

49. *Washington Post*, 27 July 1984.

Bibliography

Andreev, Kosta. "Prinosŭt na Dimitŭr Blagoev za razvitieto na marksistkata teoriia." In Kostadin Baichinski et al., eds., *Simpozium: Teoretichniiat prinos na BKP do 1944 g. i v sotsialisticheskoto stroitelstvo.* Sofia, 1982.

Andronov, Iona. *On the Wolf's Track.* Sofia, 1983.

Angelova, Trendafila. "Za reorganiziraneto na komunisticheskata i rabotnicheskata partiia, 1934–1940 g." *Izvestiia na Instituta po istoriia na BKP* 20 (1969): 455–502.

Antonov-Ovseyenko, Anton. *In Stalin's Time.* New York, 1981.

Arabadzhiev, S. S. "Borbata na BKP protiv dogmatizma i sektantstvoto na 'levite' komunisti prez perioda 1919–1922 g." *Izvestiia na Instituta po istoriia na BKP* 14 (1964): 90–99.

———. "Selski zhenski buntove vŭv velikotŭrnovsko prez 1918 g." *Istoricheski pregled* 5 (1966): 73–80.

Avramov, Petŭr. "Borbata na BKP protiv gemetovshtinata i restavratorskata opozitsiia, za krepŭk rabotnichesko-selski sŭiuz, 1944–1947 g." *Izvestie na vissha partina shkola "Stanke Dimitrov" pri ts. k. na BKP: Otdel istoriia* 4 (1959): 93–137.

———. "Organizatsionno izgrazhdane na BKP sled izlizaneto i ot nelegalnost, 9 septemvri 1944 g.–fevruari 1945 g." *Istoricheski pregled* 2 (1965): 3–31.

———. "Razvitie na vŭzgleda za Devetoseptemvriskoto vŭstanie i narodno-demokraticheskata vlast, 1944-1948 g." *Istoricheski pregled* 3 (1982): 78–94.

B. "Kommunisticheskoe dvizhenie v Bolgarii." *Kommunisticheski internatsional* 11 (1920): 1817–30.

Balkanite: Politiko-ikonomicheski spravochnik. Sofia, 1982.

Barzini, Luigi. "The Gunman in St. Peter's Square." *Washington Post Book World,* 11 December 1983.

Batalski, Georgi. "Otechestvenata voina na Bŭlgariia, 1944–1945 godina." In Tsvetana Todorova and Mito Isusov, eds., *Bŭlgarskata dŭrzhava prez vekovete*, Vol. 2. Sofia, 1982.

Beamon, A. H. *Stambuloff.* London, 1895.

Bell, John D. *Peasants in Power: Alexander Stamboliski and the Bulgarian Agrarian National Union, 1899–1923.* Princeton, N.J., 1977.

Besedi po ustava na BKP. Sofia, 1982.

Biriuzov, Sergei S. *Sovetski soldat na Balkanakh.* Moscow, 1963.

———. *Surovye gody.* Moscow, 1966.

Birman, Mikhail A. *Revoliutsionnaia situatsiia v Bolgarii v 1918–1919 gg.* Moscow, 1957.

Black, Cyril E. *The Establishment of Constitutional Government in Bulgaria.* Princeton, N.J., 1943.

———. "The View from Bulgaria." In Thomas Hammond, ed., *Witnesses to the Origins of the Cold War.* Seattle, Wash., 1982.

Blagoev, Dimitŭr. *Prinos kŭm istoriiata na sotsializma v Bŭlgariia.* Sofia, 1976.

Blagoeva, Stela. *Georgi Dimitrov: Biografichen ocherk.* Sofia, 1953.

Boev, Petko. *Kongres istoricheski.* Sofia, 1980.

———. "Kŭm vŭprosa za nachaloto na leninizatsiiata na BKP," *Izvestiia na Instituta po istoriia na BKP* 32 (1975): 345–71.

Borov, Todor, and Savova, Elena, eds. *Vasil Kolarov: Bio-bibliografiia.* Sofia, 1947.

Bozhinov, Voin, and Panaiotov, L., eds. *Macedonia: Documents and Material.* Sofia, 1978.

Brown, J. F. *Bulgaria Under Communist Rule.* London, 1970.

Bŭlgarskata komunisticheska partiia v chuzhdata literatura, 1868–1978. Sofia, 1983.

Byrnes, James F. *Speaking Frankly.* New York, 1947.

Carr, E. H. *Twilight of the Comintern, 1930–35.* New York, 1982.

Chary, Frederick B. *The Bulgarian Jews and the Final Solution, 1940–1944.* Pittsburgh, Pa., 1972.

Chastukhin, Ivan N. "Razvitie kapitalizma v Bolgarii v kontse XIX veka." *Vestnik Moskovskogo universiteta: Seriia obshchestvennykh nauk* 7 (1953): 55–70.

Cherneiko, G. A. *BZNS—Veren sŭiuznik na bŭlgarskite komunisti.* Sofia, 1980.

Chervenkov, Vŭlko. *Bio-bibliografiia, 1900–1950.* Sofia, 1950.

Constant, Stephen. *Foxy Ferdinand: Tsar of Bulgaria.* New York, 1980.

Crampton, Richard J. *Bulgaria, 1878–1918: A History.* Boulder, Colo., 1983.

Danaillow, G. T. *Les Effets de la guerre en Bulgarie.* Fontenay-aux-Roses, 1932.

Daskalov, Doncho. "Za podgotovkata na septemvriskoto vŭstanie v Sofiia prez 1923 g." *Istoricheski pregled* 4 (1983): 3–15.

Dedijer, Vladimir. *Tito Speaks.* London, 1953.

Dellin, L. A. D., ed. *Bulgaria.* New York, 1957.

————. "The Communist Party of Bulgaria." In Stephen Fischer-Galati, ed., *The Communist Parties of Eastern Europe*, 49–85. New York, 1979.

Dimitrov, Dimitŭr. "Pŭrva armiia i iugoslavskite narodoosvoboditelni voiski na Kiustendilsko-Skopskoto i Skopsko-Prishtinskoto napravlenie prez Otechestvenata voina, 1944–1945 g." *Istoricheski pregled* 1 (1983): 64–76.

Dimitrov, Georgi. *Politicheski otchet na Ts. K. na BRP(k) pred V Kongres na BRP(k)*. Sofia, 1948.

————. *Sŭchineniia*. 14 vols. Sofia, 1951–1955.

Dimitrov, Georgi M. "The Bravest Democrat of All." *Saturday Evening Post*, 6 December 1947, 28–29, 208–10.

Dimitrov, Georgi V. "Za taka narechenata 'kulturna avtonomiia' v blagoevgradski okrŭg, 1946–1948 g." *Istoricheski pregled* 6 (1979): 70–82.

Dimitrov, Ilcho. *Burzhoaznata opozitsiia v Bŭlgariia, 1939–1944*. Sofia, 1969.

————. "Smŭrtta na tsar Boris III." *Istoricheski pregled* 2 (1968): 40–59.

————, and Genchev, Nikolai. *Izgrazhdane na edinen mladezhki sŭiuz v Bŭlgariia*. Sofia, 1964.

Dimitrova, Stela. "Uchastieto na BKP v parlamentarnite izbori—noemvri 1923 g." *Izvestiia na Instituta po istoriia na BKP* 1–2 (1957): 166–201.

————. "Diskusiia po niakoi sporni vŭprosi ot istoriiata na BKP: Kharakterŭt na BRSDP prez 1894–1903 g." *Izvestiia na Instituta po istoriia na BKP* 20 (1969): 315–439.

————. "Diskusiia po vŭprosa za burzhoaznata opozitsiia i kharaktera na pravitelstvoto na Muraviev." *Izvestiia na Instituta po istoriia na BKP* 30 (1974): 165–354.

Djilas, Milovan. *Conversations with Stalin*. New York, 1962.

————. *Wartime*. New York, 1977.

Dochev, Donko. "Ofanzivata na monarkho-fashistkata vlast sreshtu antifashistkite sili, okt.–dek. 1943 g.," *Izvestiia na Instituta po istoriia na BKP* 39 (1978): 351–79.

————, "Sotsialno-klasova kharakteristika na pŭrva rodopska brigada 'Georgi Dimitrov.'" *Istoricheski pregled* 2–3 (1969): 43–60.

————. "Sotsiologicheski nabliudeniia vŭrkhu uchastnitsite v septemvriskoto vŭstanie prez 1923 g. v plovdivska oblast." *Istoricheski pregled* 4 (1983): 43–52.

Dolapchieva, I. "Nashata memoarna literatura za partizanskoto dvizhenie: Anotirana bibliografiia na knigi, izdadeni prez 1944–1961 g." *Izvestiia na Instituta po istoriia na BKP* 9 (1962): 442–75.

————. "Nashata memoarna literatura za partizanskoto dvizhenie: Anotirana bibliografiia na knigi, izdadeni prez 1962–avgust 1965 g." *Izvestiia na Instituta po istoriia na BKP* 15 (1965): 422–31.

Dragoicheva, Tsola. *Povelia na dŭlga*: Vol. 1, *Neslomimite*: Vol. 2, *Shturmŭt*: Vol. 3, *Pobeda*. Sofia, 1980.

Edreva, P. *Lenin na Bŭlgarski: Bibliografiia*. Sofia, 1970.

Ereliska, Mariia. "Geroichniiat podvig na bŭlgarskite politemigranti prez 1941 g." *Izvestiia na Instituta po istoriia na BKP* 10 (1963): 325–54.

184   *Bibliography*

———. "Protsesŭt sreshtu chlenove i sŭtrudnitsi na Ts. K. na Bŭlgarskata rabotni-cheska partiia prez 1942 g." *Izvestiia na Instituta po istoriia na BKP* 10 (1963): 313–24.

Ethridge, Mark, and Black, Cyril. "Negotiating in the Balkans, 1945–1947." In Raymond Dennett and Joseph Johnson, eds., *Negotiating with the Russians*. Boston, 1951.

Feiwel, George. *Growth and Reforms in Centrally Planned Economies: The Lessons of the Bulgarian Experience*. New York, 1977.

Free Antonov! Sofia, 1983.

Ganevich, I. V. *Deiatel' nost' Bolgarskoi kommunisticheskoi partii po ukrepleniiu diktatury proletariata, sentiabr' 1944–1948 gg.* Kiev, 1974.

Genchev, Nikolai. "Razgromŭt na burzhoaznata opozitsiia v Bŭlgariia prez 1947–1948 godina." *Godishnik na Sofiskiia universitet (ideologichni katedri)* 56 (1962): 181–273.

Georgiev, P. "Natsionalisticheska kritika." *Izvestiia na Instituta po istoriia na BKP* 3–4 (1958): 503–9.

Georgiev, Stavri. "Raztseplenieto na BRSDP prez 1903 i negovite istoricheski posleditsi." *Istoricheski pregled* 4 (1983): 34–42.

Georgiev, Velichko. "Sŭzdavane i ukrepvane na obshtiia rabotnicheski profesionalen sŭiuz prez perioda ot 9 septemvri 1944 do dekemvri 1947 g." *Profsŭiuzni letopisi* 2 (1963): 8–56.

Gerschenkron, Alexander. *Economic Backwardness in Historical Perspective*. New York, 1962.

Gianaris, Nicholas V. *The Economies of the Balkan Countries*. New York, 1982.

"Godishen otchet na Ts. K. na BKP(t.s.) za 1921–1922 partina godina, iznesen na IV kongres na BKP(t.s.)." *Izvestiia na Instituta po istoriia na BKP* 30 (1974): 357–405.

Govori radiostantsiia "Khristo Botev." Sofia, 1950.

Grigorov, Boian. "Blagoi Popov—Edin ot podsŭdimite po laiptsigskiia protses prez 1933 g." *Istoricheski pregled* 4 (1983): 74–84.

———. *Po pŭtia na reformizma: Sotsial-demokratsiiata i borbite na trudeshtite se v Bŭlgariia 9 iuni–19 mai 1924*. Sofia, 1981.

Grinberg, S. Sh. "Iz istorii razvitiia bolgarskoi promyshlennosti v kontse XIX v.: Perekhod k politike proteksionizma i pooshchreniia krupnoi promyshlennosti." *Uchenye zapiski Instituta slavianovedeniia* 30 (1956): 136–52.

Grŭncharov, Stoicho. "Bŭlgarskata burzhoazna demokratsiia, 1879–1918 g." In Vasil Giuzelev, ed., *Bŭlgarskata dŭrzhava prez vekovete*. Vol. 1. Sofia, 1982.

Henze, Paul. *The Plot To Kill the Pope*. New York, 1983.

Hoffman, George W. *Regional Development Strategy in Southeast Europe: A Comparative Analysis of Albania, Bulgaria, Greece, Romania, and Yugoslavia*. New York, 1972.

Ianev, Demir. *Svoi sred khorata*. Sofia, 1978.

Iotov, Iordan; Vasilev, Kiril; Pobornikova, Stoianka; and Koleva, Tatiana. *Dimitŭr Blagoev: Biografiia*. Sofia, 1979.

Iotsov, Iaroslav. "Sŭvetska Rusiia i Bŭlgariia, 1920–1923." In Khristo Khristov et al., eds., *Oktomvriskata revoliutsiia i Bŭlgaro-sŭvetskata druzhba.* Sofia, 1967.

———. "Upravlenieto na 'Demokraticheski sgovor.' " *Istoricheski pregled* 3–4 (1948–49): 187–203.

———. "Upravlenieto na Zemedelskiia sŭiuz, 1919–1923 g." *Istoricheski pregled* 3 (1950): 305–27, 3 (1951): 249–82.

Istoriia na BKP, 1865–1944: Bibliografiia. Sofia, 1965.

Istoriia na BKP. Sofia, 1981.

Isusov, Mito. *Politicheskite partii v Bŭlgariia, 1944–1948.* Sofia, 1978.

———. "Revoliutsionniiat protses i politicheskata sistema na narodnata demokratsiia v Bŭlgariia, 1944–48 g." *Istoricheski pregled* 4–5 (1979): 83–113.

———. "Sŭzdavane na legalnite rŭkovodni organi na BRP(k). *Vekove* 1–2 (1982): 43–52.

Kabakchiev, Khristo. "Kriticheskie zametki." *Kommunisticheski internatsional* 28–29 (1923): 7741–64.

———. "Posle perevorota." *Kommunisticheski internatsional* 28–29 (1923): 7680–7740.

Karakolov, R. K. "Kharakterni momenti ot borbata na Bŭlgarskata rabotnicheska partiia—komunisti." *Istoricheski pregled* 2 (1948): 129–56.

Kazasov, Dimo. *Burni godini, 1918–1944.* Sofia, 1949.

———. *Ulitsi, khora, sŭbitiia.* Sofia, 1959.

———. *Zveno bez grim.* Sofia, 1936.

Khadzhinikolov, Veselin. "Georgi Dimitrov, narodniiat front i rabotnichesko-selskiiat sŭiuz, 1934–1941 g." In Khristo Khristov et al., eds., *Georgi Dimitrov, rabotnichesko-selskiiat sŭiuz i BZNS.* Sofia, 1982.

———. "Niakoi problemi na koalitsionnoto pravitelstvo na Aleksandŭr Stamboliski." In Khristo Khristov et al., eds., *Aleksandŭr Stamboliski: Zhivot, delo, zaveti.* Sofia, 1980.

———. "Pomoshtta na bŭlgarskiia narod za postradalite ot glada v Povolzhieto prez 1921 g." *Istoricheski pregled* 3 (1952): 275–91.

"Kharakter na 19-tomaiskiia prevrat prez 1934 g.: Diskusiia." *Izvestiia na Instituta po istoriia na BKP* 21 (1969): 219–72.

Khristov, Filiu. "Deveti septemvri i bŭlgarskata narodna armiia." *Istoricheski pregled* 2–3 (1969): 172–93.

Khristov, Khristo. "Aleksandŭr Stamboliski v novata i nai-novata istoriia na Bŭlgariia." In Khristo Khristov et al., eds., *Aleksandŭr Stamboliski: Zhivot, delo, zaveti.* Sofia, 1980.

———. *Revoliutsionnata kriza v Bŭlgariia prez 1918–1919.* Sofia, 1957.

———. "Velikata oktomvriska sotsialisticheska revoliutsiia i razvitieto na revoliutsionnoto dvizhenie v Bŭlgariia." In Khristo Khristov et al., eds., *Oktomvriskata revoliutsiia i bŭlgaro-sŭvetskata druzhba.* Sofia, 1967.

King, Robert R. *Minorities Under Communism: Nationalities as a Source of Tension Among Balkan Communist States.* Cambridge, Mass., 1973.

Koen, David. "Provalŭt na natsistkite planove za unichtozhavane na bŭlgarskite evrei." *Istoricheski pregled* 2–3 (1969): 61–81.

Kolarov, Vasil. *Protiv liavoto sektantstvo i Trotskizma v Bŭlgariia.* Sofia, 1949.

———. *Spomeni.* Sofia, 1968.

———. "Taktika Bolgarskoi kommunisticheskoi partii v svete sobyti." *Kommunisticheski internatsional* 1 (1924): 581–628.

Koleva, Tatiana. "Bŭlgarskata komunisticheska partiia i leninizmŭt." In Tatiana Koleva, ed., *Sotsialni i revoliutsionni dvizheniia v Bŭlgariia: Rabotnichesko, komunistichesko i selsko dvizhenie.* Sofia, 1982.

———. "Oktomvriskata revoliutsiia i bolshevizatsiiata na Bŭlgarskata komunisticheska partiia, 1917–1923." In Khristo Khristov et al., eds., *Oktomvriskata revoliutsiia i bŭlgaro-sŭvetskata druzhba.* Sofia, 1967.

Konobeev, V. D. *Bŭlgarskoto natsionalno osvoboditelno dvizhenie: Ideologiia, programa, razvitie.* Sofia, 1972.

Kopylov, Anatoly. "K voprosu o funktsiiakh komitetov Otechestvennogo fronta neposredstvennogo posle 9 sentiabria 1944 goda." In Tsvetana Todorova and Mito Isusov, eds., *Bŭlgarskata dŭrzhava prez vekovete.* Vol. 2. Sofia, 1982.

Koren' kov, A. M. "Internatsionalistskaia pozitsiia Bolgarskikh Tesnykh Sotsialistov v period pervoi mirovoi voiny, 1914–1918 gg." *Uchenye zapiski Instituta slavianovedeniia* 10 (1954): 351–88.

Kosev, Dimitŭr. *Septemvriskoto vŭstanie 1923 g.* Sofia, 1954.

Kosev, Dimitŭr et al. *Istoriia na Bŭlgariia.* 2 vols. Sofia, 1955.

Kostov, Traicho. *Izbrani sŭchineniia.* Sofia, 1978.

———. *Politicheskoto polozhenie i zadachite na partiiata.* Sofia, 1945.

Lambrev, Kiril. *Nachenki na rabotnicheskoto i profsŭiuznoto dvizhenie v Bŭlgariia, 1878–1891.* Sofia, 1960.

———. *Rabotnicheskoto i profesionalnoto dvizhenie v Bŭlgariia, 1891–1903.* Sofia, 1966.

Lampe, John R., and Jackson, Marvin. *Balkan Economic History, 1550–1950.* Bloomington, Ind., 1982.

Lazov, D. *Ekzarkh Stefan I: Zhivot, apostolstvo i tvorchestvo.* Sofia, 1947.

Lendvai, Paul. *Eagles in Cobwebs: Nationalism and Communism in the Balkans.* New York, 1969.

Levintov, N. G. "Agrarnye otnosheniia v Bolgarii nakanune osvobozhdeniia i agrarny perevorot 1877–1879 godov." In *Osvobozhdenie Bolgarii ot turetskogo iga: Sbornik statei.* Moscow, 1953.

Maleeva, Vera; Vodenicharov, Tinko; and Karastoianov, Georgi, eds. *Tia obichashe khorata: Spomeni za d-r Mara Maleeva-Zhivkova.* Sofia, 1982.

Manko, Alexander. *Falshifikatori na istoriiata.* Sofia, 1980.

———. "Politika splocheniia levykh sil v strategii i taktike bolgarskoi kommunisticheskoi partii, 1918–1923 gg." In Tatiana Koleva, ed., *Sotsialni i revoliutsionni dvizheniia v Bŭlgariia: Rabotnichesko, komunistichesko i selsko dvizhenie.* Sofia, 1982.

Marinov, Ivan. "Pet dni v pravitelstvo na K. Muraviev." *Istoricheski pregled* 3 (1968): 81–102.

Markov, Georgi. *Zadochni reportazhi za Bŭlgariia.* 2 vols. Zurich, 1980.

Mashkov, Khristo. "Uchastieto na pernishkite (dimitrovskite) rudnichari v transportnata stachka prez 1919/1920 g." *Istoricheski pregled* 2 (1956): 65–71.

Mastny, Vojtech. *Russia's Road to the Cold War.* New York, 1979.

Mateev, Boris. "Za glavniia udar na devetoseptemvriskoto vŭoruzheno vŭstanie." *Istoricheski pregled* 2–3 (1969): 82–105.

Maxwell, Robert, ed. *Todor Zhivkov: Statesman and Builder of New Bulgaria.* London, 1982.

Michev, Dobrin. "Iugoslavskata istoriografiia za bŭlgaro-iugoslavskite otnosheniia, 1941–44." *Vekove* 5 (1980): 57–66.

Micheva, Zdravka. "Georgi Dimitrov i emigratsiiata na BZNS, 1923–1934." In Khristo Khristov et al., eds., *Georgi Dimitrov, rabotnichesko-selskiiat sŭiuz i BZNS.* Sofia, 1982.

Migev, Vladimir. "Izgrazhdane na razvitiia sotsializŭm v Bŭlgariia." *Istoricheski pregled* 3–4 (1981): 3–21.

———. "Politicheskite aspekti v izgrazhdaneto i razvitieto na dŭrzhavnite organi prez prekhodniia period v Bŭlgariia, 1944–1958." In Tsvetana Todorova and Mito Isusov, eds., *Bŭlgarskata dŭrzhava prez vekovete.* Vol. 2. Sofia, 1982.

———. "Za etapite na kooperiraneto na selskoto stopanstvo v Bŭlgariia, 1944–1959 g." *Vekove* 1 (1984): 47–59.

Miller, Marshall Lee. *Bulgaria During the Second World War.* Stanford, 1975.

Mitev, Iono. *Fashistkiiat prevrat na deveti iuni 1923 godina i iunskoto antifashistko vŭstanie.* Sofia, 1973.

———. "Kŭm vŭprosa za teoriiata i praktikata na BKP pri izgrazhdaneto na edinen antifashistki front sled porazhenieto na Septemvriskoto vŭstanie, 1923–1924 g." *Izvestiia na Instituta po istoriia na BKP* 11 (1964): 110–23.

Mojsov, Lazo. *Bulgarskata rabotnichka partiia (komunisti) i makedonskoto natsionalno prashanie.* Skoplje, 1948.

Moser, Charles. *Dimitrov of Bulgaria.* Ottawa, Ill., 1979.

Nakov, Angel. *Bŭlgaro-sŭvetskite otnosheniia, 1944–48.* Sofia, 1978.

———. "Bŭlgaro-sŭvestkite otnosheniia v razvitieto na sotsialisticheska Bŭlgariia." *Istoricheski pregled* 4–5 (1979): 48–62.

Natan, Zhak. "Borbata na BKP protiv 'liavoto' sektanstvo." *Izvestiia na Instituta po istoriia na BKP* 11 (1964): 124–44.

"Nepublikovani radiogrami na Georgi Dimitrov do Ts. K. na BRP(k), avgust–dekemvri 1944 g." *Izvestiia na Instituta po istoriia na BKP* 27 (1972): 5–34.

"Nepublikovani radiogrami na Georgi Dimitrov i Ts. K. na BRP(k), avgust–dekemvri 1944." *Izvestiia na Instituta po istoriia na BKP* 32 (1975): 5–62.

Ognianov, Liubomir. "Istoricheskite zavoevaniia na sotsialisticheska Bŭlgariia sled aprilskiia plenum na Ts.K. na BKP, 1956 g." *Istoricheski pregled* 2 (1981): 20–38.

Oren, Nissan. *Bulgarian Communism: The Road to Power, 1934–1944.* New York, 1971.

———. *Revolution Administered: Agrarianism and Communism in Bulgaria.* Baltimore, 1973.

Ostoich, Petŭr. *BKP i izgrazhdaneto na narodno-demokraticheskata dŭrzhava, 9 septemvri 1944–dekemvri 1947.* Sofia, 1967.

Padev, Michael. *Dimitrov Wastes No Bullets.* London, 1948.

Panaiotov, L. "Rezoliutsii na Vitoshkata partina konferentsiia, 1924 g." *Izvestiia na Instituta po istoriia na BKP* 1-2 (1957): 457–75.

Pavlov, Todor. *Protiv obŭrkvaneto na poniatiata.* Sofia, 1939.

Peikov, Ivan. "Podgotovka, provezhdane i znachenie na narodniia sŭd prez 1944–1945 g." *Istoricheski pregled* 2–3 (1964): 151–70.

———. *Razgrom na svalenata ot vlast monarkho-fashistka burzhoaziia v Bŭlgariia 9.IX.1944–IX.1945.* Sofia 1982.

Peshev, Petŭr. *Istoricheskite sŭbitiia i deiateli.* Sofia, 1929.

Petkov, Petko. "Obshtoto i spetsifichnoto v likvidiraneto na kapitalisticheskata sobstvennost v promishlenostta v Bŭlgariia." *Izvestiia na Instituta po istoriia na BKP* 20 (1969): 5–50.

Petrov, Kostadin. *Bŭlgariia po pŭtia na razvitiia sotsializŭm.* Sofia, 1981.

Petrova, Dimitrina. *BZNS prez perioda na ikonomicheskata kriza, 1929–1934.* Sofia, 1979.

———. *BZNS v kraia na burzhoaznoto gospodstvo v Bŭlgariia, 1939–1944 g.* Sofia, 1970.

———. "Obshtinski izbori v Sofiia—25 septemvri 1932 g." *Vekove* 2 (1978): 58–64.

———. "Vŭznikvane na BZNS 'Aleksandŭr Stamboliski' ('Pladne')." *Vekove* 6 (1976): 38–52.

Pobornikova, Stoianka. "Sŭzdavane na revoliutsionna marksistka partiia v Bŭlgariia." In Tatiana Koleva, ed., *Sotsialni i revoliutsionni dvizheniia v Bŭlgariia: Rabotnichesko, komunistichesko i selsko dvizhenie.* Sofia, 1982.

Popoff, Kiril. *La Bulgarie économique, 1878–1911.* Sofia, 1920.

Popov, Blagoi. *Za da ne se povtori nikoga veche.* Paris, 1981.

Popov, Petŭr et al., eds. *Borbata sreshtu otritsatelnite iavleniia v sotsialisticheskoto obshtestvo.* Sofia, 1980.

Popov, Radoslav. "Monarkhicheskiiat institut, burzhoaznite partii i problemata za konstitutsionnoto upravlenie v Bŭlgariia v nachaloto na XX vek." In Vasil Giuzelev, ed., *Bŭlgarskata dŭrzhava prez vekovete.* Vol. 1. Sofia, 1982.

Poulson, Thomas M. "Administrative and Economic Regionalization of Bulgaria: The Territorial Reform of 1959." In Thomas Butler, ed., *Bulgaria Past and Present,* 187–201. Columbus, Ohio, 1976.

Pundeff, Marin. "Church-State Relations in Bulgaria Under Communism." In Bohdan Bociurkiw and John W. Strong, eds., *Religion and Atheism in the U.S.S.R. and Eastern Europe,* 328–50. Toronto, 1975.

————. "Marxism in Bulgaria Before 1891," *Slavic Review* 30 (1971): 523–50.

————. "Nationalism and Communism in Bulgaria," *Südost-Forschungen* 29 (1970): 128–70.

————. "Todor Zhivkov: Bulgaria's Loyal Pragmatist." In Rodger Swearingen, ed., *Leaders of the Communist World*, 259–76. New York, 1971.

Rabotnichesko delo: Izbrani statii i materiali, 1927–1944. Sofia, 1954.

Rachev, Stoian. *Angliia i sŭprotivitelnoto dvizhenie na Balkanite, 1940–1945.* Sofia, 1978.

Radek, Karl. "Perevorot v Bolgarii i kommunisticheskaia partiia." *Kommunisticheski internatsional* 26–27 (1923): 7327–42.

Radenkova, Petra. "Novi danni za zhivota i revoliutsionnata deinost na Georgi Dimitrov, ianuari 1929–mart 1933 g." *Izvestiia na Instituta po istoriia na BKP* 16 (1967): 213–29.

Resis, Albert. "The Churchill-Stalin Secret 'Percentages' Agreement on the Balkans, Moscow, October 1944." *American Historical Review* 83 (1978): 368–87.

Rothschild, Joseph. *The Communist Party of Bulgaria: Origins and Development, 1883–1936.* New York, 1959.

Savova, Elena, ed. *Georgi Dimitrov: Letopis na zhivota i revoliutsionnata mu deinost.* Sofia, 1952.

Searles, Joel N. "The Emergence of the Leadership Element in Bulgaria: A Social and Political Investigation, 1877–1881." Ph.D. diss., University of Washington, 1976.

Semerjeev, Peter. *Dimitrov and the Comintern: Myth and Reality.* Soviet and East European Research Centre, Hebrew University of Jerusalem. Paper no. 7, 1976.

————. *Sudebny protsess Traicho Kostova v Bolgarii, 7–12 dekabria 1949.* Soviet and East European Research Centre, Hebrew University of Jerusalem, 1980.

Seton-Watson, R. W. *Europe in the Melting Pot.* London, 1919.

Shishiniova, M.: Litsova, Z.; and Stoianov, E. *Vrŭzki i edinodeistvie na BKP i BZNS v pazardzhiski okrŭg v perioda 1894–1925 g.* Pazardzhik, 1973.

Skerlev, Stratiia. *D-r G. M. Dimitrov: Lichnost, delo i idei.* Paris, 1977.

Slavcheva, Ganka. "Evoliutsiia na politicheskiia krŭg 'Zveno' kŭm antifashistko sŭtrudnichestvo s BKP v navecherieto na Vtorata svetovna voina." *Izvestiia na Instituta po istoriia na BKP* 25 (1971): 75–112.

Slavov, Atanas. *The "Thaw" in Bulgarian Literature.* New York, 1981.

Spasov, Boris. "Bŭlgarskite konstitutsii." In Vasil Giuzelev, ed., *Bŭlgarskata dŭrzhava prez vekovete.* Vol. 1. Sofia, 1982.

Stavrev, Peniu. "Nachalo na sŭprotivata na bŭlgarskiia narod protiv khitleristkoto khozainichene." *Istoricheski pregled* 2–3 (1969): 30–42.

Sterling, Claire. *The Time of the Assassins.* New York, 1983.

Stoilkova, Aneta. "Tretiiat plenum na Ts. K. na BKP i niakoi vŭprosi ot borbata sreshtu 'liavoto' sektanstvo." *Izvestiia na Instituta po istoriia na BKP* 32 (1975): 372–98.

Stoinov, Boris. *Boinite grupi, 1941–1944.* Sofia, 1969.

A Subversion of the Neo-Crusaders. Sofia, 1983.

Subversive Activities of the Evangelical Pastors in Bulgaria: Documents. Sofia, 1949.

Tanchev, Ivan. "Sŭstavŭt na Ts. K. na BRSDP prez 1894–1897 godina," *Vekove* 1 (1979): 38–42.

• Tishev, Dimitŭr. "BZNS i vŭoruzhenata borba na bŭlgarskiia narod protiv monarkho-fashistkata diktatura, 1941–1944 g." *Istoricheski pregled* 3(1966): 3–32.

Tobias, Robert. *Communist-Christian Encounter in Eastern Europe.* Indianapolis, Ind., 1956.

Todor Zhivkov: A Biographical Sketch. Sofia, 1980.

Todorov, G. D. "Deinostta na vremennoto rusko upravlenie v Bŭlgariia po urezhdane no agrarniia i bezhanskiia vŭpros prez 1877–1879 gg." *Istoricheski pregled* 6 (1955): 27–59.

Todorov, Kosta. *Balkan Firebrand.* New York, 1943.

Todorov, Nikolai et al. *Stopanska istoriia na Bŭlgariia, 681–1981.* Sofia, 1981.

Todorov, Stanko. *Usilni godini.* Sofia, 1980.

Topalov, Vladislav. "Osnovavane na Bŭlgarskiia zemedelski sŭiuz." *Izvestiia na Instituta za istoriia* 8 (1960): 153–204.

The Trial of Fifteen Protestant Pastors-Spies, Sofia, 1949.

The Trial of Nikola D. Petkov. Sofia, 1947.

The Trial of Traicho Kostov and His Group. Sofia, 1949.

Trotsky, Lev, and Kabakchiev, Khristo. *Ocherki politicheskoi Bolgarii.* Moscow, 1923.

Trŭnski, Slavcho. *Neotdavna 1942–1943–1944.* Sofia, 1979.

Tsankov, A. Ts. "Bŭlgariia prez vionata i sled neia." *Spisanie na Bŭlgarskoto ikonomichesko druzhestvo* 1–2–3 (1921): 36–55.

Turlakov, Marko. *Istoriia, printsipi i taktika na Bŭlgarski zemedelski naroden sŭiuz.* Stara Zagora, 1929.

Ulam, Adam. *Titoism and the Cominform.* Cambridge, Mass., 1955.

Vasilev, Orlin. *Vŭoruzhenata sŭprotiva sreshtu fashizma v Bŭlgariia.* Sofia, 1946.

Vekov, Angel. "D. Blagoev and G. V. Plekhanov." *Izvestiia na Instituta po istoriia na BKP* 36 (1977): 83–118.

Vidinski, Kiril. *Podvodnicharite.* Sofia, 1963.

Weissman, George, and Williams, Duncan, eds. *The War Correspondence of Leon Trotsky: The Balkan Wars, 1912–13.* New York, 1980.

Wolff, Robert L. *The Balkans in Our Time.* New York, 1967.

Zarchev, Iordan. "Bŭlgarskiiat zemedelski naroden sŭiuz, 9 septemvri 1944–1948 g." *Izvestiia na Instituta po istoriia na BKP* 32 (1975): 107–53.

―――. "Bŭlgarskiiat zemedelski naroden sŭiuz i sotsializmŭt, 1944–1971. *Istoricheski pregled* 4–5 (1979): 63–82.

Zhivkov, Todor. *Otchet na Tsentralniia komitet na Bŭlgarskata komunisticheska partiia pred Dvanadesetiia kongres i predstoiashtite zadachi na partiiata.* Sofia, 1981.

Zhivkova, Liudmila. *Za usŭvŭrshenstvuvane na choveka i obshtestvoto.* Sofia, 1980.

Zinoviev, Grigori. "Uroki bolgarskogo perevorota." *Kommunisticheski internatsional* 26–27 (1923): 7341–54.

Zlatev, Zlatko. "Sotsialno-ikonomicheski preobrazovaniia v Bŭlgariia, 1944–1948 g." *Istoricheski pregled* 1 (1981): 3–21.

Index